Capturing Children's Meanings in Early Childhood Research and Practice

Capturing Children's Meanings in Early Childhood Research and Practice draws together contemporary research and established theories to produce a unique take on the meanings children express through a range of creative tools. Drawing on Reggio Emilia and the Mosaic approach, this book provides readers with a range of strategies for accessing, recording and interpreting young children's perceptions of and responses to their experiences.

Providing a synthesis of the multiple imaginative ways we can capture young children's meanings through observations, art, photo elicitation, mindfulness, music and other creative methods, Halpenny covers topics such as:

- Negotiating challenges presented by researching with children
- Frameworks for seeing and hearing children's intentions
- Accurately documenting and interpreting research findings
- Promoting children's meanings and their performance of them
- Moving forward with new understandings

This book is an indispensable resource for students of early childhood education, especially for courses focusing on the lived experiences of children from early to middle childhood. It is also a useful reference for those working with young children in educational and caregiving settings, and for those advocating for young children.

Ann Marie Halpenny is a lecturer in Psychology and Research Methods at the School of Languages, Law and Social Sciences in the Technological University, Dublin, Ireland.

Capturing Children's Meanings in Early Childhood Research and Practice

A Practical Guide

Ann Marie Halpenny

LONDON AND NEW YORK

First edition published 2021
by Routledge
2 Park Square, Milton Park, Abingdon, Oxon, OX14 4RN

and by Routledge
52 Vanderbilt Avenue, New York, NY 10017

Routledge is an imprint of the Taylor & Francis Group, an informa business

© 2021 Ann Marie Halpenny

The right of Ann Marie Halpenny to be identified as author of this work has been asserted by her in accordance with sections 77 and 78 of the Copyright, Designs and Patents Act 1988.

All rights reserved. No part of this book may be reprinted or reproduced or utilised in any form or by any electronic, mechanical, or other means, now known or hereafter invented, including photocopying and recording, or in any information storage or retrieval system, without permission in writing from the publishers.

Trademark notice: Product or corporate names may be trademarks or registered trademarks, and are used only for identification and explanation without intent to infringe.

British Library Cataloguing-in-Publication Data
A catalogue record for this book is available from the British Library

Library of Congress Cataloging-in-Publication Data
Names: Halpenny, Ann Marie, author.
Title: Capturing children's meanings in early childhood research and practice : a student guide / Ann Marie Halpenny.
Description: Abingdon, Oxon ; New York, NY : Routledge, 2021. | Includes bibliographical references and index.
Identifiers: LCCN 2020043315 (print) | LCCN 2020043316 (ebook) | ISBN 9780815350033 (hardback) | ISBN 9780815350040 (paperback) | ISBN 9781351163965 (ebook)
Subjects: LCSH: Early childhood education--Research. | Reggio Emilia approach (Early childhood education) | Perception in children.
Classification: LCC LB1139.225 .H35 2021 (print) | LCC LB1139.225 (ebook) | DDC 372.21--dc23
LC record available at https://lccn.loc.gov/2020043315
LC ebook record available at https://lccn.loc.gov/2020043316

ISBN: 978-0-8153-5003-3 (hbk)
ISBN: 978-0-8153-5004-0 (pbk)
ISBN: 978-1-351-16396-5 (ebk)

Typeset in Melior
by SPi Global, India

Contents

	Acknowledgements	vii
1	Researching young children's experiences and meanings	1
2	Negotiating challenges in doing research with young children	25
3	Documenting children's meanings	46
4	Ways of seeing: Observation skills in research with young children	78
5	Ways of listening: Supporting children's conversations	102
6	Making children's meanings visible	126
7	Mindful moments and performance of meanings	161
8	Capturing meanings and moving forward with new understandings	197
	References	225
	Index	248

Acknowledgements

My sincere thanks to Dr. Liz Nixon, Dr. Sheila Garrity and Dr. Margaret Kernan for their very helpful comments on commencing work on this publication. A very special thank you to my colleague Anne Fitzpatrick for her expertise and support throughout the process of completing this book. Many thanks also to Alison Foyle and Alex Butterworth in Routledge and to all those involved in editing and bringing the book to publication. Sincere thanks to Aisling Ni Dhuibhlinn for contributing sample artwork carried out by children in her early years setting. Finally, a special thank you to all the early childhood educators and researchers whose creative and inspirational work with children provided excellent illustrations of capturing children's meanings in early childhood research and practice.

Researching young children's experiences and meanings

Capturing children's perceptions of their lived experiences is an active process of communication involving listening to children, interpreting their expression and co-constructing meanings through these dialogues (James, 2007). A key principle underpinning this process is acknowledgement of young children's personal accounts of their experiences as a fundamental element to understanding their worlds. The motivation to do research involving young children is reinforced by a desire to generate knowledge and greater understanding of childhoods and children's meanings in the context of their everyday lived experiences. This chapter outlines and discusses some of the key ideas and principles underpinning the rationale for doing research with young children. The value of child-centred research has been well documented, and the chapter further emphasises the importance of giving young children the opportunity to express their meanings and perspectives in research and practice. Such an approach foregrounds the particular expertise of young children in terms of their knowledge about childhood, their role as skilful and competent communicators and their right to participate in and contribute to decision-making in matters that affect their lives. The importance of refining research methods and drawing attention to innovative and creative ways to work with children in research, in order to capture in a meaningful way the worlds and perspectives of children, has been highlighted in recent decades (Clark, 2017).

Key aspects of children's development in the early years will be summarised later in the chapter, with a view to guiding and informing the research methods and strategies adopted in order to capture young children's meanings. Drawing on some of the established approaches to doing research with young children, creative strategies appropriate for engaging young children in the research process are outlined.

Researching young children's meanings

The uniqueness of children's perspectives on experiences of their everyday lives has been evidenced in prior research, such as where, how much and with whom they play (Colliver, 2017; Einarsdóttir, 2003; Rogers & Evans, 2008). Young children's perspectives contribute substantially to our knowledge of what they process and prioritise in terms of aspects of their experiences (Miles, 2018). Significantly, children's unique perspectives can also contribute to challenging adult assumptions around these experiences (Ruscoe, Barblett & Barratt-Pugh, 2018). Young children's perspectives are, thus, an essential consideration for democratic representation of all citizens in a society (Broström, 2012; Sommer, Samuelsson & Hundeide, 2010). Including children's perspectives in meaningful ways in research has the potential to transform what is currently known about early childhood education by providing perspectives that have not been captured in more traditional research approaches (Mayne, Howitt & Rennie, 2018). Notwithstanding these views and arguments, Colliver (2017) draws attention to the fact that many researchers around the world ascribe little weight to young children's perspectives.

In their valuable resource *Steps for Engaging Young Children in Research* (Volume 1 & 2), Johnson, Hart and Colwell (2014a), draw attention to six key steps that should be included in any research process that seeks to engage young children's participation. The first step to consider is whether there is a commitment to including young children in research, and moreover, whether the data gathered and the knowledge generated from the research will be acted on and have influence. The second step prioritises the importance of developing appropriate ethical protocols and processes. The necessity of being able to build trusting, supportive and professional relationships with young children in the research process is highlighted in the third step. Selecting appropriate methods to engage with children in research and identifying sensitive and child-friendly strategies for communication are emphasised in the fourth and fifth steps set out by Johnson et al. (2014a). Finally, consideration of the context and relevance of the research to young children's lives is prioritised in the sixth step in engaging children in research.

> **Steps for Engaging Young Children in Research**
>
> **Johnson, Hart & Colwell (2014a)**
>
> **Step 1:** Consideration of capacity and capability: commitment to including young children in research and acting on the knowledge generated
> **Step 2:** Developing ethical protocols and processes
> **Step 3:** Developing trust and relationships
> **Step 4:** Selecting appropriate methods
> **Step 5:** Identifying appropriate forms of communication
> **Step 6:** Consideration of context and relevance of research

How adults conceptualise children and childhood influences the extent to which they can engage with children effectively in the research process. In the section below, current understandings of childhood and how these concepts have evolved over time are briefly outlined and discussed.

Constructions of children and childhood

Current understandings and constructions of children and childhood are informed, among other influences, by postmodern views of children and childhood, the sociology of childhood, and the children's rights movement (Alanen, 2001; Corsaro, 1997; Einarsdóttir, 2007; Harcourt & Gray, 2013). Perspectives that emphasise childhood, viewed as a social construction from a sociological perspective, place an emphasis on children as social actors and citizens, rather than as deficient adults. Childhood and children are, therefore, considered as worthy of investigation in their own right, separate from their parents or caregivers (Corsaro, 1997;

Christensen & James, 2008a; James & Prout, 1990). In the past, traditional understandings of childhood emphasised developmentally appropriate practices, informed exclusively through a reliance on developmental theories, which tended to view children's development as moving towards adulthood, at times with greater emphasis on what a child was not yet able to do, rather than highlighting the child's ability and competence. As summarised by Mayall (1994, p. 1):

> Children's lives are lived through childhoods constructed for them by adults' understandings of childhood and what children are and should be.

Such a perspective contributed to a view of childhood that overlooked childhood agency and prioritised regulating children's learning to what is considered to be normal development (Atwater, Carta, Schwartz & McConnell, 1994). More recent perspectives conceptualise children as strong, capable and knowledgeable experts on their own lives, possessing knowledge, perspective and interest that is best gained from the children themselves (Malaguzzi, 1994; Mashford-Scott & Church, 2011). Underpinning this perspective is recognition that children have agency, defined as 'the power to make decisions that impact on self and others and act on them' (Sancar & Severcan 2010, p. 277). Children's exercise of agency can best be understood in relation to the social, cultural and political contexts in which it occurs, and in connection with adult agency. Recognising children's agency in research posits a view that children are individuals who experience their worlds in unique ways and that these unique experiences are a valued focus of study (Greene & Hill, 2005). Research using creative, diverse methodological approaches has provided evidence that young children are reliable informants, capable of contributing unique and valuable information (Clark, 2017; Clark & Moss, 2001; Mayne et al., 2018).

Competing paradigms and values have informed our understanding of childhood in recent decades. Childhood is now understood primarily through the lens of social constructionism and children are viewed as active participants constructing their own learning (Mayall, 2000; Smith, 2007). Notwithstanding the variety of contexts and frameworks in which children's perspectives and views are sought, a common aim that draws together all such research is that it strives to generate greater knowledge and understanding about the richness of children's lives (Kellet, 2011). Research with young children has been influenced by discourses of children's rights and citizenship. Children's competence to participate in research and their ability to express their opinions has also been clearly articulated in the UNCRC (United Nations, 1989).

General Comment 7 (Office of the High Commissioner for Human Rights (OHCHR), 1989), emphasises the rights of all children, including young children, to be consulted in matters that affect them. Specifically, Article 12 of the convention emphasises the right that a child who is capable of forming his or her own view should have the right to express these views freely on all matters affecting the child and that those views should be given weight in accordance with age and maturity (United Nations, 1989). Four key dimensions, which are relevant to designing and carrying out research with young children, are highlighted in Article 12 as follows: *space* to generate opportunities for children's expression of their views; *voice*, to ensure that these views are expressed effectively; *audience,* to ensure that children's views are listened to; and *influence*, to ensure that young children's views are listened to and acted on.

> **Four key dimensions to conceptualize the provision of Article 12 (UNCHR, 1989); Lundy (2007, p. 933 cited in Tay-Lim & Lim, 2013)**
>
> **Space:** Creating opportunities for children to express their views
> **Voice:** Facilitating the expression of these views
> **Audience:** Actively listening to these views
> **Influence:** Responding appropriately to these views

Young children's participation in research

Acknowledging children's right to participate in research requires developing meaningful ways and strategies through which children can be involved in research projects. Mayne et al. (2018) draw attention to a hierarchical model of children's (3- to 8-year-olds) research participation rights that builds on work by Roger Hart and integrates key dimensions of participation rights drawn from Article 12 of the UNCRC. More specifically, the authors emphasise that attention must be focused on the ways in which information is communicated to children, the level of understanding that is achieved, generating opportunities for children's opinions to be voiced, and what, if any, influence can be exerted, resulting from participation. The importance of recognising that researchers and children have differing agendas and, in practice, all research with children requires some level of adult direction, is foregrounded in these arguments (MacNaughton, Smith & Davis, 2006; Mayne et al., 2018). Hart's (1992) ladder of participation has been used extensively to identify different possibilities in terms of the level of children's research participation, ranging from a basic level of participation in which little or no agency is afforded to children, to the highest level of participation where children are involved in gathering data and in discussion about aspects of research design and dissemination, and ultimately, can share decision-making equally with adults (Greig, Taylor & MacKay, 2007). The hierarchical model of participation developed by Mayne et al. (2018) extends the ladder of children's participation as described by Hart (1998) and introduces the four elements of children's participation rights: *information, understanding, voice* and *influence* to reflect the requirements of Article 12 of the UNCRC. Information provided to children can range from being negligible, where little or no information is provided to children, to being significant, and, at the highest level, being created by children themselves. Understanding refers to how appropriate the information and participation is to the child's competencies and capacities, and this can range from being negligible or facilitating very limited understanding for the young child, to facilitating an understanding that is equal to or greater than that of the adult. The element Voice refers to the extent to which children can express their views and relate their experiences. This element can range from practices where children are provided with no opportunity to express their views at all to the highest level where children's voice and expression are equivalent to that of adults. Finally, the element Influence refers to the extent to which children's views carry weight in terms of influencing decision-making processes and can range from situations where children's participation will have no influence to the highest level where significant influence is exerted.

A more nuanced understanding of children's opportunities to participate in research and practice in ECE (Early Childhood Education) can be achieved through using a combination of the criteria developed by Hart (1992) and extended by Mayne et al. (2018). So, for example, a young child may be scaffolded by adults to participate in a research activity and this might correspond to Level 6 on Hart's Participation Ladder where the participation involves *adult-initiated, shared decisions with children*. However, this level of participation can be further assessed and evaluated when we consider to what extent children are provided with meaningful information and possibilities for equal understanding with adults in the participation process and, importantly, the level of expression and influence that children's voices will be assigned through this process. The diverse nature of research with children means that children's participation will vary widely and is likely to be expressed in a unique manner in each research project (Mayne et al., 2018).

Wyness (2012) points out that in Hart's model, children's authentic voice is located near the top of the hierarchy of participation and greater adult involvement near the bottom, whereas it may be more useful to classify children's participation and the involvement of adults horizontally rather than vertically. Adult involvement in children's participation in research is often necessary and serves to enable and empower the child's voice and to collaborate with young children in the co-construction of meanings. The hierarchical model of children's participation developed by Mayne et al. (2018) allows for such a horizontal dimension to extend our understanding of the many possibilities and considerations to take on board, when designing methods and tools for young children's participation in research. Wyness (2012) highlights, with reference to children's perspectives, that the concept of participation and voice cannot be fully understood unless we take on board the complexities involved and reflect on the nature of child-adult relationships.

While there has been a positive increase in emphasis on hearing the voices of children in research since the early 1990s, the focus on accessing the views of young children, under the age of 8 years, has been less significant (Johnson, Hart & Colwell, 2014a). Mayne and Howitt (2014, 2015) published a systematic review of published empirical research involving children under 8 years of age, which indicated that 97% of articles included young children in non-participatory roles as objects of research (65%) and in semi-participatory roles as subjects of research (32%). Less than 4% of studies included young children in inclusive, highly participatory roles as social actors (3%)

and co-researchers (0.4%). Reasons for this absence of focus on younger children may be that an increased awareness of ethical issues in working with children and the need to protect children from inappropriate questioning may be seen as insurmountable obstacles. Other possible reasons are that it may not always be appropriate or desirable to include young children in research and researchers may not always be aware of or skilled in appropriate research methods and strategies.

Young children's construction of meanings

Seeking meaning is a central aim and objective of all research and, from a developmental perspective, meaning-making is an important part of understanding how children make sense of the world and construct meaning (Duncan, 2013). Meaning-making is typically associated with cognitive and social processes, involving the use of symbol systems (Brooks, 2009). The term meaning-making is also used frequently in constructivist approaches to education because, from this perspective, meaning is considered as being constructed from knowledge generated through interactions with people, places and objects in the environment. These notions of meaning-making are also often linked to socio-cultural models of understanding the ways in which young children develop. Children construct meaning from their experiences and, for this reason, will have their own theories and interpretations of the world. Furthermore, it has been argued that children's ability to engage in multimodal meaning-making, as, for example, through the use of visual, aural and spatial media, increases their capacity to use many forms of representational thinking and to mentally manipulate and organise images, ideas and feelings (Wright, 2007).

Deficit narratives: The value of accessing young children's meanings in research and practice

Reconceptualisations of children and childhood, informed by postmodern perspectives and the adoption of the United Nations Convention for the Rights of the Child (United Nations, 1989) have contributed, to some extent, to a reframing of our understandings of childhood and increased focus and activity around young children's participation in research relevant to their lives. These developments have raised awareness that knowledge generated through conversations with adults alone may result in what can be termed 'deficit narratives' (Nicholson et al., 2015, p. 1569). Consequently, there may be disconnections between how children experience childhood and how adults perceive it to be experienced (Harcourt, 2011). An interesting illustration of the potential divergence between children and adults' perspectives on children's play is presented in the Focus on Research below, by Nicholson, Kurnik, Jevgjovikj and Ufoegbune (2015).

FOCUS ON RESEARCH

Deconstructing adults' and children's discourse on children's play: listening to children's voices to destabilise deficit narratives

Nicholson, Kurnik, Jevgjovikj and Ufoegbune (2015)

Study aims

Compare the discourse adults use to discuss children's play and the language children use as authors of their own experiences to make visible points of alignment and dissension.

- A substantial body of research on play opportunities for children in the early years tends to foreground a focus on loss and deficit perspectives when exploring this topic from the perspective of adults.

- Many research studies and reports have concluded that opportunities for children to engage in child-initiated free play at home and at school are declining in contemporary American society.

- Factors believed to influence this trend include hurried family lifestyles, the burgeoning accountability movement expanding pressure on young children to exhibit academic skills and knowledge associated with school readiness and achievement, the decrease in safe neighbourhoods and outdoor play environments accessible to children, children's expanding use of technology and the increased supervision of children.

(Continued)

- Given this socio-political narrative describing the loss of play for children, it seems especially important to understand children's perspectives about play in their everyday lives.
- Significantly, we need to understand whether adults' assumptions about children's play are mirrored in children's descriptions of their own play and, if not, how these discourses differ.
- The Children's Play Narratives (CPN) project was designed to gather information from children about their perspectives on their own play as children. CPN data reported in this study include interviews with 98 children, 64 females and 34 males. The children were between the ages of 3 and 17 years, although the majority of the participants were between the ages of 3 and 10 years. Twenty-six children were pre-schoolers (3–4 years).
- Interview questions were developed with a goal of documenting children's ideas about play across the lifespan, positive and negative memories of play, contextualised stories of play experiences and theories/beliefs related to children's and adults' play.
- The Global Play Memories Project (GPMP) was carried out in order to collect play memories from adults around the world. Combining interview and survey data, information from 135 adults (100 females and 35 males) from 21 countries was collected and analysed.

Findings below highlight the divergence in adult and children's views on play in the early years.

Deconstructing adults' and children's discourse on children's play: listening to children's voices to destabilise deficit narratives

Adults' descriptions of children's play	Children's descriptions of their favourite types of play
Kids nowadays are constantly submerged in a console.	I make things with mud, playdough and stuff.
Children today have to be guided. They are not as creative as we were as children.	Me and my friend we were playing football, we made up a game called awesome catches.
Children do not make up games to play and I doubt if they have make believe friends like we did.	I like to play games with my friends and we can race and we like playing made up games.

Children do not play outdoors.	It is fun playing in the sandbox outside.
The children now get tired with their materials and say they are bored.	My favourite toys is playing with my friends in the dollhouse and playing with Playdough.
Girls have mostly become selfish.	I play on my iPad.
They are not taking risks ... I do not see them having that initiative to do the risky stuff.	I like to go on the grass and do flips.
They seem to want adults to tell them what to do or to entertain them.	I like to play with puzzles.
Children these days cannot make up any plays.	We pretended that we ran a summer camp and all the kids were being naughty.
They do not know how to play now.	I like playing in the park. Play with my sister ... we play superheroes.
I feel like they are not reacting to what is going on in the real world.	[My favourite play], well, inside, word games with my sister or... if I am playing outside, ride my bike. Play wall ball.
Creativity has gone out the window in general which I think is very sad.	I like to hang out with my friends, play soccer, play tag, go to parks and stuff.

What is striking about these findings is the divergence in the views of the children and the adults when reflecting on children and play in contemporary American society. Unlike the narratives and views reflected when focusing exclusively on adult perspectives, children's views on their own involvement in play demonstrate ongoing excitement, engagement, taking risks, physical exertion, creative and imaginative dimensions and many of the features of play that we might associate with past contexts. By undertaking further research whereby adults and children are invited to share their expertise, new understandings about children and childhood may emerge.

Hearing first-hand from children, in research contexts in which children are authors of their own experiences, highlights the benefits and drawbacks of limiting our representation of children's subjective experiences through an exclusive focus on adults' perspectives. By juxtaposing the findings from two distinct studies – one where children discuss their own play and the other where adults describe play across their lifespan including their perspectives on children's contemporary play – we gain insight into how these perspectives may diverge, and indeed converge at times. Findings from the study carried out by Nicholson et al. (2015) presented above draw attention to the fact that it is essential to include children's own voices in attempts to convey information about aspects of children's lives. Children's expertise and lived knowledge of their experiences should be given equal representation, where appropriate and possible, to that of adults who assume this knowledge and expertise.

Children's meanings as co-constructions

The value and importance of listening to young children is clearly illustrated when we compare children's views with adult views on particular issues. However, in reality, it is essential to acknowledge that children's meanings are typically co-constructed through actions and interactions with key adults in their lives (Mannion, 2007; Schiller & Einarsdóttir, 2009). Mannion (2007) emphasises the critical part adults play in the dialogical process around the negotiation of children's participation. The author further warns that without a focus on the relations between adults and children, and the spaces they inhabit, we are in danger of providing a restricted and narrow view of how children's voice and participation are produced. Wyness (2012) argues for a more interdependent and intergenerational approach to including young children in research. As emphasised by Wyness (2012, p. 12):

> children's perspectives, participation and voice cannot be fully understood in its complexity unless we tease out the nature of relations between children and adults.

Reframing children's participation to emphasise further the co-construction of children's meaning in research goes some way to addressing these issues.

Understanding of the ways in which social interaction is co-produced between children and adult researchers is framed by the concept of generational relations between children and adults (Breathnach, Danby & O'Gorman, 2018). Generational relationships identify the social positions that children and adults hold in relation to each other, and within specific social structures such as homes and schools (Alanen, 2001; Bae, 2009; Jenks, 2005; Mayall, 2002). Much of the work that happens on a daily basis in early childhood education settings involves innovative and effective ways of enhancing children's communication and engagement. A key aspect of this meaningful communication is the role that the adult early years practitioner plays in promoting, supporting and facilitating young children's expression of their meanings.

Differences between research with children and research with adults

Researching children's perspectives on their lives through engaging with them as active participants requires researchers to be creative, responsive and flexible (Christensen & James, 2008a). Creative games and prompts can be introduced to enhance possibilities for sustaining children's focus and attention. Visual and narrative approaches may hold the attention of both adults and children of all ages, but particular approaches, such as using three-dimensional visual methods, may be developed to take into account the different thinking and communicative capacities of children. Regardless of the level of participation and agency afforded the child in the research process, there are particular ethical issues that need to be considered in order for research to be in the best interests of the children (Punch, 2015). In the framework developed by Johnson et al. (2014a) to support the engagement of children in research, it is not only the range of engaging methods that can be used with young children that are prioritised but also the importance of considering the capabilities of the researchers, ethical protocols and procedures, and building trust and relationships with the children. Power relationships may exist in all research. However, between adult or even older child researchers and child participants it may be a central concern and facilitating collaboration and co-construction of meanings with children and early childhood educators goes some way to addressing this power differential.

Focus on development in childhood and research with young children

A substantial proportion of the material focusing on doing research with children has tended to focus on children in middle childhood and early adolescence. Less emphasis has been placed on doing research with children in the early years, with the exception of some notable authors such as Clark and Moss (2001) and Clark (2017) who, in developing the Mosaic approach, contributed extensively to our knowledge and understanding of how to use creative and meaningful strategies in order to understand young children's feelings and responses to their lived experiences. Given the focus in this book on capturing young children's meaning, specifically children in early childhood, it is worth delineating as far as possible significant features of young children's development that have particular relevance for doing research with young children. Key features of young children's development that inform and guide the development of effective strategies for capturing young children's meanings are considered in the sections below.

Any activity requiring a response from young children needs to be mindful of the issue of *language,* both in terms of the complexity of the explanation of the task and with regard to the linguistic ability of the child. Criteria to inform the development of appropriate methods include a focus on developing activities that could firstly be explained to children in simple terms, and secondly an activity that required a response that was not dependent on language (Marshall & Shibazaki (2011)). The ability of young children to hold substantial knowledge in *memory* may be limited. Activities that are relatively short in duration and that do not rely excessively on the use of memory are, therefore, preferred. Marshall & Shibazaki (2011) also draws attention to issues of *concentration* and *distraction* in young children's participation in research. Research carried out in naturalistic settings such as the home or the early childhood education setting are likely to reduce the likelihood of difficulties arising related to focus and attention. Young children may be more likely to feel *intimidated* by the presence of others, especially those with whom they are not familiar, and by places that are not familiar to them.

Providing children with opportunities to participate on an individual basis may be beneficial for some children, such as facilitating access to quiet spaces where children feel less conscious of being judged or evaluated on what they say. *Lack of familiarity* with a researcher may also constrain a young child's participation. Early years practitioners are typically well placed to scaffold young children's participation, given the trusting, supportive relationships that have often been established between the child and the adult.

Capturing a sense of curiosity

Curiosity, wonder and mystery typically characterise the toddler and early childhood years and are primary motivational forces driving the acquisition of knowledge in young children. Among the different dimensions of curiosity, the epistemic nature of curiosity, or the quest for knowledge, is worth emphasising in children's learning (Chak, 2007). Young children's curiosity and exploration, which are expressions of their eagerness to know, if nurtured, can be a key motivational force for the acquisition of knowledge. Understanding curiosity as a motivational force, as expressed through exploratory behaviour, may serve as a focus for understanding the characteristics of young children's curiosity and for better understanding how we can foster and nurture children's curiosity and desire to know more. With specific reference to doing research with young children and accessing children's meanings, strategies that attract children's curiosity and enhance children's sense of wonder are likely to be more successful in engaging young children in research and sustaining their motivation to participate. Parents and early years practitioners, as people who are significant in creating and organising the environment for young children, play a significant role in promoting their curiosity and exploratory behaviour (Chak, 2007), thereby mediating and maintaining the intrinsic motivation of children.

Documenting children's meanings in early childhood research and practice represents a particular approach to understanding young children's experiences and their motivation to explore and learn. Wien (2013) highlights that pedagogical documentation invites us to be curious and to wonder with others about the meaning of experiences and events to children. Through such an approach, we become co-learners together, focusing on children's expanding understanding of the world as we interpret that understanding with children and others.

Moments of wonder – children's working theories

In developing effective research methods with young children, it is essential to take account of the fact that each child is unique and complex. Consequently, challenges arise when facilitating a means of expression that allows us to better enter into dialogue with young children and to capture and comprehend the meanings they attribute to their surroundings and the world around them. Given that young children may not readily engage with us in dialogue, observation provides us with an invaluable stepping stone into children's wonderment, which we can then explore further with appropriate and creative tools. Capturing a sense of wonder in young children has been achieved through the use of participatory observation in previous research. The concept of children's working theories encompasses the notion that children have ideas that are developing over time through their everyday interactions and experiences with people, places and things (Areljung & Kelly-Ware, 2017). Related to this, Forman and Hall (2005) highlight how observing children provides us with a key to exploring the particular theories that children construct about the meaning in their world. The authors emphasise that these theories are based on *our* speculations about children's meanings, words and actions:

> As we observe children, we need to consider their goals. What effects are they trying to create? We observe their actions and listen to their comments to determine the strategies they choose to attain those goals. The relation between the strategy and the goal will reveal a possible theory, a theory about how to make the desired effect occur.
>
> (Forman & Hall, 2005)

Early years practitioners and researchers identify and speculate on the theories constructed by children, informed by what they know about children's experiences and consistent with child development research (Forman & Hall, 2005). Through documenting children's meanings, we can further reflect on how children's theories can be extended within and across various contexts. Furthermore, through such documentation, we can give children the tools necessary to represent their theories and communicate them to others.

> **Conversations with children**
>
> **(Forman & Hall, 2005)**
>
> If we truly want to have high-level conversations with children about their beliefs, expectations and assumptions, we need to know their beliefs, assumptions and expectations so that we might enter the conversation with a paraphrase or counterpoint.
>
> We need to know what the child thinks can be done in real situations, and we need to know the procedures the child believes will make things happen. If we have watched and listened long enough to determine the child's goals and strategies for attaining those goals, then we have both a resource for understanding the child and an interesting basis for a high-level conversation.

Navigating the social world in early childhood

In understanding how to develop creative and effective methodologies for capturing young children's meanings, it is useful to reflect briefly on the range of skills that are developing in the early years, with a particular focus on cognitive and social development. Children are most like us in their feelings and in their emotions, and least like us in their thoughts (Elkind, 2007). Piaget's early work (e.g. Piaget, 1951, 1952) revealed the richness and complexity of young children's thought. Vygotsky built his early theory around the idea that social communication provides the input for the child's developing mental functions (Vygotsky, 1978 (Vygotsky, 1986)). Piaget's concept of *egocentrism* refers to certain difficulties that some young children may have in being able to adopt the perspective of another person. However, we know that young children competently identify with the feelings of adults or of other children, when provided with some perceptual clues to the other person's feeling state (Carpendale, Lewis & Muller, 2018). A young child will, for example, be able to comfort another child who is crying because the other child's tears are a clear sign of distress.

Research on theory of mind has reshaped our understanding of cognitive growth and development in early childhood, with important implications for social and cognitive development (Banaji & Gelman, 2014). Theory of mind research addresses the development of young children's understanding of the intentions, goals and emotions of people and the ways those mental states are affected by others' actions. Together with research on joint attention, pointing, and collaborative problem solving, studies by Warneken and Tomasello (2006, 2007) indicate that toddlers are sensitive to the goals and intentions underlying others' behaviour and that they can enter into those intentional states in helpful and cooperative acts during their second year (Carpendale et al., 2018).

Cognitive development and social development are profoundly intertwined, although in recent decades, with the emergence of computers and technology, cognitive development in the area of child development has typically focused more exclusively on what is inside the child's mind and has become less explicitly relevant to children's functioning and wellbeing in the real world (Banaji & Gelman, 2014). Banaji and Gelman (2014) highlight that most of the research on cognitive development in the early years shifted to an exclusive focus on the processes that unfolded in children's minds. However, in the past decade, the authors highlight and celebrate a 'renaissance' (p. 4) in the reunion between social and cognitive psychology. Key concepts emphasised and prioritised in contemporary early childhood education include the development of metacognitive skills in children, promotion and support of emotional and self-regulation skills, and many of the skills associated with what has been termed executive function in neuropsychology (Alduncin, Hoffman, Feldman & Loe, 2014). These skills are associated with mental processes that enable children to plan, focus attention, remember instructions and juggle multiple tasks successfully.

Many of the theories of cognitive development now place children in their social environment (Gelman, 2009; Meltzoff, 2007) showing how much they already know as infants about other people's goals and intentions (Carpendale et al., 2018). The profound importance of early years practitioners facilitating cognitive and social self-regulation and promoting metacognitive skills has been demonstrated in recent literature in the early years (Hayes, 2013; Whitebread, 2012 (Whitebread, 2013)). Guided and informed by this knowledge, early years practitioners and researchers are, therefore, well positioned to enter into dialogue with young children through research and to scaffold children in expressing the meanings they attribute to their surroundings and the world around them. Getting closer to young children's thinking is more likely to be achieved through a focus on how children live, on how they experience the world around them and on what children's responses to these experiences are. Such a focus aligns well with researching children's views in early childhood settings, with early years practitioners facilitating meaningful and creative approaches to generating better understandings of young children's thoughts and feelings.

Creative ways of researching young children's perspectives

Multi-modal approaches to researching children's perspectives

From a pedagogic point of view, a multi-modal approach to researching young children's perspectives recognises that all modes – not just language and verbal and textual expression but also visual, dramatic, storytelling, learning stories and other approaches – enable and empower children to articulate their feelings and responses in a manner that is familiar and natural for them. Multi-modal approaches 'open up full and productive access to the multiplicity of representational and communicational potentials' (Bock, 2016; Kress, 2000, p. 159).

Recognising meanings and thoughts inherent in children's behaviours may be challenging for adults; children '...have an autonomous world, independent to some extent of the worlds of adults' and their behaviours, meanings and thoughts can be 'incomprehensible to adults' (Hardman, 1973, p. 95). Equally, young children tend to present their actions, meanings and thinking through '...play, body language, facial expression, or drawing and painting' (Lansdown, 2010, p. 12). Key research approaches and associated resources, which offer rich opportunities for developing and refining creative strategies for doing research with children, are briefly outlined below.

The Mosaic approach

The Mosaic approach (Clark & Moss, 2001) was originally developed and used in England, through a project with 3- and 4-year-old children in an early childhood education setting. Clark (2005, p. 29) describes it as 'a strength-based framework for viewing young children as competent, active, meaning-makers and explores of their environment'. The approach draws on participation research methods that do not require literacy or numeracy skills. A predominant influence in the development of the Mosaic approach is the pedagogical approach of Reggio Emilia, in which ideas of the competent child and the pedagogy of listening and of relationships are foregrounded. Key elements that are included in the Mosaic approach include a *multi-method approach*, combining a range of multi-modal approaches and creative strategies; a *participatory* approach, which conceptualises children as experts and agents in their lives; a *reflexive approach*, emphasising the need for all participants and researchers to reflect on and negotiate interpretations; an *adaptable approach* that can be used with children of different ages and backgrounds in early childhood; an approach that focuses on *children's lived experience* rather than abstract knowledge; and an approach that is *embedded in the practice of early childhood education*. Central to the Mosaic approach is the practice of documentation. Documentation provides 'traces/documents that testify to and make visible the ways of learning of the individuals and the group' and allows the group and the child to 'observe themselves from an external point of view' (Rinaldi, 2005, p. 23). A more detailed focus on documentation and, in particular, pedagogical documentation, is provided in Chapter 3. Key elements included in the Mosaic approach are outlined below.

> ### The Six Elements of the Mosaic Approach
> ### Clark (2017, p. 24)
>
> - **Multi-method:** recognises the different 'voices' or languages of children
> - **Participatory:** treats children as experts and agents in their own lives
> - **Reflexive:** includes children, practitioners, and parents in reflecting on meanings, and addresses the question of interpretation
> - **Adaptable:** can be applied in a variety of early childhood settings
> - **Focuses on children's lived experiences:** can be used for a variety of purposes including looking at lives lived, rather than knowledge gained or care received
> - **Embedded into practice:** a framework for listening that has the potential to be used both as an evaluative tool and to become embedded into early years practice

Clark (2011, p. 27) draws attention to the importance of a multi-method approach in order to be as inclusive as possible and to 'play to young children's strengths'. Significantly, a multi-method approach can generate opportunities for children to experiment with a range of different roles, some of which will be familiar to the children, while other roles are more typically experienced as adult roles (Clark, 2008, 2010). Figure 1.1 details the range of roles that children took on during a study called *The Living Spaces*, which aimed to place young children's experiences of their early childhood environment at the centre of plans for designing new spaces. Further possible roles identified in research that has included children as participants have been added in shaded boxes.

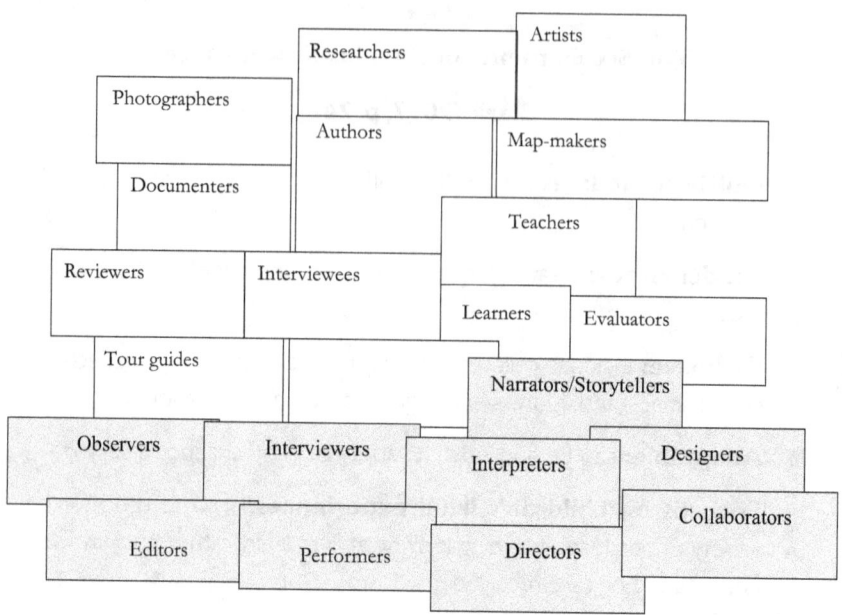

Figure 1.1 Potential roles that children adopt through participating in research. Adapted from the range of children's roles during The Living Spaces study (Clark, 2010).

Steps for Engaging Young Children in Research

Steps for Engaging Young Children in Research is a framework, and a compendium of creative methods, which was developed through collaboration with a team of international researchers funded by the Bernard van Leer Foundation and edited by Vicky Johnson, Roger Hart and Jennifer Colwell in 2014. Volume 1 (the guide) provides useful information and guidelines on engaging young children (available at: https://bernardvanleer.org/publications-reports/steps-engaging-young-children-research-volume-1-guide/). Volume 2 (the researcher toolkit) provides a comprehensive overview of many different and appropriate strategies and activities for carrying out research with young children (available at https://bernardvanleer.org/publications-reports/steps-engaging-young-children-research-volume-2-researcher-toolkit). The framework addresses key issues facing researchers wishing to engage young children in research processes and offers ways to overcome some of the challenges researchers may face. A selection of useful and insightful case studies is also included to demonstrate how experts working in a wide range of international contexts have worked with children to facilitate young children's engagement in the research process.

Reggio Emilia and Project Zero

In 1997, educators from the Municipal Preschools and Infant-Toddler Centres of Reggio Emilia (a small city in northern Italy) and Project Zero (a research organisation at the Harvard Graduate School of Education) came together to investigate the group as a learning environment and to explore documentation as a way to make visible and shape how and what we learn. Since the late 1960s, Project Zero researchers have studied the development of learning processes in children, adults and organisations. The Reggio pre-schools originated from the efforts of parents in local communities to rebuild their schools after the devastation of World War II. For more than forty-five years, educators in this exceptional set of thirty-four municipal pre-schools and infant-toddler centres have carefully researched, documented and facilitated children's learning, bringing international attention to children's capacities as individual and group learners. In 2001, a framework was published for understanding, documenting, and supporting individual and group learning in the book *Making Learning Visible: Children as Individual and Group Learners,* co-authored by Project Zero researchers and Reggio educators. Since the publication of *Making Learning Visible,* these researchers have worked to document children's learning through notes, photographs, video, transcripts and student work. *Visible Learners: Promoting Reggio-Inspired Approaches in All Schools* was published more recently in 2013.

Young Children as Researchers Study

The Young Children as Researchers (YCAR) study adopted a qualitative 'jigsaw' methodology (Murray, 2017, p. 224) to co-research with children aged 4–8 years ($n = 138$), their parents, practitioners, and professional researchers. The study identified key epistemological factors and epistemological categories that may support young children's research behaviours in everyday activities. Supporting young children's participation in research, and being guided and informed through a focus on these factors, contributes to increasing potential to reposition young children away from the margins of research into an intrinsic position in research concerning matters that affect them and secures their rights as researchers. Significantly, Murray (2017, p. 224) states, 'such research can inform early childhood policy and practice in a deeply grounded manner that values young children as competent thinkers with expertise concerning their own lives.'

Negotiating challenges in doing research with young children

In doing research with children, a number of critical issues concerning ethical challenges and appropriate methodological approaches need to be negotiated and resolved. In this chapter, significant ethical considerations in doing research with young children are underlined. Some of these considerations include finding appropriate ways of ensuring young children are fully informed and give their consent to take part in research; accessing consent from appropriate gatekeepers; protecting children's right to confidentiality and privacy in the research process while, at the same time, being mindful of and attentive to the ethical implications of a child's disclosure revealing potential risk or harm. The task of balancing power differentials in the child-adult researcher relationship is also addressed and explored. Challenges with regard to participatory research with children identified by Waller and Bitou (2011) are focused on and further examined. Specifically, the effectiveness of child-centred research tools in engaging young children is explored, along with consideration of the extent to which participatory research actually empowers children. The chapter concludes with a focus on the dilemma that arises when, despite our efforts to design and develop effective, child-centred approaches to researching young children's perspectives, the ultimate interpretation of children's meanings and perceptions are from an adult researcher's perspective. Early childhood educators develop sensitive and accurate knowledge about the individual children they work with. One response to the dilemma of accurately interpreting young children's meanings is to encourage early years practitioners, many of whom have developed professional, reciprocal relationships with the children they work alongside, to engage in scaffolding and co-constructing meanings with young children in research. In the following chapter, this issue is further explored through a focus on conceptualising pedagogical documentation in early childhood education as research with children.

Positioning children as equal partners in research

A key challenge in doing research with children in the early years is being able to position children as equal partners in the research process. The close and trusting relationships, which many early childhood educators build with the children they work alongside, helps to address this challenge to some extent. Research activity is a relational activity and is dependent on building close and trusting relationships with participants, especially when doing research in the context of early childhood education with children as participants. Ethical issues need to be addressed as an ongoing process as part of this relational activity by, for example, including children themselves in the process of making the language used meaningful and accessible. Any critical discussion on the challenges of doing research with young children must begin with a focus on the theoretical underpinnings that frame research undertaken with young children. As highlighted in Chapter 1, the new sociology of childhood focuses on children as experts on their own lives (Clark & Moss, 2001; Mayall, 2002) and as being competent to share their views and opinions (James & Prout, 1997). Underpinning this perspective is recognition that children have agency, defined as 'the power to make decisions that impact on self and others and act on them' (Sancar & Severcan, 2010, p. 277). Such perspectives foreground the notion that it is the responsibility of researchers to ensure that children are considered as research partners in a meaningful way, with shared power in the process of the research.

As outlined in Chapter 1, qualitative research methodologies and diverse, creative methods in capturing children's meanings have enabled us to gain valuable insights into how to best approach doing research with young children. Child appropriate methods and strategies have contributed significantly to our understanding that young children are reliable informants, competent and capable of expressing their views and providing valuable and useful information (Clark, 2011; Clark & Moss, 2001; Murray, 2017). However, allied to this knowledge is an understanding that doing research with young children necessitates adopting different methodological approaches to accessing children's views and expression of their meanings. Increasingly, research involving young children has generated a variety of participatory and creative methods to ensure that children's views can inform research outcomes in a meaningful way (Bell, 2008).

Given the present focus on early childhood educators as researchers with young children, we may also assume a theoretical underpinning informed by a children's rights discourse and the inherent understanding that children have the right to express their views about matters that are significant in their lives. Children's rights also influence all aspects of research with young children (Mayne, Howitt & Rennie, 2018) with positive participation in research dependent on affording children sufficient 'space' to express their views, 'voice' where their opinions are heard, 'audience' in which more powerful others are prepared to listen, and 'influence' where action is taken on their behalf (Mayne et al., 2016, p. 675; Lundy, McEvoy & Byrne, 2011). In addition to the complexity of selecting and developing appropriate methods of gathering data from young children, the methodological and ethical challenges associated with interpreting and representing children's meanings are substantial and significant.

Negotiating ethical challenges in doing research with young children

Ethical challenges in doing research with young children are multiple and complex. The following sections provide an overview of some of the key issues that need to be addressed when designing research projects with children in the early years, with a specific focus on gaining assent from young children, gaining consent from appropriate gatekeepers, protecting young children's right to confidentiality and privacy and being mindful and attentive to the ethical implications of a child's disclosure revealing potential risk or harm.

Engaging in research with young children provides practitioners and researchers with a window of opportunity to develop an appropriate research space for children in which they can share deep thinking rather than superficial responses, which are generated in more token participatory methods (Mayne et al., 2018; Robbins, 2003). Key to developing such an appropriate research space is establishing a shared meaning about the purpose of the research to be undertaken. If opportunities are provided for responsibility and initiative through attempts to share power more equally between children and adults in a research process, there is the potential to generate meaningful insights into children's unique and unanticipated perspectives (Miles, 2018; Robbins, 2003). The notion of capturing children's meanings collaboratively requires researchers to provide opportunities for consideration with children of how adult and child might work together to support each other's meaning making (Mayne et al., 2016; Wyness, 2012). Several levels of gatekeeping are also involved in research projects involving children in the early years, including the child's assent and the permission of their parents and other relevant gatekeepers.

Meaningful ways of seeking assent from young children

Research that reflects a participatory rights perspective and that positions children as agentic and capable of active citizenship emphasises the importance of children making informed decisions about their participation (Dockett & Perry, 2011). Though children do not have the legal capacity to consent to participate in research, they should be involved in the process if they are able to assent to participate by being given relevant and comprehensive material in language that is easily accessible. Beyond a simple focus on agreement to participate, however, assent is best understood as embedded, on an ongoing basis, within the relationship between the researcher and child (Dockett & Perry, 2011). Specifically, assent from children to participate in research is meaningful when the researcher's presence is accepted positively by the child and when the researcher is attuned to the child's actions in such a way as to be able to identify and respond to any sense of uneasiness or disinterest (Harcourt, Perry & Waller, 2011). Seeking informed assent from children is, therefore, an invitation to children to be partners in the research project and involves a relational process whereby children's participation decisions arise from ongoing negotiation between child and researcher.

Inviting assent from children in meaningful ways includes facilitating discussion and exploration of the roles and responsibilities of those participating in the research project as an important initial step in engaging children in the process (Mayne, Howitt & Rennie, 2018). Ensuring that children have a good grasp of and input into the different methods that may be used to collect and analyse data, and ensuring a clear understanding of the fact that the data may be shared with others, must also be emphasised (Dockett & Perry, 2011). Communicating information in a language that is appropriate and accessible, in order to allow young children to make an informed decision about participation, is also essential. The importance of monitoring young children's willingness to participate on an ongoing basis, rather than simply carrying out a theoretical exercise at the beginning of the research process, is highlighted by Johnson, Hart and Colwell (2014a). Key details to communicate to children are the precise expectations that researchers have of the children's participation, along with the consequences and possible risks of taking part. Of primary importance in this communication is explaining to young children that participation is voluntary and that they are free to withdraw at any time (Ericsson & Boyd, 2017; Mayne, Howie & Rennitt, 2016).

> **Key features of seeking meaningful assent from children**
>
> - Providing children with comprehensive, meaningful, accessible information about what the research is about and what will be expected of the child as a participant.
> - Inviting children to be partners in the research project.

- Ensuring educator/researcher's presence is accepted positively by the child.
- Ensuring educator/researcher is attuned to the child's actions in such a way as to be able to identify and respond to any sense of uneasiness or disinterest.
- Facilitating discussion and exploration of the roles and responsibilities of those participating in the research project.
- Ensuring that children have a good grasp of and input into the different methods used to collect and analyse data.
- Ensuring children understand the data may be shared with other people.
- Communicating information in a language that is appropriate and accessible, to allow young children make an informed decision.
- Monitoring young children's willingness to participate on an ongoing basis.
- Communicating to children the precise expectations that researchers have of their participation, along with the consequences and possible risks of taking part.
- Explaining to young children that participation is voluntary and that they are free to withdraw at any time.

Challenges in seeking assent from young children

One of the most significant challenges in developing effective strategies for obtaining young children's assent to participate in research is the fact that all children are individual and unique and, therefore, strategies for seeking assent may need to be tailored to suit these individual differences. Characteristics such as temperament, personality factors, and the child's learning dispositions all require the researcher to be sensitively attuned to the varied needs and abilities of young participant children (Conroy & Harcourt, 2009). Early years practitioners working closely with children are in a uniquely privileged position in terms of being familiar with these individual characteristics. Young children's varying cognitive abilities, particularly the range of abilities with regard to children's language comprehension and expression, can represent a very significant challenge to overcome. Contradictions may exist between using a child-centred approach to research and the traditional consenting processes that virtually exclude children's voices (Ford et al., 2007). Informative and creative ways of seeking assent are highlighted by these authors, who emphasise the benefits of involving young children themselves in the process of developing meaningful ethical forms. Specifically, discussions and conversations with children facilitate better insight into appropriate phrasing, familiarity with vocabulary and length of sentences that work best to communicate meanings to young children. In turn, when children who are invited to participate in research are able to fully understand what is being asked of them, they are empowered in their decision-making processes. Valuable and helpful guidelines in developing meaningful ways of seeking children's assent to take part in research are outlined below by Johnson et al. (2014b).

Steps for engaging young children in research
Johnson, Hart and Colwell (2014b, Vol 2)

Purposes: To provide an opportunity for the children to indicate whether they are happy or otherwise with the process/activity or explanation you have provided about the research.

- Take time to ensure that the children feel able to indicate their true thoughts/feelings, i.e. they feel able to indicate they are unhappy and they are awsare that there will be no negative consequences for not wishing to take part in research.

- This activity can be easily slotted into the time needed to discuss the research process and/or activities with the children. It will take around 10 minutes the first time and then two minutes as the children get used to the process. If the children are indicating they are unhappy or unclear about the process, time will be needed to rectify the issues.

- Time to make the flags or paddles will also be needed. The materials needed for this activity can be made by the researcher or the children.

- Each child must have access to a flag or paddle, which has two sides. One side must indicate that the child is happy, e.g. a smiling face, a sunshine, or a tick. The opposite side must indicate that the child is unhappy or unclear, e.g. a sad face, a thunder cloud, or a cross.

- The children and the researcher must select the most appropriate sign for the children they are working with. These materials can be re-used throughout the research process.

- As you describe the research process and/or activities it is important that you check that the children understand and are happy to proceed.

- Once you feel the children understand the process you can ask them to raise their flag or paddle to answer questions. For example, you could explain the activity you have planned and ask the children to indicate if they are happy to participate in that activity using the flag or paddle. You could then inform the children about who you will share the data with and ask them to indicate with the flag or paddle if they are happy for that to happen.

- Time may be needed to ensure that the children feel able to show their true feelings. This method can provide a very quick and simple way of checking if the children are happy with the process.

- Once the children are able to use this method it can be used to gauge the children's feelings very quickly and alert you to any potential problems.

Key features of seeking assent from young children to participate in research include providing appropriate information, creating ample opportunities to discuss this information and to expand on it if necessary, and ensuring there is time for children to make their decision (Dockett, Perry & Kearney, 2013). Prior research favours sharing this information with children using formats that combine images and text, as this makes information more easily accessible to young children. Such a format is also more likely to attract children's interest and promote understanding (Kress & Van Leeuwen, 2006). A simple child assent form developed by Dockett et al. (2013), which combines information about the research project, is presented below in the Focus on Research, which is based on a review of a number of strategies designed to facilitate providing children with opportunities to make choices about research participation.

FOCUS ON RESEARCH

Promoting children's informed assent in research participation

Dockett, Perry and Kearney (2013)

Study aims

To facilitate children's choices about research participation, the authors reviewed a number of information sheets, assent forms and/or statements that had been developed in previous research (Bruzzesse & Fisher, 2003; Einarsdóttir, 2007; Ford et al., 2007; Hurley & Underwood, 2002; Moore, McArthur & Noble-Carr, 2008).

- From these, the authors constructed an information/assent form and an information form accompanied by a separate text document, which mirrored that seeking parent/guardian consent.
- The different versions of the form were developed with the aim of appealing to children across the range of pre-school to upper primary and secondary school settings.

(Continued)

34 Negotiating challenges in doing research

■ Teachers of pre-school and early years of school groups chose the combined information/assent form below.

Child assent form

We would like to find out about your town. We would like to talk to you about the things you like to do in your town and what it is like to live in your town.

We might ask you to have a conversation with us, take some photos, draw some pictures, make a model or tell us in some other way about your town.

We would like to record these activities.

We will look at and listen back to what you tell us about your town so we can tell other people the types of things you would like to have in your town.

When we tell other people what you think about your town we won't use your real name.

Would you like to choose another name for us to use?

_____

You can tell us anything you like about your town, but if you tell us something that makes us worried about your safety we will tell someone who can help you.

We have asked your parents if it is ok if we talk to you and they have said yes. Now we want to know if you would like to talk to us about what you like about your town?

If you would like to talk to us please write your name just here.

_____

And /or you can circle the face that tells us how you feel about talking to us.

If once you have started to talk to us and you decide you no longer want to talk to us that is ok, you can stop, we won't mind.

If you have any questions or would like to talk about this, ask your Mum, Dad or teacher to phone us on 02 6051 9403 or email Sue

sdockett@csu.edu.au

Thank you for your help

An interactive narrative approach to informing young children about research

An interactive narrative approach to informed consent/assent for young children is proposed by Mayne et al. (2016) and is reinforced as a successful and appropriate method for engaging children in discussion about issues that affect them (McIntosh & Stephens, 2011). This approach is similar to that outlined above but focuses on using a storytelling approach to providing information on the proposed study. For many young children, storytelling and narratives are a familiar part of young children's everyday lives. A key strength of such an approach is that it is built on interactions between the child and the adult researcher or practitioner. This narrative approach to seeking assent from children adopts the use of a storybook, which draws on both text and images to communicate the details of the research project that children are being introduced to. The narrative part of this approach involves two sections – the first section provides information to the child about the research project and the second section focuses on what participation would involve and how the child might actually convey their assent/dissent. The final pages of the story provide value-neutral information about making a participation choice and signifying consent (Mayne et al., 2016).

The extent to which images, such as photographs of people involved in the research and the research setting, are included can be decided on by researchers and others involved in the study. Computer technology can be used in such an approach and children's engagement with the story and the details of the story may be enhanced using interactive technologies such as a touchscreen and sound effects. This approach can also be achieved through the use of a more traditional hard copy document. The research story can be read to individual children or to small groups of children (Mayne et al., 2016). In the Focus on Research below, an example of this approach is provided in a study carried out by Martin and Buckley (2018) on including children's voices in an initiative to improve quality in an early years setting.

FOCUS ON RESEARCH

Including children's voices in a multiple stakeholder study on a community-wide approach to improving quality in early years setting

Martin and Buckley (2018)

Study aims

To include the voices of young children in an ongoing evaluation of a community-based prevention and early intervention programme.

- Children's voices were included in the project evaluation through participatory research methods including 12 young children (aged 3–4 years) in a pre-school setting.
- Informed consent was sought from the children through two steps: informing and consenting. Children can only provide their consent if they understand their role in the study and the purpose of the study.
- To inform the children about the study, the researcher developed a picture book about the research project, which introduces the researcher and the purpose of the study in a visual and child friendly way.
- This follows the approach of 'narrative non-fiction', which has been established as a means of ethical informing where the researcher 'establishes the research context and purpose, rules of participation, and information in the form of a factual narrative, supported by photographs of real people, places, and events' (Mayne, Howitt & Rennie, 2016, p. 683).
- The storybook was developed in conjunction with the pre-school staff to make sure it was appropriate to the children's age and cultural understanding.
- Once the informing step was complete, consent was sought from the children verbally and children could also answer yes or no or give a thumbs up and thumbs down sign.

(Continued)

- The child was given the opportunity to ask questions and the researcher took the opportunity to explain anything that was not clear.
- Additionally, children who did not want to participate were to be offered an alternative activity by pre-school staff and they could demonstrate their consent non-verbally by moving to a different part of the room and participating in another activity.
- The children's ongoing assent was monitored by the researchers and by the pre-school staff who were very familiar with the children and work with them on a daily basis.

(a)

(b)

Figure 2.1 Extracts from picture books for seeking informed assent with children (Martin & Buckley, 2018; Merewether, 2018)

Gaining consent from appropriate gatekeepers

Gaining assent from children is challenging and requires careful and ongoing monitoring of individual children's responses throughout the research process. Negotiating access to and consent from a number of other gatekeepers in research projects is equally important.

Research involving children in early childhood education settings requires informed consent to be obtained from children's parents and, where relevant, from early years practitioners working alongside young children. The primary gatekeepers for obtaining such consent will be staff in the early childhood setting and, in particular, the manager of the setting. When seeking consent from parents or even managers and other gatekeepers, it is important to be mindful of the potential risk of causing anxiety or distress to parents who may find it difficult to refuse to allow their children to take part in research projects, due to fear of possible negative consequences for their child or the service their child receives (Dockett et al., 2013; Flewitt, 2005). Due to the potential sensitivity of these relationships, it is necessary that parents and other potential participants are provided with both formal and informal opportunities to express their wish to *not* participate in the research.

Protecting young children's right to confidentiality and privacy in the research process

Ensuring privacy and confidentiality to participants in research with young children can also be particularly challenging. Young children may express the wish that their identity is not anonymised in publications resulting from the research. Harcourt (2008) provides an example of this with reference to a study carried out on children's views about quality in ECE. The author reported a group of children, aged 5 years, requesting that their real names be used, because they indicated that using their real names says who they really are (Conroy & Harcourt, 2009). Sensitive issues may also arise where other people, including parents, may be interested in having access to data collected. However, the researcher is obliged to respect children's wishes should they not wish for this information to be shared and to ensure that the information remains confidential. The importance of allowing children to express their views privately, if they so wish, in a secure space and without being overheard is also important to include in planning for research with young children.

Disclosures revealing potential risk or harm

The primary importance of ensuring confidentiality and anonymity in research with children cannot be overestimated. However, research with young children is unique in terms of not being possible to ensure and guarantee such confidentiality (Einarsdóttir, 2007; Hill, 2005). Profound difficulties can arise in cases where a researcher becomes aware of issues concerning child safety and child protection. Unanticipated issues may be identified in a situation where a child includes information that gives rise to concern, or, more directly, where a child reports incidents causing potential harm or abuse. As Graham, Power and Taylor (2015) point out, respect for the child's autonomy and right to confidentiality may directly conflict with the researcher's ethical responsibility to ensure that children are protected from harm. Researchers in the dual role of early years practitioner and researcher may find this dilemma particularly challenging. In the child and parental information sheets and consent forms distributed to families, a clear statement of the early years practitioner's and researcher's ethical responsibility to ensure the child's protection should be clearly highlighted. Key ethical issues to be considered when involving young children in research are summarised below, adapted from Graham, Powell and Taylor (2015).

Ethical research involving children: Encouraging reflexive engagement in research with children and young people

Graham, Powell and Taylor (2015)

Guiding issues

Potential harms and benefits

Assessing potential harms/benefits in research involving children

Minimising/eliminating potential harm/distress

Researchers' responsibilities if children show signs of harm/distress

Appropriate follow-up services for children/parents

Ensuring children's participation in research is equitable

Informed consent/assent

Child's capability of providing consent

Parental/adult consent required

Ensuring children are fully informed

Ensuring children's consent is freely given

Respecting children's dissent

Privacy and Confidentiality

Ensuring privacy if not a social/cultural practice

Selecting location that guarantees privacy

Ensuring confidentiality with groups/focus groups

Limits to confidentiality when safety/wellbeing concerns arise

Children (or parents) may not wish to be anonymous

Privacy and confidentiality challenges related to technology

Negotiating methodological challenges in research with young children

Can participatory methods really empower young children in research?

Critiques of terms such as 'participatory methods' and the notion of empowerment through participation have been raised in the literature on research methods with young children. Gallacher and Gallagher (2008) argue that participatory approaches, rather than enhancing children's opportunities for spontaneous involvement, may involve children in processes that tend to regulate and possibly constrain them. Given that many of the participatory research methods are designed by adults, the authors suggest that such research might be understood as a process of socialisation through which children are taught to conform to adult norms and to value 'adult cultures' over their own.

The use of participation has also been contested in early years literature (Tisdall, 2015), with preferences for terms such as *listening* over participation being highlighted. Listening can be considered to be part of the act of participation, but it also goes beyond participation alone and can be better understood as an 'ethic of relating to others' (Moss et al., 2005, pp. 8–9, cited in Tisdall, 2015). Waller (2006) argues that rather than just thinking about engaging children's views to inform research (or influence curriculum planning and design) we need to rethink participation also in terms of 'spaces for childhood', within which children can exercise their agency to participate in their own decisions, actions and meaning-making, which may or may not involve them engaging with adults.

Waller and Bitou (2011) explore the use of participatory techniques with young children in research with a particular focus on the following questions: (1) Does using 'participatory' tools (such as cameras) necessarily engage children? (2) Does the adult research agenda inevitably change children's experiences? And (3) How does participatory research empower children? With regard to the first of these questions, the authors point out that, while the value of developing effective, creative and appropriate research methods for working with young children is undeniable, there may be an assumption that the tools themselves can automatically guarantee participation. However, the primary implication that has been generated from the literature is that it is both the research design *and* relationships that facilitate and generate children's meaningful participation and engagement. Providing children with effective tools to access their meanings can be greatly enhanced if we ensure that children themselves are centrally involved in the selection of the tools to be used. As highlighted previously, the importance of the adult researcher's presence being accepted by children is essential to enable meaningful participation. The challenge of how adults become accepted as a member of children's groups in order to understand and interpret children's experiences and perspectives is a significant one, and as previously highlighted, early years practitioners are well positioned to take on this role due to their familiarity with the individual children they are working with Children may also exercise agency with the cameras provided by adults but choose not to contribute to the research agenda (Gallacher & Gallagher, 2008).

The second issue that Waller and Bitou (2011) draw attention to is whether the adult research agenda will inevitably change children's experiences as they engage in the research process. For example, providing children with cameras to take photographs, in order to access their views, may have an impact on and ultimately change their normal activity and place more emphasis on the adult agenda of the researcher. What children choose to take photos of may have more to do with the novelty of having cameras to engage with rather than the particular meanings that children themselves wish to express. In terms of responding to the third issue raised by Waller and Bitou (2011), the authors conclude further that these photographic and video images do not empower children on their own, but it is the shared construction of knowledge around conversations with the children based on their photographs that can enable children's meaning to prevail. As Cook and Hess (2007) argue, joint discussion of photographs between children and adults involves a deeper analysis and can generate further insights.

Terms such as empowerment and transformation have typically been used alongside the notion of participation. Yet, the extent to which participatory approaches actually manage to empower in practice is less known. Tisdall (2015) further points out that children's participation can be manipulated to enable those with power to maintain the status quo. Other authors draw attention to the fact that participation *techniques* have been emphasised in research with young children, rather than the *meaning* of participation (Leal, 2010). Related to this it can be argued that some research activities concentrate on engaging people rather than putting efforts into ensuring accountability to participants.

Interpreting children's meanings

Three key aspects of analysing and interpreting young children's data are briefly addressed in the following sections. These include: the risk of impeding an understanding of children's meaning through a primary focus on adult assumptions; the need to adopt an open attitude and to take into account children's non-verbal signals, where relevant and possible; and placing an emphasis on adults co-constructing meanings with young children, which includes consulting with children in terms of how best to represent their meanings.

Awareness of adult assumptions

A key challenge for researchers working with young children is knowing how to interpret, understand and represent children's meanings in a way that reflects the child's authentic views. In the literature on participatory methods there is a broad consensus that the interpretation of children's perspectives is generally made from an adult point of view (Waller & Bitou, 2011). Moreover, the literature on analysing and interpreting young children's data provides insufficient guidance to help researchers move from listening to young children to understanding them (Colliver, 2017). The value of researchers analysing young children's data with a critical view of their own assumptions about key concepts is underscored in research by Miles (2018) where children's responses to an event or a phenomenon being explored through a particular research focus may not coincide with adult researcher expectations, and, at times, researchers need to be able to step back from an overly narrow focus on the research agenda. Fleer (2016, p. 16) emphasises the importance of aspiring to achieve a 'contextual intersubjectivity', whereby the adult shifts her/his understanding towards that of children, in order to be able to capture children's meanings more accurately. As Cook and Hess (2007, p. 44, cited in Waller & Bitou, 2011) argue, young children's perspectives are 'fragile', and 'can easily be crushed by adult researchers who cannot move from their own version of experience.'

Adopting an 'open attitude' to listening to young children

In doing research with young children, it is also necessary to be aware that while the content of what children say or communicate visually through drawing and photographs and other creative methods is important, the value of attending to children's non-verbal expression, where this is relevant and possible, is also underlined by researchers in the field of early childhood education. If we only pay attention to verbal expression and neglect to take into account non-verbal, bodily communication, there is a risk of limiting our capacity to fully understand children's perspectives (Akin, 2011). Examples of such non-verbal messages include a child walking away instead of responding to a question or an activity. Researchers in the field of early childhood education have emphasised that such responses on behalf of children can signal how (un)interesting or (un)comfortable the research might be for participating children (Dockett, Einarsdóttir & Perry, 2017; Pálmadóttir & Einarsdóttir, 2015).

Co-constructing meanings in research with young children

Co-constructing meanings with children focuses on the inclusion of children's voices as an integral part of the research process and prioritises collaboration with adult facilitators. The actual participation of children within a research process is, for all parties, an experience in co-construction of meaning (Conroy & Harcourt, 2009). Facilitating children's meaningful partnership within the research process requires the re-conceptualisation of some of the existing practices and attitudes. To what extent do adult interpretations of children's expressions and representations influence, or alter, the meanings identified in research? To what extent do they misrepresent the original meanings that children wish to convey? The imbalance of power within the relationship of adult-child co-researchers, and the way we 'see' children, would seem to be critical barriers to research processes and protocols that respect children's competence.

3 Documenting children's meanings

In this chapter, the focus is on documenting children's meanings in early childhood research and practice. The chapter opens with a broad contemplation on the role and nature of documenting children's meanings in the early years. The focus then moves more specifically to the role of pedagogical documentation as research, with a particular emphasis on early childhood educators' skills and dispositions in accessing children's views and their ability to accurately interpret and co-construct young children's meanings. The term 'pedagogical documentation' is defined and the associated aim of making development and learning visible in early childhood education through documenting young children's everyday experiences is emphasised. Drawing on principles of the Reggio Emilia approach to early childhood education, pedagogical documentation emphasises the practitioner's role in inquiring into, recording, reflecting on and sharing data that communicates and displays aspects of children's learning and development alongside their thoughts, feelings and values. Finally, the chapter moves to focus on the importance of pedagogical documentation as a generative process of learning in action (Roosevelt, 2007) where, through reviewing and re-organising thought and action, a transformation of thinking can take place. This transformation of thinking may include new ways of understanding the world from a child's perspective, thereby contributing to reducing the gap between the child and the adult world. A key feature of such a process is the co-construction of meaning between the child and the adult practitioner or researcher. The benefits of such a process include reciprocal learning for children and adults, which, through facilitating greater 'symmetry between the two viewpoints ... can give rise to a more equitable reality of childhood' (Harcourt, 2011, p. 343) and a more balanced understanding of children's worlds.

Documentation in the traditional use of the term includes a focus on gathering information, through textual, visual, or audio artefacts, in order to demonstrate or provide evidence of a particular event, process or phenomenon. A shift in the emphasis of the meaning of the term 'documentation' is implicit in the practice of pedagogical documentation. Whereas previously the term denoted a gathering of documents and records to build and provide evidence, the term has been animated in its more recent usages to include a focus on observing, recording, interpreting and sharing thought (Krechevsky et al., 2010, p. 65) – activities that are core practices in any research process. Pedagogical documentation is described by Dahlberg, Moss and Pence (2007) as playing a central role in the discourse of meaning-making. Most significantly, pedagogical documentation places a greater emphasis on possibilities for *generating* rather than simply *collecting* and presenting static knowledge. An essential dimension to the process of pedagogical documentation is that of interpretation and analysis, allowing us to extend and expand our understandings through shared explorations of documentation. The concept of pedagogical documentation is most frequently associated with the Reggio Emilia approach to early childhood education and learning. The concepts and principles underpinning the Reggio Emilia approach have been captured and summarised across many publications. A well-established publication that tends to be cited with reference to these key principles is *The Hundred Languages of Children* (Edwards, Gandini & Forman, 1998). Other terms that tend to be used synonymously include *pedagogic documentation, educational documentation* and *pedagogical narration* (Fleet, Patterson & Robertson, 2017, p. 14).

Capturing and documenting meanings through slowing down

An important feature in an effective pedagogical approach to learning and development is a calm, slow pace in which children have space and time to lead their learning (Dalli, White, Rockel & Duhn, 2011). However, the ability to give space and time to observe and document as the basis of a responsive pedagogy is dependent on supportive structural conditions, such as adequate ratio of educators to children (Dalli et al., 2011).

Young children are developing within contexts that typically involve an emphasis on speed – getting things done – and that often involve information overload and multiple distractions (Hayes, 2013). These hurried environments are also populated by adults and educators who deal with the stress of working under pressure to meet significant deadlines. Young children need time to wonder, time to take a closer look and to pay attention to those things that their curiosity naturally draws them toward. The value and importance of calm and predictable early experiences that provide children with encouragement and sufficient time and space to develop the necessary skills to live in and adapt to their changing contexts is emphasised. Hayes (2013, p. 34) states that a key contribution of quality early years practice to these developments is the provision of unhurried learning environments where practitioners themselves are calm and understand and respect the central developmental features of early childhood that need to be developed and refined during this first stage of education.

A significant feature of documentation, and pedagogical documentation in particular, is the prominence it accords to encouraging and enabling a slowing down of the process of observing children's interests and activities through its emphasis on wondering and collaborating with other practitioners (Wien, Guyevskey & Berdoussis, 2011).

> Pedagogical documentation stops the train of standardized expectations and slows down our thinking processes to consider some topic with exquisite care.
>
> (Wien et al., 2011)

The pressure on early childhood educators to deliver an early years curriculum involves stress and speed, including the demands of filling in paperwork without always having a clear rationale for why this is needed and meeting the multiple requirements of an early childhood education curriculum. However, through engaging with meaningful documentation, early years practitioners 'placehold' events in order to study and interpret children's meanings, together with other children and adults and, most importantly, with these children themselves (Wien, 2013, p. 2). In this way, over time and through collaboration, children and practitioners generate and further develop theories about children's social, intellectual, physical, and emotional strategies of communication.

> Out of that slowed-down process of teacher research, we have the potential to discover thoughtful, caring, innovative responses that expand our horizons. We discover what we did not yet know how to see. Pedagogical documentation inserts a new phase of thinking and wondering together between the act of observation and the act of planning a response.
>
> (Wien, 2013, p. 2)

The importance of slowing down and tuning into children's learning and development is reinforced through findings from an exploratory study on the *why* and *how* of learning for infants and young children (Dalli et al., 2011, p. 6), where a strong emphasis is placed on having a calm, slow focus to facilitate 'watchful attentiveness'. Specifically, researchers worked with twelve practitioners from five infant and toddler centres in Auckland and Wellington to clarify the *what, hows and whys* of infant and toddler pedagogy. Dialogue between the researchers and the educators identified a range of ways in which they constructed the child as a learner, including the child as discoverer, as sense-maker, as embodied learner and as a future world citizen, but also as vulnerable and seeking security. A key message to emerge from this study was the value and importance of providing a space for children to create and play, and of generating opportunities for educators to follow children's current interests, thereby enabling access to greater depth and breadth of knowledge.

Specific practitioner skills identified that were required to achieve this attentiveness included the ability to attain emotional attunement and orientation to the child's experiences (Dalli et al., 2011). Notwithstanding the emphasis on spontaneity and naturalness that pedagogical documentation implies, the value of systematic and methodical planning, reflection and reviewing cannot be over-emphasised in this approach. Meticulous consideration of and deliberation on the aim of the documentation, the specific participants around which documentation is focused, and the audience the data generated is targeting all shape the design of the documentation tools and methods.

Making learning and meanings visible through documentation

The importance of making learning visible both inside and beyond the classroom has been well established in a large body of literature, much of which was inspired and generated in response to the Reggio Emilia approach to learning and development in the early years (Clark, 2017; Clark & Moss, 2001; Krechevesky, Rivard & Burton, 2010; Krechevsky, Mardell, Rivard & Wilson, 2013; Wien, 2011). The Making Learning Visible project (Project Zero) has focused on supporting and nurturing powerful learning communities through a precise focus on the dynamics of individual and group learning processes. Project Zero researchers collaborated with educators from the Municipal Preschools and Infant-toddler Centres in Reggio Emilia, Italy. During the first decade of the 2000s, Project Zero researchers worked with educators across the US to develop ways to support children and adults' individual and group learning by collecting and reviewing documentation of how and what children learn.

The concept of making learning visible foregrounds the notion of 'being accountable to progressive ideals in an age of skills-based learning and standardized testing' (Krechevsky, Rivard & Burton, 2010, p. 64). These authors further highlight three particular forms of accountability that are important to address in our research and practice with children in the early years, and more broadly across the wider educational contexts.

The first of these, *accountability to self*, involves being reflective as an early years practitioner and, moreover, being aware of the extent to which there is genuine commitment to achieving and realising aspirations in practice. Documenting children's learning facilitates an ongoing review and revisiting of work and activities. Reflective documentation provides a means for a comparison between what is aspired to and what is achieved in practice. In this way, documentation enables early years practitioners to collaborate with children in order to deepen their understanding of their own learning and to become better observers of learning in the process. *Accountability to each other* involves contributing to collective learning as well as to one's own learning. Krechevsky et al. (2010) highlight that documentation plays a key role both in supporting individual and group learning and in building a collective identity. Sharing meanings and practices through documentation facilitates collaboration between early years practitioners both within and beyond settings. Parents and other family members can also contribute effectively to this sharing of children's meanings and learning. Finally, the importance of *accountability to the larger community* is emphasised by Krechevsky et al. (2010) as a means of extending the learning experience to the wider public and contributing to the collective knowledge about how children learn. The authors conclude that documentation does not set out to assess children's progress but rather it provides a portrait of a group of children and adults as a learning community. Documentation opens up possibilities for building and deepening both individual and collective understanding of how children learn in, and as, a group.

Conceptualising pedagogical documentation as research with children

Early childhood is an area of increasing focus in the research field – research that includes explorations with young children, with their families and with relevance for their communities (Farrell, Kagan & Tisdall, 2016). Research in early childhood education, as an empirical driver of the development of policy initiatives with the aim of enhancing young children's learning and development, cannot be overestimated. The Effective Provision for Preschool Education (EPPE) study was the first major European longitudinal study of a national sample of young children's development between the ages of 3 and 7 years (Sylva, Melhuish, Sammons, Siraj-Blatchford & Taggart, 2004). The EPPE team collected a wide range of information on 3,000 children in order to investigate the effects of preschool education. The study also looked at background characteristics related to parents, the child's home environment and the pre-school settings children attended. While children's perspectives were not included as a focus in the EPPE study, it has become well known for its contribution to evidence based policy in early years education and care. Findings are robust because they are based on sound and innovative research methods. Significantly, the findings of the EPPE project and the associated implications for policy have been acted on at national and local level. EPPE set out to contribute to the debate about the education and care of young children; the EPPE mixed-method research design targeted issues that could 'make a difference' to the lives of young children and their families (Sylva et al., 2009, p. 9).

Specifically, the EPPE research explored preschool education and concluded that high quality preschool education had an impact on positive developmental outcomes for children; EPPE's qualitative studies *'gave detailed information for practitioners on aspects of effective practice and highlighted areas which might provide quality experiences for young children'* (Taggart, 2010, p. 214). Allied to this expanding field of research in the early years is the increasing participation of early childhood educators or 'practitioner-researchers' (Farrell et al., 2016, p. 5). In the UK, research carried out by early years practitioners has expanded, supported by the emergence of the Mosaic approach, developed by Clark and Moss (2001) and Clark, Kjorholt and Moss (2005). The conceptual underpinnings of respect for childhood, children's rights, children's agency and competence have generated methodologies that expand opportunities for children's participation in both the processes of designing and planning the research (Farrell et al., 2016a) and for accessing and facilitating the expression of children's meanings.

As part of the longitudinal study of early years professional status, a study was carried out to ascertain how Early Years Professionals (EYPs) use and respond to children's perspectives to inform their practice and improve the quality of their provision (Coleyshaw, Whitmarsh, Jopling & Hadfield, 2010). Three distinct stages of development in the use of children's perspectives in early years settings were identified. The first of these represented a relatively naïve view of children's perspectives, primarily focused on facilitating children's *choice* and access to resources and activities. These settings demonstrated more limited awareness of how to support children in expressing their views and how to encourage, facilitate and respond to children's perspectives in practice. A second level of expertise in facilitating children's perspectives in ECE settings adopted a more *consultative* approach. These settings set children's perspectives in the context of choice and access to resources and activities, but also recognised the need to restrict choice in certain contexts, for example to allow quieter children to have a voice. Early years practitioners in these settings had also begun to encourage children's criticality in terms of expressing negative views of provision, but this remained limited. Finally, EYPs and settings with mature approaches to children's perspectives demonstrated a critical understanding of how to facilitate and co-construct their participation with the children and provide feedback to them. They regarded as essential the development of children's ability to be critical and recognised the importance of giving them a safe space and the language to do this. These settings had also embedded an ethos of using children's perspectives into their practice, regarding them as both a quality assurance process *and* an outcome of quality.

In Australia, early childhood practitioner research is featured in the Research in Practice series published by Australia's professional body Early Childhood Australia (Goodfellow, 2009; Goodfellow & Hedges, 2007). In a number of early childhood educational research projects in New Zealand, everyday documentation of EYPs forms the backbone of the data. The transformative potential of research to support and enhance change and development in the research setting, and in those involved in those research contexts (Farrell et al., 2016), is emphasised in these examples. Carlina Rinaldi, in her final presentation to the United States delegation during a study tour in March 2003, stated:

> I would like to underscore something that has been, and continues to be, one of the most significant elements among those that we have tried to highlight for you during these days ... an element that has been fundamental to our experience: the concept of the teacher as a researcher ... Only searching and researching can guarantee us that which is new, that which is moving forward. Yet, this normality excludes research as an everyday approach and, therefore, excludes doubt, error, uncertainty, curiosity, marvel and amazement as important values in our daily lives.
>
> (Rinaldi, 2003, pp. 1–2)

Pedagogical documentation, in particular, describes the many ways of capturing young children's meanings, of getting close to children's lived experiences, and of attempting to understand what matters in children's worlds, while seeking meaningful and innovative ways to achieve these aims. In the Focus on Research below, pedagogical documentation is explored as an approach for teacher-researchers' listening in outdoor early years settings.

FOCUS ON RESEARCH

Listening to young children outdoors with pedagogical documentation

Merewether (2018)

Study aims

To explore children's perspectives on outdoor spaces in pedagogical settings through pedagogical documentation.

- The study informing this article was conducted over a 12-month period at a metropolitan early learning centre (hereafter, 'the Centre') in Western Australia, which welcomes thirty-five 2- to 4-year-old children. The researcher visited the Centre at least one full day per week, and often on other occasions.

- Children were not separated by age in the Centre; all were free to move between the indoor and outdoor areas, apart from during rest and for most meetings and mealtimes, which happened inside.

- The research focused on seventeen 2- to 3-year-olds, but other children also contributed as part of the Centre's milieu.

Observations

- Most of the observations took place when the researcher joined children in their everyday activities, often at their behest, although she also requested permission to join children's activities on some occasions. The researcher sometimes just sat and chatted with children as they worked with things like paint, clay, water, construction, and gardening, but she frequently became a fellow participant.

Conversations

- Conversations with children in the early stages of verbal development are not dominated by children's words. Therefore, listening to them requires listening not just with our ears but with all our senses.

- Children's contributions to conversations were frequently gestural – they nodded, shook their heads, smiled, frowned, pointed, looked away or towards, showed, etc.

Documenting children's meanings

Photography

- The study used both adults' and children's photography. Photos formed part of the field notes, as a camera enabled the researcher to quickly record details of the environment and events whilst participating in activities with children. The researcher used the photos to prompt memory when writing in the research journal.

- From the outset, children showed great interest in the camera, so the researcher suggested they too might like to use it. This was greeted with much enthusiasm, so children were invited in pairs to take the researcher on 'tours' (Clark & Moss, 2001) around the outdoor space at the Centre and to photograph what they thought to be 'good'.

- During these tours, children wore audio recorders suspended on lanyards around their necks; recordings were later transcribed.

- The researcher learned much from children on the tours, in which they participated with gusto. She printed photos from each child's tour and later invited them to look at them and place stickers on three photos showing things that were 'really good' (Figures 3.1 through 3.3).

Figure 3.1 Leaf design

(Continued)

Figure 3.2 Looking at photos

Figure 3.3 Lylah's photo

Writing

- Writing took various forms that not only provided ways to record observations but also allowed the researcher to see more clearly relationships amongst people and materials. Writing began well before the researcher's work at the Centre. Beforehand, for example, short recollections were written of being outside as a child and a teacher, and accounts of everyday outdoor experiences, such as gardening

In the study outlined above, Merewether (2018) emphasises that writing is at the heart of pedagogical documentation and is an essential component of the analysis and method of discovery, foregrounded in such research with children. Handwritten field notes were also an essential element of the pedagogical documentation process in this study. The researcher also indicated that writing in a notebook tended to attract the attention of the participant children, who were curious about what was being documented. Children frequently asked the researcher what she was writing or instructed her as to what to write in it, as captured in the extract below:

> 'Write we like swinging' (Amber, 3 years, 8 months); 'I like it when we take photos. Write that' (Izze, 3 years, 8 months). Younger children often sidled up to me as I wrote. Then, having captured my attention, they would insist I watch as they appeared to perform for the notebook. 'Should I write that down?' I would enquire, invariably to an affirmative response.
> (Merewether, 2018, p. 272)

Key elements in this study also included a research journal in which the researcher typed up field notes at a later point and added reflections, questions, photos and other images, along with plans for the emerging study. Moreover, a documentation book was developed including snippets of conversations, photographs and the researcher's interpretations and it was made visible to children, teachers and families associated with the research project.

Significantly, Merewether (2018, p. 273) stresses the importance of what she terms the 'material-discursive entanglement' of pedagogical documentation – the ongoing reviewing and revisiting of an assemblage of materials and methods, shared and discussed with colleagues, in order to interpret and extend meanings. What distinguishes pedagogical documentation from more linear approaches to research with children is the assemblage of all elements – observations, notes, photos, words and children's work, alongside the practitioner/researcher's strategies, which operate in an ever-unfolding relationship with each other.

Learning stories in pedagogical documentation

Learning stories are a particular form of pedagogical documentation, in which early years practitioners formulate details of a child's learning process, which are articulated as a letter to the child and supported with photos and other visual representations of the selected situation (Zhang, 2017). As a form of documentation, learning stories are designed to enable consideration of and deliberation on children's educational processes, with a particular focus on the strengths of the child. A learning story draws attention to where the learning occurred, the context of the learning moment, who was involved and how it began (Carr & Lee, 2019). Each learning story may be crafted and created in different ways, with some including a lot of direct interactions and verbalisations from the participant children. Such an approach has dominated the documenting of early years learning in New Zealand over the past decade (Knauf, 2019). Carr and Lee (2012, p. 2) conceptualise learning stories primarily as an assessment tool where 'adults and children tell and retell stories of learning and competence, reflecting on the past and planning for the future'. The profound value of learning stories for developing and reinforcing learner identities in early childhood education is emphasised in this perspective. Diane Kashin (2016) sees learning stories as more than a means of assessment when she states that:

> Documenting learning and sharing the documentation with children is a way for teachers to show children that they are valued. When children see and hear learning stories, where they are the featured main character, it must be a validating experience. Sharing with families adds more opportunity for added perspectives.

Documenting children's meanings **59**

In essence, learning stories are a particular form of pedagogical documentation (Southcott, 2015), and therefore share the main features of pedagogical documentation such as making learning visible (Carr & Lee, 2019). Carr and Lee (2019, p. 157) draw attention to what they term as 'the progressive filter of early years teaching', represented in Figure 3.4 below. The authors point out that, in the course of just one day, early years practitioners are noticing, recognising and responding to children many times. These responses may include a smile, a gesture, such as thumbs up, or a comment. A few of those events and experiences will be noted down or held in memory in order to be recorded as part of a learning story. These may be very ordinary events or episodes but, for the child who becomes the focus of the story, these are significant moments or episodes of learning, as perceived and documented by early years practitioners. Recognising moments that are significant in terms of how the child experiences them requires a special understanding of individual children – the kind of knowledge that is most frequently generated through ongoing interactions with these children within their families and in early years settings.

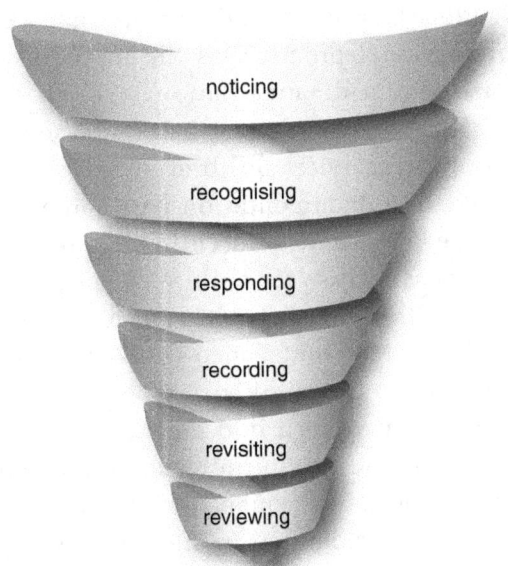

Figure 3.4 Progressive Filter of Early Years Teaching (Carr & Lee, 2019)

Effective documentation in pedagogical documentation

Pedagogical documentation has the power within and beyond ECEC practice to transform ways of seeing and thinking about children and parents. In order to achieve this potential, however, pedagogical documentation must be used as an active tool (Dahlberg, Moss & Pence, 2007), rather than a method of recording static evidence on children's learning and development. Significant distinctions have been made between the effectiveness of documents that generate opportunities for collaboration and sharing, and that have the power to impact, to some extent, a change on the social reality in which it is generated, and documentation that can be considered merely as a registration of facts (Ferraris, 2013). As outlined above, in previous research, Rintakorpi, Lipponenand Reunamo (2014) studied the tool of documentation from the perspective of a toddler and his parents during the child's transition from home to kindergarten. Such documentation was not only useful for the registration of facts, but also had value in extending knowledge on children's learning at home and in kindergarten. Defined according to Ferraris's (2013) terms, these documents had a strong impact on teachers' professional practice, as the teachers were empowered through use of the documentation method. Moreover, the teachers reported that documentation had increased opportunities for their communication with children and parents. The teachers also expressed that documentation had helped them process and engage to a greater extent with child-centered pedagogy, and had created more possibilities for children's participation. Similar findings for the benefits of documentation have been reported in the literature of Dahlberg, Mossand Pence (2007, p. 145) and Rinaldi (1998, p. 121). However, the study also revealed how easily pedagogical documentation may turn into a simple registration of facts without generating possibilities for influencing and enhancing communication and practice. Consequently, the children's views may not be invested with the potential to significantly influence ECEC practice.

A number of key questions to focus on when creating or viewing documentation are outlined below.

> **Questions to focus on when creating or viewing documentation**
>
> **(Krechevsky, Rivard & Burton, 2010)**
>
> - In what ways does the documentation focus on learning, not just something we did?
> - How does the documentation make visible the learning process as well as product?
> - Does the documentation promote conversation or deepen understanding about some aspect of learning?
> - Is there evidence to support the interpretations made in the documentation?
> - Is there other information the viewer needs in order to follow the account of learning represented in the documentation?

Children can participate in making their learning visible for a wide range of reasons. Through their expressions, they are communicating their ideas, expressing their feelings, developing their imagination and creativity, and testing their hypotheses about the world. These opportunities for making thinking visible are fundamental to children's learning and development – opportunities of which all children have a right to avail (DCSF, 2008).

Creating opportunities for revisiting and deepening understandings

Further unpacking of the term 'pedagogical documentation' emphasises the learning and educative dimension to documenting – specifically, documentation becomes pedagogical as a result of the learning that is facilitated through making children's thinking and feeling visible, thereby generating knowledge about the many ways in which children learn (Alcock, 2000).

I find it interesting to underscore how the concept of documentation, which has only recently moved into the scholastic environment, and more specifically into the pedagogical-didactic sphere, has undergone substantial modifications that partially alter its definition. In this context, documentation is interpreted and used for its value as a tool for recalling, that is, as a possibility for reflection.

(Rinaldi, 2006, p. 62)

Four key practices of documentation are emphasised as follows: observing, recording, interpreting and sharing (Krechevsky, Mardell, Rivard & Wilson, 2013). These different features of pedagogical documentation are further explored in the sections below.

Observing and recording: Capturing the processes and products of young children's learning

As in any kind of research, the design of the study, the research tools and the instruments adopted to carry out an inquiry will influence and shape the kind of data that are crafted from a research approach (Mukherji & Albon, 2018). A wide range of materials and tools can be used in pedagogical documentation to capture and record traces of learning and development, such as: photographs; illustrations; dialogue; children's observations; children's work, either in progress or completed; comments and interviews; videos of children and practitioners involved in activities; feedback from parents; and written transcriptions of children's natural responses and perspectives (Alcock, 2000; Fiore & Suarez, 2010). Central to effective documentation is the element of spontaneity, which can only be achieved through making documentation a habit within daily routines in early childhood education.

Strategies, instruments and tools used for documenting (e.g. digital cameras, video recorders, audio-taping devices, ECE service smartphones and tablets, notepads and other tools), if made available at all times, can be used to capture learning when and where it happens. Embedded within the context of routine activities, pedagogical documentation becomes more than simply a practice, but rather an attitude towards teaching and learning. Pedagogical documentation, in this way, further reinforces the notion that early childhood educators are well placed to facilitate action research approaches to capturing young children's meanings and messages. Moreover, pedagogical documentation positions practitioners as co-learners and co-researchers with children, with the potential to provide valuable insights into both pedagogy and practice (Giudici, Rinaldi & Krechevsky, 2001).

> We discover what we did not yet know how to see. Pedagogical documentation inserts a new phase of thinking and wondering together between the act of observation and the act of planning a response. Rather than looking for what is known through assessment, pedagogical documentation invites the creativity, surprise and delight of educators who discover the worlds of children.
> (Wien, 2013, p. 2)

Tangible artifacts of children's meanings

An evocative concept which Krechevsky et al. (2013) draw attention to, with a view to describing the data that may be collected through pedagogical documentation, is that of 'tangible artifacts' (p. 79), which enable tangible traces of an experience to be captured and recorded. Tangible artifacts refer to images, narratives, textual descriptions, or video or film extracts that serve to make tangible and available to memory experiences and feelings which may otherwise be difficult to reflect on and revisit with any precision or accuracy. Children can begin by representing what they know through drawing and creating three-dimensional art. For example, clay, wire, wood, and recycled materials may be used to help children express what they know. Tangible representations of children's meanings may open up the potential for children to revisit memories and experiences, which otherwise may be cognitively challenging for them without such a concrete record of these experiences. Through interacting with and revisiting the textual and visual data generated through documentation, children can be supported and provided with helpful prompts to facilitate greater expression and articulation of their meanings. For early years practitioners, these tangible objects and representations provide meaningful ways of deepening and extending their understandings of children's meanings. Collecting documentation in different media allows for multiple kinds of listening, eliciting different recollections, insights and feelings about the experience (Krechevsky et al., 2013).

Interpreting meanings through pedagogical documentation

Interpreting documentation is essential to the practice of documentation and is one of the key features that distinguishes documentation from display (Krechevsky et al., 2013). The authors go on to highlight three specific strategies to help early years practitioners interpret and make meaning from documentation:

- Grounding individual reflection and interpretation in documentation
- Interpreting documentation with colleagues
- Interpreting documentation with learners

With regard to the first of these strategies, documentation can be used to support and extend reflexivity in educational practice. Documentation facilitates early years practitioners to revisit and review learning experiences and, moreover, to identify possible misconceptions which otherwise could go unnoticed. A second strategy is interpreting documentation with colleagues. Krechevsky et al. (2013, p. 84) further state that documentation 'allows teachers to bring the eyes and ears of critical friends into their classroom and benefit from other perspectives'. Involving colleagues to collaborate in interpreting documentation is a powerful means of enhancing professional development and can generate novel responses and strategies for moving learning forward. Collaboration with other practitioners can also facilitate greater understanding of the developmental trajectory of the children in their settings.

Finally, interpreting documentation with learners and, in the context of early childhood education, with the young children whose learning is documented, contributes to making children's learning and meanings more broadly visible to children and to the adults who are centrally involved in their lives. Educators in Reggio Emilia refer to documentation as 'visible listening' because it creates the physical traces of listening and because the very act of documenting communicates to children that educators are listening to them (Krechevsky et al., 2013, p. 86). Notably then, pedagogical documentation goes beyond merely providing a record of children's learning and development to make visible children's thinking through providing a process for listening to children. This process is typically ongoing through a focus on generating insights into children's meanings, creating effective tools for exploring children's views, and for sharing interpretations of the knowledge crafted from documentation. This emphasis on pedagogical orientation as being process-oriented aligns well with the concept of the early years practitioner as researcher and pedagogue (Rintakorpi, Lipponen & Reunamo, 2014). It should be emphasised that uniformity of analysis and interpretation is not the primary goal of a pedagogical documentation approach. Alcock (2000) highlights the fact that different people may interpret the same document in diverse ways and it is a vital element of this approach that diversity is reflected and respected through the inclusion of unique perspectives. Similarly, different documentation techniques and tools may create and generate different messages and meanings. Pedagogical documentation as process-oriented, collaborative and interpretative can, therefore, through the interpretation of images and words, facilitate shifts away from more traditional pedagogical approaches, making it possible to provide education as a source for change and connection within a community (Turner & Gray-Wilson, 2009).

Sharing meanings through pedagogical documentation

Drawing on principles of the Reggio Emilia approach to early childhood education, pedagogical documentation emphasises the practitioner's role in inquiring, recording, reflecting on and *sharing data* that communicate aspects of children's learning and development alongside their thoughts, feelings and values. The notion of sharing data can refer to the collaboration between practitioners and children in interpreting the meanings of children's expressions, which, as mentioned previously, contributes to a deepening and expansion of understandings of children's meanings. Sharing, as a concept within pedagogical documentation, goes beyond this, however, and refers to the potential for building collective knowledge across different rooms in ECE settings and across different ECE settings, building and reinforcing connections with parents and families, and engaging with public audiences through making children's meanings visible. Krechevsky et al. (2013)

highlight three strategies for facilitating the sharing of meanings generated through pedagogical documentation. These strategies include:

- Building collective knowledge within and across classrooms
- Engaging families through documentation
- Creating public exhibitions and products for a wider audience

Within and across classrooms

Pedagogical documentation enables early years practitioners to collaborate within and across classrooms in an early childhood education setting. Sharing documentation on children's learning and development, and on children's interests and activities with other early years professionals, extends possibilities for understanding and advancing knowledge on children's development in the early years. Reviewing material collaboratively, developing and refining professional perspectives in partnership with other practitioners, contributes to achieving best practice in early childhood education, enhancing opportunities for effective communication and planning (Flottman, McKernan & Tayler, 2011). Pedagogical documentation also creates greater possibilities for critical reflective practice within and across different classrooms.

Working in partnership with other early years practitioners, and in collaboration with early childhood researchers, may also contribute to developing stronger links and connections between research and practice, thus facilitating a more significant role for early years practitioners in knowledge generation (Buysse, Sparkman & Wesley, 2003).

Engaging families through documentation

Parent involvement, or partnership with parents, refers to the relationship and associated interactions between early years practitioners and the parents and families of the children who attend early years settings. Parents make significant contributions to sharing valuable information with early years practitioners, which, in turn, enhances practitioner knowledge about individual children's development and academic learning. Fostering and nurturing relationships between the home and the early years setting (Fitzpatrick, 2012) is an essential dimension to understanding children's learning and development. Parents' involvement in early learning experiences of their children also has potential benefits for the parents, the practitioners, and, most importantly, the child. Sharing documentation is a meaningful way of deepening the connection between home and school and engaging parents as intellectual partners (Krechevsky et al., 2013). In this way, both family and practitioners' understanding of how to support learning is enhanced. Many early years settings communicate in natural and spontaneous ways with parents and families in order to share information. Apart from the everyday routines of dropping off and collecting children, parents may be invited to document children's interests and activities through a daily diary or regular record of care for their child (NCCA, 2009). Building strong partnerships between early years settings and parents through documentation also opens up possibilities for parents to discover new ways of interacting with their children.

Creating public exhibitions and products for a wider audience

The importance of early childhood education reaching beyond the early childhood setting has been emphasised in recent research and literature (Krechevsky et al., 2013). Exhibitions of children's learning and the artwork and materials created through activities in early childhood education provide rich opportunities for early years settings to make valuable connections with the wider neighbourhood and community in which they are located. Sharing documentation and children's creations beyond the early years setting generates possibilities for making learning visible and interrogating some of the assumptions, values and beliefs about how and what children learn (Krechevsky et al., 2013). Connecting to the wider social context and the larger community has also been highlighted as a positive feature of facilitating public exhibitions of children's work in early childhood education. An example of this is provided in annual exhibitions of children's artwork, generated by young children in an early childhood setting in Dublin, and exhibited in a nearby public library (Figure 3.5).

This early years setting works in partnership with parents and the wider community to share knowledge and details of children's learning and development, in order to emphasise the profound importance

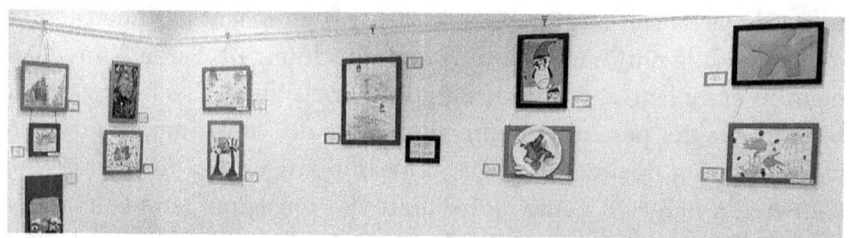

Figure 3.5 Children's artwork created in early years setting exhibited in public library

of these formative years. The rationale behind making children's art visible to the wider community is the opportunity it provides for children to represent and symbolise their experiences, and for these representations of children's experiences to be openly communicated to the wider public. Children also feel encouraged by being allowed to publicly exhibit their work, and empowered to experiment, create and make decisions, all of which help them to make sense of the world around them (Figure 3.6).

Exhibitions of children's learning and activities may also help to foster a sense of belonging and connectedness to the community through valuing and endorsing children as active members of the community, and thereby perhaps supporting children to realise their potential (Joerdens, 2014).

The collaborative feature of pedagogical documentation, with its emphasis on sharing and making documentation visible, facilitates both creative and effective ways of listening to children's own views and perspectives, while at the same time allowing and inviting educators to reflect on, interpret sensitively and share these views with children and other adults (Wien, 2013). In this way, insights and understandings of children's meanings deepen, expand and become refined over time through collaboration and ongoing reflection. This collaborative aspect of the documentation process encompasses reflection, discussion and action, based on acknowledging diverse interpretations of the documentation products. Children's agency and competence is also valued in such an approach, as documentation that does not encompass the views and perspectives of children may undermine children's belief in the relevance of their views. Alcock (2000) points out that, without this shared and collaborative pedagogical process, documentation may

Documenting children's meanings **69**

Figure 3.6 Children's artwork created in early years setting exhibited in public library

deteriorate into a meaningless paper-collecting exercise. A thought-provoking and noteworthy illustration of key features of effective documenting with regard to listening to and understanding children's meanings is illustrated in the Focus on Research below, which outlines details of a study exploring strategies for listening to young children, aged 2–4 years of age.

FOCUS ON RESEARCH

Horses in the sandpit[1]: photography, prolonged involvement and 'stepping back' as strategies for listening to children's voices

Stephenson (2009)

Study aims

A key aim of this article is to report on strategies that emerged from research with children, aged 2–4 years, in a New Zealand early childhood education centre. The context for the use of these strategies was a wider ethnographic study which explored the scope of curriculum as children experienced it, and enacted it, within an early childhood education centre.

- Activities using photographs of an early childhood education centre, and children's own photographs of that environment, were found to be effective ways of enabling young children (aged from 2–4 years) to share their thoughts about their experiences.

- Many children were keen to spend time with an adult who wanted to listen to them, and so the challenge was to search for ways of talking with them that they would find engaging, and that would allow them to articulate their ideas. Experience in this study reinforced the effectiveness of using a range of approaches (Clark, 2004; Clark & Moss, 2001); the approaches that used photographs and/or photography seemed particularly appealing to the children.

- **Photographs** were used with children in four possible ways:
    - The first strategy consisted of an A4 folder of 11 colour photographs of different rooms and spaces in the centre environment and this was used as a focus for conversations with children.
    - The second strategy, focused on a set of photographs of activities and events within the centre (such as water play, dough play,

---
[1] The use of photographs in this study is further explored in Chapter six with reference to making children's meanings visible.

- collage, mat-time, rest-time and meals) which was used to initiate conversations with children and as a focus for exploring what aspects of centre life they liked, or disliked.
  - The third strategy involved children being invited to photograph their favourite places, the places they liked around the centre, as a form of the photo tour developed by Clark and Moss (2001).
  - In the fourth strategy, photographs were used when children were showing the researcher their learning portfolios. Portfolios are records of children's learning recorded in words and photographs and with pieces of children's work included.
- However, in reflecting on the data, it was recognised that two other features had contributed significantly to a deeper understanding of children's perspectives: the prolonged and sustained data collection period and 'stepping back' from the research agenda.

Stephenson's research reinforces the argument that early years practitioners are uniquely well placed to engage with children in research on their lived experiences. While the strategies used in the study, photographs and other research tools were effective in helping to elicit and scaffold the young children's expression of their perspectives, being immersed in the early years setting for prolonged periods of time and over an extended period, were highlighted as key features that powerfully influenced the extent to which children's meanings were identified and understood. A prolonged and sustained data collection enabled all children to participate if desired, facilitated prolonged and sustained interactions with children, and made it possible for children to choose the activities they wished to participate in, repeating these over and over again in some cases. As emphasised by Stephenson (2009), significant implications in what children said and did would have been missed if relationships had not been built up over this extended time in the setting. The deeper contextual knowledge accessed through spending extensive periods of time in the setting made it possible to interpret, in a meaningful way, the children's expressions and responses.

A second feature emphasised as significant in achieving a deeper understanding of the children's meanings was being able to step back and create some distance from the research agenda, in order to be able to hear what children were saying in a more nuanced manner.

Being able to step back from the narrow research focus also allowed other messages to be heard – messages that were not answers to the questions being asked. Stepping back in this way facilitated hearing children's views within the wider context of the interactions that had already been shared, which, in turn, led to the researcher's assumptions being challenged (Stephenson, 2009). Early years practitioners carry out research within this context of prolonged and sustained interactions with the children who participate, with the capacity to draw on the knowledge and insight generated from these repeated interactions and exchanges. While the focus of a particular research agenda will shape and influence what practitioners observe, record and document, their agenda will naturally extend beyond the scope of the research focus, being sensitive and responsive to children's nuanced expression of their meanings.

The documentation above provides an illustration of how pedagogical documentation aims to achieve much more than reorganising and putting materials together in order to achieve a descriptive linear story. Neither is documentation about finding answers and drawing conclusions but rather about generating new knowledge that sparks further curiosity and inquiry (Turner & Gray-Wilson, 2009). It is also important to note that pedagogical documentation and its usage are never neutral; rather, the function and understanding of it is always relative to the social situation in which it is applied. The recordings or contents of the documentation do not represent empirical truths or reality, as the meaning of any recording is negotiated and renegotiated within the situated discourse of a particular institutional practice (Rintakorpi et al., 2014). Thus, negotiating and contesting are important aspects of capturing young children's meanings through pedagogical documentation. Below, key features of learning associated with the pedagogical approach of making learning visible are briefly outlined. Krechevsky et al. (2013, p. 54) call attention to five principles of learning associated with the pedagogical approach of making learning visible.

> **Principles of learning associated with the pedagogical approach of making learning visible**
>
> **Krechevsky, Mardell, Rivard & Wilson (2013)**
>
> - **Learning is purposeful:** Organised around understanding, knowledge and skills relevant to the child, educator, discipline and the larger community.
>
> - **Learning is social:** Accessing multiple points of view and interpretations through engaging with children, families and the wider community – through these acts of sharing, reflecting and revising, meanings emerge.
>
> - **Learning is emotional:** Going beyond intellectual knowledge to incorporate an *emotional* dimension to learning – where the emotional principle of learning is valued, opportunities to reveal and reflect on feelings of wonder, surprise and pleasure are supported.
>
> - **Learning is empowering:** Engaging with multiple audiences to craft meanings promotes the qualities of agency and self-direction in young children.
>
> - **Learning is representational:** Photographs, texts and visual and audio recordings of children's learning and expression contribute to building collective knowledge and providing memories for children and educators.

Benefits and challenges to using pedagogical documentation

In Finland, early childhood educators have been directed to use documentation to assess and develop pedagogy and practice by the social pedagogical curriculum for early childhood education. Rintakorpi (2016) carried out empirical research to examine the perceived challenges and benefits experienced by a group of Finnish preschool teachers when they learned to document their work. The study participants (n = 35) produced a total of 88 negative and 229 positive conceptions about using documentation in ECE. A substantial majority of all conceptions were positive.

Key challenges that were identified in the study included time constraints, technical issues, and challenges in terms of learning the methods. More specifically, challenges related to time constraints focused on the fact that educators felt that documentation was not valued sufficiently, with particular reference to being counted into working hours. Time needed to facilitate children taking photos and developing other visual methods, processing and interpreting this documentation and finding time to share this documentation with colleagues and children's parents, were noted as key barriers to implementing this approach to learning and to capturing children's meanings. The second challenge identified was the lack of experience and technical knowledge on the part of educators, which was required to engage with technical equipment. This obstacle arose particularly in the case of settings where there was an absence of up-to-date equipment necessary to facilitate an ease in documenting children's meanings. Finally, learning to document was experienced as an ongoing process – a challenging process that demanded time, technical resources and effective support in order to allow educators to be able to implement this approach.

A substantial number of benefits were also highlighted by educators in the Finnish study (Rintakorpi, 2016) including the benefits for professional development, making education in the early years visible, identifying and highlighting pedagogical processes, and facilitating child-centredness and participation for children in early childhood. With regard to benefits for professional development, educators reported that their work and the activities generated with the children had become more meaningful and inspiring as a result of engaging with pedagogical documentation approaches. A major benefit highlighted was the role that effective documentation can play in transmitting ECEC-related knowledge and experiences to children's parents, and others, beyond the classroom. Benefits related to designing, assessing and conducting pedagogical work were also noted by educators in the study. Specifically, the importance of planning how to document children's learning and being able to re-visit and review past activities and records were highlighted by educators. Pedagogical documentation was viewed as a very effective means of accessing children's meanings and of gaining insight into what children prioritised and valued. However, the importance of being able to act on these insights and to implement the necessary changes in practice remained a challenge to many of the educators. While educators perceived pedagogical documentation to increase possibilities for greater participation on the part of young children, the researchers and authors believed that the resulting conceptions did not reflect a very strong use of participatory methods but rather described these conceptions as 'frail openings' (Rintakorpi, 2016, p. 407). A simple tool for accessing young children's meanings, from parents' and practitioners' perspectives – the fan of the child – is illustrated in the Focus on Research below.

FOCUS ON RESEARCH

The Fan of the Child Rintakorpi, Lipponen and Reunamo (2014)

Study aims

- This study is a case analysis drawn from an extensive qualitative study at a private kindergarten in Finland. Data were gathered on site for the period from June to December 2012 (Figure 3.7).

- The parents were encouraged to take photos of things and situations that they considered important and meaningful to their child, or

Figure 3.7 The fan folder

(Continued)

situations that could give some important information to the educators about the child's experiences in the transition phase from home to kindergarten.

- The parents were asked to look through their home photo albums, make notes about the photos they had taken, and insert the photos and notes into small ready-cut leaflets. The leaflets were then taken to the kindergarten, where they were bound together by the educators to form the fans.

- The educators carried out the same procedure in school as the parents had at home. The situations, people, and items that they considered important for the child or the family were documented with a camera and placed in the leaflets with written notes. These leaflets were bound into the children's Fan folders along with the leaflets that had been made at home.

- Table 3.1 below presents findings related to Leo as documented by the educators and Leo's parents.

Table 3.1 The content of Leo's leaflets

	LOVING	HAVING	BEING
Home leaflets (n = 6)	Important and loved brothers	Funny animals, owls and squirrels	Swinging, songs, learning words
Kindergarten leaflets (n = 20)	Having breakfast with mother Hugging with brother Playing with father Making friends Crying and getting comfort from an educator	Favourite things (animals) Daily routines (sleeping, eating) Music instruments and drama play accessories Leo has quick brain and movements	Playing and singing Learning words
Institutional practices	Comforting Building personal relationships	Sharing physical, social, and psychological environments Building learning environments	Communication Integrating home and kindergarten pedagogy and care Trips to the forest

Source: Rintakorpi et al., 2014

Documentation moves us beyond an interest in outcomes and moves us to an exploration of the relationships and feelings that form the context and stuff of educative experience (Yu, 2008). As Rinaldi (2003, p. 3) states:

> Documentation ... is not simply a technique that can be transported but a way of guaranteeing that our thinking always involves reflection, exchange, different points of view, and differences in assessment or evaluation. The documentation materials we use attest not only to our path of knowledge regarding children but also to our path of knowledge about the child and humanity, and about ourselves. They also attest to our idea of the teacher as researcher, of school as a place of research and cultural elaboration, a place of participation, in a process of shared construction of values and meanings.

4 Ways of seeing
Observation skills in research with young children

Observation as a tool emphasises the importance of going beyond seeing to actively recording and documenting data on the phenomena we are exploring. This chapter provides a focus on the multiple and varied methods of observation with young children, from covert to overt, depending on the aims and objectives of the research focus and the associated role of the researcher. Roles can range from non-participant, to participant observer, to complete membership (Baker, 2006, pp. 174–178), and a number of roles may be assumed within the one research inquiry. The unique contribution that can be made by early childhood educators when observing young children, with reference to the close, personal relationships they develop with these children, is also a key focus of this chapter. Young children are most likely to make their feelings known in the context of a trusting relationship and, in turn, early years educators are well placed to read and interpret children's meanings through their body language and non-verbal and verbal behaviour (Dunphy, 2008). The particular benefits of observation as a tool for accessing young children's meanings are outlined and discussed with a focus on the rich and textured descriptions of young children's interactions, and on documenting instances of children's co-construction of knowledge in early years settings.

The chapter then moves to a review of particular observation tools which that have been developed.

Observation in the early years

Carrying out and recording observations of young children has a long-held tradition in early childhood practice (Giardiello, McNulty & Anderson, 2013). Susan Isaacs's influence on the field of early childhood has perhaps been the most significant through her emphasis on the value of observation-led records for understanding children's learning and development (Giardiello, 2011; Robson, 2006). Observation as a research method is a broad term encompassing a range of methodological approaches and types of instruments through which data can be collected (Baker, 2006). For the purposes of the present chapter, the focus is primarily on unstructured and naturalistic observations and, more specifically, on observation as a valuable tool to activate and animate the documentation of children's meanings. Gorman and Clayton define observation studies as those that 'involve the systematic recording of observable phenomena or behaviour in a natural setting' (2005, p. 40). Other authors define observation within the broader context of ethnography or indeed provide a narrower focus on participant observation. What is consistent in all these definitions, however, is the need to study and understand people, and in this context, children within their natural environment.

Observation plays a central role in early childhood education practice. Practitioners in early childhood education settings develop precise skills in observing in order to be able to record objectively and accurately – knowing what and when to observe, knowing what type of observation to use and being able to interpret effectively the documentation generated through observations (Baker, 2006). The importance of observing and gathering information and interpreting that information in a planned and systematic manner is also highlighted (Fawcett & Watson, 2016). Using the skills and knowledge implicit in and acquired through practice in early childhood education, observations carried out by early years practitioners play a valuable role in facilitating a holistic view of children. Consistent with this view, Fawcett and Wilson (2016) emphasise the value of observation in capturing the different features of children's development, which are inextricably bound up together and must all be taken into account.

Observations have been used extensively in research on child development, typically using pre-determined categories in order to indicate developmental milestones, alongside checklist-style recording methods. These methods of observation were guided, informed and influenced predominantly by theories and principles encompassed by Developmental Psychology. A primary focus of this more traditional type of observation is to assess, categorise and classify children's behaviour and development with reference to prescribed developmental outcomes. More recently, as outlined in Chapter 1, early childhood education has moved away from an exclusive focus on children's developmental outcomes and adopted a post-modern perspective, which places emphasis on the notion of childhood as a social construction, culturally located and historically and politically shaped (Bronfenbrenner, 1986). In early childhood education, the role of observation is no longer simply to assess and classify children according to pre-determined norms but rather to capture the complexity and spontaneity of children's interests, activities, experiences and insightful features of their learning and development, in order to inform child-centred, relational practice in early childhood education (Schulz, 2015).

Early childhood educators as observers

Early years practitioners are uniquely placed to be able to engage in a meaningful way with young children through observations, and to minimise the potential effects of the presence of the observer on the child's behaviour and responses. Central to the particular skill of the early years practitioner as observer is the close and trusting relationship that early childhood practitioners build with young children. A key aspect of this relationship is the notion of attunement – being aware of and responsive to another (Perry, 2000). The importance of effective communication with young children – of developing insight into how children feel and respond to their experiences, and how best to engage and to listen in multiple ways to children – is highlighted in the concept of attunement. Early years practitioners are faced with the challenge of having to become attuned, as far as possible, to the many different strengths, vulnerabilities, sensory preferences and styles of exploration of the children they work with on a daily basis.

Hedges and Cooper (2018) argue for a complex understanding of experienced early years practitioners' engagement with children's learning through relational pedagogy.

Relational pedagogy is 'an evolving concept' that requires an 'exploration of understandings, interpretations and practices' (Moyles & Papatheodorou, 2009, p. 228). Such a pedagogy is underpinned by sociocultural theories derived from the work of Vygotsky (1978, 1986) and prioritises the roles of relationships – relationships with practitioners, contexts and culture – in determining learning. The importance of interactions and conversations that support complex learning activities are also emphasised. With particular reference to observing and children's play, and participating in the complexity of children's interests and learning, early years practitioners are encouraged to move:

> from being *passive observers* at the periphery of play, or didactic instructors in sessions that do not involve play, to being *knowledgeable participants* alongside children during and inside play.
> (Hedges & Cooper, 2018, p. 371)

Within the context of early childhood education, the purposes of observations will vary. However, a key purpose and focus of observations for early years practitioners is to document and identify aspects of children's learning and development and gain insight into the particular interests, curiosities and abilities of the children they work alongside (Fawcett & Watson, 2016). Regardless of the purposes of observations, the importance of gathering information through observations in a systematic, detailed and precise manner cannot be overestimated. Key skills necessary for carrying out observations in early childhood education include the ability to understand precisely what one wants to observe, to be able to select the most appropriate and effective type of observation and observation tool to use, to be clear about and comfortable with the way in which the observation data will be recorded (e.g. narrative accounts, video, photos) and knowing how to interpret and share, if appropriate, the data generated through observational methods. Further skills include being able to give full attention to the object and focus of the observation, and having the capacity to step back and avoid intrusion or interference, which might in some way influence the flow of events. It is also essential for early years practitioners to be able to assess the quality and validity of the observation, in terms of remaining impartial as far as possible and being able to engage in objective, critical reflection and discussion with others.

Why observation matters in accessing young children's experiences

Observations have been used extensively in research both on and with children for a wide variety of aims and objectives. Early years practitioners who are working alongside young children and are familiar with individual characteristics of these children engage with young children in natural and spontaneous contexts, thereby potentially opening a window into young children's interests, feelings and responses to their everyday experiences. Through regular observations, new understandings about the way children learn and develop can be generated and shared with colleagues and with children's parents and families. The value of observation cannot be overestimated, as a child's spontaneous interaction with their environment and those within their environment provides rich opportunities, on an ongoing and sustained basis, for practitioners to deepen and extend their understanding and reflection on practice.

Giardellio et al. (2013) draw attention to the need for both planned and spontaneous observations in order to generate a more holistic picture of the child. In the sections below, key concepts and benefits associated with observing young children are briefly outlined and discussed.

Observing: The heart of documentation

In engaging with the concept of *making learning visible*, early years practitioners endeavour to slow down the fast-flowing pace of activities and events in order to step back, to be able to focus in depth on the details of everyday routines, and to be open to the unexpected and unanticipated content of children's meanings (Krechevsky et al., 2013). An important aspect of documenting children's meanings is being able to record actions, interactions, and familiar and routine events within early childhood settings and reflecting critically on these records of everyday life and experiences. Observation is at the heart of such documentation (Roberts-Holmes, 2018). Being open to seeing things in a new way and learning to observe actively and critically facilitates a holistic and effective documentation.

Gateway to children's interests

The concept of capturing young children's meanings was greatly progressed in the late 90s and early 2000s, with particular reference to the development of The Mosaic approach (Clark, 2017; Clark & Moss, 2001). The Mosaic approach is a multi-method approach to understanding young children's perspectives, which was developed and adapted through four funded research studies based on listening to young children. Three of these studies were empirical: Listening to Young Children (1999–2000), Spaces to Play (2003–2004) and the Living Spaces study (2005–2007). As one significant piece of the mosaic of children's meanings, observations played a central role throughout many of these projects, and allowed researchers to identify children's key interests and to follow up on children's interests using a multi-modal approach. A multi-modal approach involves including multiple methods and encompasses a variety of media including drawings, photos, map-making, child-led tours and other research tools. Rinaldi's (2006) circle of listening guided and informed the observations, emphasising the following steps:

- Observe/notice/find interest in something regarding children's activities;
- Stop and document small events from the children's play;
- Discuss the observation/critical reflection – the creating of new ideas, perspectives and interests;
- Act in new ways before the circle of listening begins again with new observations.

The aim of the Listening to Young Children study (Clark 2004; Clark and Moss 2001), carried out with children aged 3–4 years, was to include young children's perspectives in the evaluation of a group of services for children and families. In the Focus on Research below, an extract from an observation of a group of 3- and 4-year-olds playing together is presented. Clark (2017) provides an account of a narrative form of observation of young children at play in order to capture what children liked most about their play experiences.

> **FOCUS ON RESEARCH**
>
> **Listening to Young Children (1999–2000)**
> **Clark (2017, p. 35)**
>
> Gaby was often involved with a group of friends in organising complicated imaginative play. One session took place in the afternoon by the computer table on a very wet day in June. It was a game of hospitals and houses in which Gaby was one of the major players. Gaby had a baby (a doll) who wasn't well. She lay the doll on the mouse mat for the computer and used the mouse to pump the baby's chest and make her better. "Daddy is coming home soon. The baby is ok. She is moving".
>
> - Extract from observation of a group of 3- and 4-year-old children playing together.

Clark (2017, p. 35) points out that this 'snapshot' provides a record of play in progress, which can be discussed with children, practitioners and parents as an example of time spent in the setting. This particular example highlighted the importance of role play to Gaby's enjoyment of being in the setting, which was later confirmed through conversations with her keyworker and her mother as part of the study.

Capturing curiosity and wonder through observation

In Chapter 1, the value of fostering and stimulating curiosity and wonder in childhood was foregrounded. Curiosity motivates and enables children to explore topics of special interest and, at the same time, allows for the development of broader skills necessary for competent social interactions with peers and adults (Schmidt & Lahroodi, 2008). Early years practitioners are well positioned, as a result of their experience and training, to document children's natural curiosity and, thereby, to shape exploration in meaningful contexts. Central to this ability to document and record children's spontaneous explorations through expressions of their curiosity and wonder is the skill of understanding how and when to avoid intervention – to step back and meaningfully observe without hindering children's enquiry – and having motivation to follow their curiosity. As young children wonder, are curious, and learn about the world around them, they gather ideas from their own experiences or those provided for them.

Haiman (1999, p. 8) states that wonder becomes possible when children 'can risk being themselves without there being any risk at all'. Key characteristics of early years practitioners who can enhance and extend children's sense of wonder include those who typically *ask,* rather than those who more often *tell* or *instruct*. Moreover, the ability to be flexible enough to postpone planned activities from time to time and allow a child's creative idea or reflection to lead the way is also essential. Observations allow practitioners to slow down the hurried pace typical in everyday early childhood settings, to zoom in on children's wonder and curiosity and to identify key features that can be used in order to extend children's learning through wonder and curiosity and, thereby, to enhance practice.

> Children are unique and complex and thus often difficult to comprehend. And they do not readily engage us in dialogue in order to explain the reasons for their caprice as they explore the world that surrounds them. Yet, as teachers, it is important for us to know our children deeply, to flow with their currents, and to extend their nascent theories about how the world works ... Given the delightful yet often enigmatic characteristics of young children, we learned decades ago that in order to comprehend children we must begin by observing them as they play. But what do we see as we observe, and how do we use our observations to enhance our effectiveness as teachers?
>
> (Forman & Hall, 2005)

Guiding and informing practice and research in early childhood education

Regular observations provide practitioners with a window into all aspects of children's learning and development and typically serve as a means of extending and expanding on children's interests and initiating new and desirable practices. Observation of children in symbolic play, in which objects are used to represent places and things, can be particularly useful in research for gaining insights into children's knowledge and experience of the physical environment (Johnson et al., 2016). Specific behaviour patterns and difficulties can also be highlighted through systematic and carefully designed observations, thereby enabling practitioners to tailor practice to the needs of certain children. Observation is an invaluable tool which can serve to increase understanding about what elements are important for young children with regard to creating an active and inviting learning environment. Practitioners who are committed to regular and meaningful observation are typically motivated to provide pleasurable and challenging learning experiences for children. The role of observations in guiding research in early childhood education is also significant. Located within the field of professional practice and typically conducted in early childhood settings, the work of the early childhood practitioner-researcher has generated a substantial and significant body of data (Farrell et al., 2016) and many of such studies have included observation as central to their research methods and often combined with other supplementary research tools.

Observations with younger children aged 1 and 2 years

As previously outlined, the Mosaic approach has been adopted and adapted by practitioners and researchers across a range of contexts and countries (Clark, 2017). In most of the studies adopting this approach, observation as a research tool has had prominence. One example of such research carried out in Norway explored how indoor play spaces could become a more meaningful environment for young children (aged 1 and 2 years), in order to support their sustained, self-initiated play (Clark, 2017). The project was led by the pedagogical leader, with three teaching assistants, over a nine-month period. Four children out of a group of thirteen were chosen to participate in the project, as each had older siblings in the same setting. The following account provides a simple but effective illustration of the power of observation in interrogating and troubling some of the assumptions of early childhood practitioners:

> We started with observation on children and found that the children were wandering around a lot and that our thoughts for the indoor environment did not comply with the children's use of their environment. By reflecting on our observations, we found that the children did not play for long before they changed activity.

Therefore, we had to find out how the indoor spaces could develop into more meaningful spaces for the 1- and 2-year-olds (Reiden Larsen, pedagogical leader; Clark, 2017, pp. 141–142).

The Mosaic approach was chosen as a way of engaging different perspectives and of enabling the youngest children to play an active role in meaning-making in their environment. A number of research tools and strategies were adopted in addition to the observation research tool. These included: further discussion and reflection on observations; child-led tours, which included older siblings taking on the role of photographing their younger siblings; book making and map making; interviewing older siblings; and using the Magic Carpet[1] – all facilitating further exploration of and responses to different environments. Using each of the different tools involved generated possibilities for identifying how the youngest children inhabited the space (Clark, 2017). The importance of being flexible and adjusting the research methods for working with young children aged 1 to 2 years are highlighted in the following extract:

> I found the approach with its multiple ways of listening to toddlers, a good opportunity to really listen to their perspectives and let the children participate, not only by observation on children, but *with* children (Reidun Larsen, pedagogical leader, cited in Clark, 2017, p. 142).

Observational methods and practice in research with children in the early years

Strategies and research methods for working with children in the early years draw on and are informed by a range of methodological approaches and paradigms, and observational methods are no exception to this. As outlined earlier, observation in early childhood education practice draws primarily on qualitative, less structured approaches to observing children, with the aim of capturing children's interests, thoughts, feelings and responses to aspects of their lived experiences, rather than measuring and quantifying behaviours with a view to identifying outcomes. In the sections below, a brief overview of structured observations, typically used in some early years settings, are outlined.

Structured observations

Structured observations tend to have a precise focus and aim and are underpinned by principles associated with quantitative methodological approaches (Mukherji & Albon, 2018). Examples of structured observation types are event sampling, time sampling, and using checklists and rating scales to observe and document children's behaviours.

Event sampling

An event sampling observation focuses on a particular type of behaviour with the key aim of providing a detailed account of these target behaviours as they occur. Continuous, narrative observational records of pre-determined, specific behaviours are detailed in narrative accounts, observed and documented by practitioners. For example, an early years practitioner may wish to find out *precise detail* about a child's aggressive behaviour, including what kind of aggressive actions are manifest, what are the *triggers or antecedents* of such behaviour and what are the *consequences* of this behaviour (Mukherji & Albon, 2018). Event samples can be carried out over an agreed period of time and, in some cases, throughout the day, in order to build a rich and in-depth profile of the specific behaviour being explored. Key issues for the practitioner to keep in mind are that, in order to be able to identify a particular behaviour, it is essential to have operationalised the behaviour in a way that is meaningful and facilitates inter-rater reliability across different observers. Developing a list of behaviours and the particular attributes that go towards constituting that behaviour help to achieve inter-rater reliability (e.g. kicking, shouting, hitting out, etc. could be attributes included in operationalising the behaviour of aggression). Such an approach to observation also necessitates alertness and attentiveness on the part of the observer. The key benefits of such an approach are that an observer will learn more about the potential causes of certain behaviours and the characteristics of the behavioural event, and potentially gain insight into how such behaviours can be positively addressed and resolved (Table 4.1).

Table 4.1 Excerpt from an event sample of aggressive behaviours

Time	Record of event	Antecedent	Consequence
9.15	Jamie pushes Adam forcefully, shouting at him "leave it" and grabs Lego pieces, shifting them out of Adam's reach.	Jamie had been playing on his own with Lego pieces when Adam quietly approached and pointed towards a particular piece.	Adam walks away startled at Jamie's reaction. Sarah (EYP) approaches Jamie and gently enquires as to why he does not want to play with Adam.
9.40	Several children at the table where a high rise building is being constructed with Lego. Jamie reaches out suddenly and knocks the construction to the ground where it breaks apart.	Kate (child who had been observing) bends down to pick up the pieces. Jamie walks away.	Sarah (EYP) helps Kate to pick up the pieces. Sarah then moves to interact with Jamie in order to encourage him to play more co-operatively with other children.

Time sampling

A time sampling observation, sometimes called an interval recording, is used when educators wish to find out how frequently a particular behaviour is occurring. Individual children or groups of children are observed at regular intervals during the day and the frequency of the specific behaviour is observed and recorded. The observation period may last from several minutes at different times throughout the day to an hour or more every day for several weeks. For example, having identified that a child or children are engaging in solitary behaviour and play, a time sampling observation will help to identify precisely how often this behaviour is occurring. As with an event sampling technique, it is essential that, before the observation takes place, observers have a clear understanding of the aim of the observation, who or what is being observed, what information will be recorded, how often the recording will be made and how long will each observational recording last (Mukheri & Albon, 2018). Key issues for observers to keep in mind include the importance of carrying out time samples at different times of the day and on different days of the week, to enable practitioners to identify consistent patterns over time. Time samples can be very useful

Table 4.2 Excerpt from a time sample observation

Time	Frequency of solitary behaviours	Detail of solitary behaviours
9.00	2	Withdrawing from group of children to be alone
9.15	0	Playing alone in home corner
9.30	1	Moves away from home corner and goes to library corner alone
9.45	1	Turns away from child who approaches and asks a question

for gaining insight into the extent to which a certain behaviour is occurring and also for capturing changes in the frequency of target behaviours, which may result as a consequence of intervention. Forms are usually quite simple, typically divided into smaller intervals of 15 seconds to 1 minute, and behaviours may be detailed and specified in advance on the form so that the observer can record what is occurring during each interval. In Table 4.2 a sample time sample observation is presented with reference to the frequency of occurrences of solitary behaviours.

Checklists and rating scales

Typically used widely in the past in early childhood education to document aspects of children's learning and development, checklists and rating scales are no longer used exclusively in early childhood education settings but can be used to supplement other less quantitative observational methods in order to determine the presence or absence of a particular skill or behaviour or to rate the quality of the behaviour or setting. Checklists can be very useful for educators to gain a sense of the extent to which a particular child is achieving, or failing to achieve, particular developmental milestones. For example, children are observed at play to determine which skills they have mastered, which are emerging, and which remain to be learned (Table 4.3).

Unstructured observations

Capturing young children's meanings in early childhood research and practice typically draws more on less structured types of observation.

Table 4.3 Excerpt from a checklist to observe children's development

Behaviour	Yes	No
Can distinguish primary colours by name		
Can distinguish between light and dark colours		
Can distinguish between objects combining colour and shape		

Unstructured observations require the observer to 'go with the flow' of the setting in which it is being conducted (Roberts-Holmes, 2018, p. 132). In such an observation, it may not always be possible to write down what you are observing at the time, so the importance of reflecting and making notes of all you have seen and observed is emphasised.

Continuous narrative records

Continuous narrative records are qualitative methods in which the observer aims to write down and record what the participant says or does. 'Naturalistic observations' is another term used for narrative observations, running records and written observations (Mukherji & Albon, 2018). These observations are commonly used by practitioners in early childhood settings as part of their everyday work. Although this is a reasonably straightforward method and often the one that early childhood education practitioners tend to use, it is a complex method, which needs precision and systematic planning in order to be effectively carried out. Observations are usually recorded using a notebook and pen and written up as soon as possible in order to maximise on what is fresh in memory (Table 4.4).

Participant and non-participant observations

In participant observation, a researcher participates and joins in with the children in their daily routine and activities. The researcher is an *insider* in participant observations (Roberts-Holmes, 2018, p. 138) and participates at different levels in the event and the context being

Table 4.4 Excerpt from a continuous narrative observation

Date 10.3.2019	Time observation started: Time observation ended:	10am 10.30am
Child's name SOPHIE	Gender Female	Date of Birth 16.8.2016
Age	2 years, 7 months	
Primary language of child	English	
Context	Playing in home corner – 6 other children are present in the room. Three EYPs present.	

Sophie has been crying as she was distressed when her mother left the setting. Her mother explained to Hannah (EYP) that Sophie had been out of sorts the previous night and that morning. Hannah walks over to Sophie and picks out Sophie's favourite picture book (title). She walks with Sophie over to the quiet corner where they sit together on cushions. Sophie reaches to take the book from Hannah's hands. Hannah asks her "Do you want the book, Sophie? Would you like me to read it to you?" Hannah begins to cry quietly and shakes her head. "What's wrong, Sophie? You're not yourself today". Hannah opens the book and quietly begins to read the story to Sophie. Sophie calms a little and rests her head against Hannah, listening to the story being read.

observed. The depth of involvement will vary between researchers and research projects (see further Table 4.1. which details possibilities for different levels of participation) but common to all participant observers is the substantial time needed in order to observe effectively (Roberts-Holmes, 2018). By observing the situation or event while simultaneously participating in it, the observer is better able to understand the research topic first-hand. One of the primary reasons for doing participant observations is that important aspects of the environment and the context being observed may not be accessible or visible to those who are not part of or participant in the setting. Participant observation also facilitates greater access to observations of complex interactions among the setting members and with the physical environment. Brief summaries of two observational studies are outlined below in the Focus on Research extracts. In the first of these studies, Salamon and Harrison (2015) carried out observational research exploring early years practitioners' understanding of infant capabilities and of how these conceptions influence their practice with babies. As the researcher was not a staff member but visited the setting regularly to observe both the children and the practitioners in practice, the researcher took on the role of *observer as participant*.

OBSERVER AS PARTICIPANT

FOCUS ON RESEARCH

Early childhood educators' conceptions of infants' capabilities: the nexus between beliefs and practice

(Salamon & Harrison, 2015)

Study aims

Explore EYPs understandings of infant capabilities and how these beliefs impact on practice.

- The site for the study was an infant room programme within a larger organisation in Sydney.
- Five ECE professionals participated, working with children aged 6–15 months.
- Seven infants participated, aged 6–12 months when the data collection period began.
- The lead researcher attended the site three half-days a week for six months to observe the typical practices of educators (and infants).
- Data were generated in a variety of forms in order to fit in with and best represent the regular practices at the site.
- Written field notes, digital photographs, and audio and video recordings served as a stimulus for group discussions at monthly team meetings.

As outlined above, the lead researcher was not part of the staff team but visited the setting three half-days a week for six months to observe the typical practices of educators (and infants). In this case, the researcher is best categorised as *observer as participant*, according to levels of participation outlined in Table 4.5 below. Findings which were highlighted through participant observations in the study above emphasised that infants were considered capable of independently directing their own physical and cognitive learning. Educators' belief in infants' physical and cognitive competence motivated their practice in ways that supported and enhanced independent physical and cognitive development (Salamon & Harrison, 2015). A transactional cycle of influence and development was observed in terms of infants' developing physical and cognitive capabilities, in turn reinforcing and sustaining educators' further beliefs (and practices) regarding these capabilities. Such a cycle was also observed in an inverse manner as illustrated in the following quote:

> If we believe children aren't able to engage with, say, dramatic play and then we don't give them the opportunity, then of course they aren't able to engage in dramatic play because they haven't had the opportunity to engage in dramatic play, and so it becomes this cycle.

A further interesting finding to emerge from the observational study above was that infants were considered less independent in their emotional and social development than in their physical and cognitive learning (Salamon & Harrison, 2015).

A second observational study used participatory observations that involved a combination of *participant as observer*, with researchers visiting and documenting through observations on a regular basis, and *complete participation*, where data were gathered by practitioners working in the setting, through observations and data generated through other forms of documentation (Yelland, 2018). The data reported in the Focus on Research below formed part of a larger case study with children from 2–12 years of age that took place over four years. Specifically, the study focused on providing empirical evidence of using multimodal experiences to support young children to become literate in the 21st century. The data reported here were generated through observations with children in the age range 4–8 years in Australia.

PARTICIPANT AS OBSERVER AND COMPLETE PARTICIPATION

FOCUS ON RESEARCH

A pedagogy of multi-literacies: Young children and multi-modal learning with tablets

Yelland (2018)

Study aims

Consider the potential for new learning with new technologies and supporting teachers to use tablets to reconceptualise pedagogies and practices in the early years.

Three sources of data.

- First, daily reflective notes in which we recorded events as we recalled them as a narrative.

- Second, teachers/educators in the schools and centres shared their planning documents and observations by making them available to us and in conversations with them when we made the visits.

- We also interviewed all teachers/educators in their schools/centres.

- Here, we focus on daily reflective notes which we typed up at the end of each day and shared in conversations with annotated remarks and photographs.

Three key areas were identified in which working with tablets contributed to new learning for children. Used alongside other more traditional methods, tablets helped to support building the foundational skills that are central to the development of literacy skills. Secondly, tablets provided opportunities for supporting the development of creative, multimodal texts, which also allowed for documentation of learning processes. Thirdly, tablets created opportunities for providing explicit scaffolding and support of learning, through including a focus on authentic activities and communicating ideas with real audiences.

Central to effective participant observation is spending a lot of time with children and practitioners if you are a researcher and not a member of the setting staff. As pointed out by Merewether (2018), conversations with children in the early stages of verbal development are often not dominated by children's words so that listening to them requires 'listening not just with our ears but with all our senses (sight, touch, smell, taste, orientation)' (Rinaldi, 2006, p. 65). The better a researcher knows the context, practitioners, children and parents, the richer the quality of the data and evidence collected. Where a researcher is well-known, they are more likely to be able to understand the detail as well as being more familiar with the subtleties and complexities of a situation. Developing these relationships takes considerable time and, therefore, a researcher should be prepared to spend large amounts of time inside and outside the research setting, developing these all-important relationships. The focus of the research and the aims and objectives of the research project will determine the choice of either participant or non-participant observational methods. Table 4.5 below outlines four possible dimensions of participation for researchers, including complete participation, participant as observer, observer as participant and complete observer, adapted from Mukherji and Albon (2018).

Non-participant observation is a way of observing behaviours and events within a particular setting without interacting directly with the participants. Researchers may be present with the participants in the setting but, in other cases, may not be present in the setting. The extent to which the researcher engages with the participants in the study will be minimal by comparison with participant observations. Early childhood education practitioners as part of their daily routines engage in both participant and non-participant observations. Non-participant observations may be more appropriate and viable in situations where the observer does not know the children well enough to be present in the room without their presence exerting an influence on the child's behaviour and responses. In the Focus

Table 4.5 Levels of participation in observational research

Complete participation	Observer is a full member of the group being studied. If the researcher is a complete participant, it is not usual to inform the group about the research aim, as this may alter the group's behaviour towards the researcher. This aspect of complete participation is considered unethical as it involves deception and the participants have not been given the right 'not to participate'.
Participant as observer	Observer spends a considerable amount of time with a group and attempts to become a full member of the group but explains to the group from the beginning that they are conducting research. This is similar to practitioner research in early years settings. The staff team will be fully aware that the researcher is undertaking observations (and for what purpose) and may give insightful comments on what has been recorded or even help with data collection. If observing children, it is important to gain the written permission of parents too.
Observer as participant	Observer spends only a limited amount of time with the group they are observing, seeking permission from the participants to join in only with the activities that they wish to observe. This is similar to a student on a course attending a nursery setting for a limited amount of time a week. The advantage of this is that it is easier to remain objective, but a complete understanding of what is happening may be difficult to attain because the observer remains an outsider.
Complete observer	Observer does not involve themselves with the group being observed at all. She/he remains anonymous and endeavours not to be noticed by the participants. An example of this may be a researcher observing children playing in a public place. Johnson and Christensen (2012) consider that the participants do not need to be informed that they are being observed. The advantage of this type of observation is that the participants' behaviour is less likely to differ from their usual behaviour, but the information obtained will lack the insider's point of view.

on Research below, an example of an observational strategy involving observer as both participant and non-participant is illustrated. The study focused on how role-play offers possibilities for the development of children's cultures, common values, beliefs, knowledge and practices. Participating within their cultures enables children to develop a common framework in their attempt to make sense of their world and themselves in it (Papadopoulou, 2012).

> **FOCUS ON RESEARCH**
>
> **Participant and non-participant observations**
>
> **The ecology of role play: intentionality and cultural evolution**
>
> **Papadopoulou (2012)**
>
> **Study aims**
>
> Explore several role-play activities that were orchestrated and performed by children themselves and thus might be considered as reflecting only their intentions and perceptions.
>
> - The research took place in a Greek state school and employed participant and non-participant observation of the children's role-play sessions.
> - The researcher observed instances of children's pretend play and kept notes of the scenario, participants, negotiations, roles and narratives.
> - When invited, the researcher participated in the play setting but refrained from suggesting or initiating any activities or modes of performing.

Including both participant and non-participant strategies in the observations allowed the researcher to move between these levels of involvement in a fluid and non-intrusive manner. Where further clarification was needed, the researcher initiated conversations with the children who were keen to explain why certain roles were carried out in certain ways and what the characteristics of different roles should be. Participant observations also facilitate a less visible role for the observer, who may be involved in the regular routines with children but also recording and documenting what is happening without the children being distracted by such activity. At times, the researcher must acknowledge the potential impact their presence may have on children's behaviours and interactions. As pointed out by Papadopoulou (2012, p. 584), the intention of the researcher was not to be 'a fly on the wall' but rather to minimise any potential disruption to interactions. Findings identified from the observations carried out by Papadopoulou (2012) were classified under four key themes, which emerged in the role-play of young children. These included the themes of *sheltered families, the battle between good and bad, disobedience and punishment,* and *the world of protectors and their protégés.* More detail on these findings is outlined and discussed in Chapter 5.

Observing and recording with technological media

There are many electronic recording devices that can be used to enhance observations. A brief overview of some of the types of technological media that can be used to enhance observations are outlined and discussed below. The early childhood practitioner's knowledge, skills, experience and creativity using technology expands with practice but should never replace the intimate one-on-one interactions with a child (Dockett & Perry, 2007). Over many decades, photographs have been used as research evidence, stimuli to generate further data, and documentation of research processes (Rose, 2016), eliciting not only information but also affect and reflection from participants and researchers (Knowles & Sweetman, 2004). Digital technology has further contributed to making photography more accessible in everyday routines. Observation more generally enables the capturing of moments in order to reflect on these further at a later point. Photography facilitates a particular kind of observation – one that might involve 'snapping up passing moments' (Nilsen, 2017, p. 340). Photography may also be particularly valuable as an observation tool in capturing children's expressions in order to gain insight into their precise responses to events and people in their environment and to pinpoint environmental stimuli that may be triggers for problematic behaviour.

Digital video recorders have the advantage that observational recordings can be played back for children to view, review and respond to.

Breathnach et al. (2018) point out that paradigm shifts over the past two decades in childhood research have resulted in an increasing recognition of engaging children as research participants (Alderson, 2008; Mason & Danby, 2011; Prout & James, 1997; Theobald, Danby & Ailwood, 2011; Theobald et al., 2015). Engagement in research is a right that tends to be granted to adults, older children and young people but that is not typically afforded to children in a way that acknowledges them as competent participants in research and as 'experts in their own lives' (Clark & Moss, 2011, p. 35). In the Focus on Research below, the co-production of child–researcher interactions with children aged 5 years in their first year of primary schooling in Australia was explored. The study was informed and underpinned by principles of the sociology of childhood with a particular emphasis on the social competence of young children. The study provides an illustration of how early years educators, researchers and children collaborate actively to access and express children's feelings and responses to their experiences. In negotiating visits to the classroom, the classroom teacher suggested a schedule that provided the researcher with opportunities to observe teacher-directed episodes, spend morning tea and lunchtime with the children, and accompany the children to specialist lessons (such as science and physical education). Researchers were also invited to observe and participate, where and when children invited them, in child-led, free-choice activities, such as craft, puzzles and pretend play.

FOCUS ON RESEARCH

Children as researchers and co-researchers

Becoming a member of the classroom: supporting children's participation as informants in research

(Breathnach, Danby & O'Gorman, 2018)

Study aims

Explore the co-production of child–researcher interactions with children aged 5 years in their first year of primary schooling in Australia.

- Participants included 1 primary school teacher, 2 part-time teacher assistants and 25 children (13 girls and 12 boys).
- Fieldwork occurred over five months. The researcher engaged with children inside and outside of the classroom. Researcher participation in children's activities was at children's request or invitation.
- Video-recorded participant observation and informal conversations formed the basis of data collection. Inside the classroom, 65 hours of video-recorded participant observations and conversations with children were recorded.
- Outside the classroom, 40 hours of audio-recorded participant observations and conversation with children were recorded.

Breathnach et al. (2018) draw attention to a number of points which are worth highlighting in the research process that the study above involved. Inviting the researcher to observe and, at times, engage with the children in their activities, was a practice the children were familiar and comfortable with, as teachers, teacher assistants and parents were involved regularly in classroom activities. Including the researcher as sometimes observer, sometimes participant ensured that the researcher's role was not singular or fixed but was multi-faceted and one which adapted with flexibility to the contexts and participants in the setting. Such an approach is well aligned with ethnographic research, where the researcher is positioned as a research instrument and the children as research participants. Adopting fluid and flexible roles and positions in the research process facilitates the collaborative construction of relationships, knowledge and identities. Significantly, children played a central role in this collaborative construction of knowledge as the data collection was guided by each child's interests and their inclination to engage with the researcher. Video recording of children inside the classroom captured key aspects of their interactions as they engaged in their everyday classroom activities and practices. Audio recordings were used in outside spaces to avoid capturing images of children from adjoining classes who were not part of the study.

Findings related specifically to the research process in the study above included a challenge to the typical generational social order of the classroom and an exchange of typical roles, with children represented as expert informants and the researcher represented as learner.

Specifically, with regard to challenging the generational social order, the researcher noted that children tended to respond to her with gestures that communicated their distinction between adult- and child-typical behaviours. An example of this was identified when the researcher joined the children in conversations outside while they were sitting on the grass. When she sat down alongside the children, one child brought her a chair to sit on. The researcher asserted she would prefer to sit on the grass, thereby asserting her position as equal to the children in terms of body positioning and relationship. Moreover, the researcher did not work within the teacher positioning typically taken on by other adults in the setting but rather took a stance of learner, which presented opportunities for the children to assume roles as the expert insiders and informants about their school practices.

Note

1 The Magic Carpet is further detailed as a research method in Chapter six.

5 Ways of listening
Supporting children's conversations

In this chapter, the value of listening is emphasised as an essential part of establishing respectful relationships with young children and of accessing and sharing their meanings. The chapter draws on and further explores material generated through the Mosaic Approach (Clark, 2005; Clark & Moss, 2001) in order to better understand listening to children as an active process of receiving, interpreting and responding to communication. The concept of a pedagogy of listening is expanded on, acknowledging the significance of listening as a strategy for children to make sense of their world. A pedagogy of listening foregrounds the need for researchers and educators to go beyond listening alone and to facilitate a reflexive process in which young children can review and reflect on meanings, make discoveries and new connections and express understandings (Clarke, 2005). The researcher's role as facilitating 'internal listening' and 'multiple listening' is also highlighted in this chapter. A range of strategies and research tools for supporting children's conversations, based on empirical work, are outlined and discussed. One such strategy involves using focus-group interviews, following a model of circle time, which allow children to express their views within a format that is a familiar part of their everyday routines. Other strategies, building on the Mosaic Approach, include: child-to-child interviews; interviews through child-led tours; storytelling and narrative approaches, including small world play interviews and persona doll interviews; and finally a focus on listening to children through dramatic play activities. These strategies will be further elaborated on, with a particular focus on visual research methods with young children in Chapter 6. Analysing and interpreting data will focus primarily on identifying themes and patterns occurring in the data.

A fundamental part of understanding what children are feeling and an effective means of tuning into and gaining insight into children's early years' experience is knowing how to listen to children. Listening to children is an integral part of early childhood education and early years practitioners regularly tune in to individual children's interests, activities and competencies as part of everyday routines. Practitioners are, therefore, well positioned to bring these skills to their work with young children, with particular reference to the knowledge and competences required for effective listening to children. Key aspects of listening, according to Clark (2004), involve being open to *actively* receiving, interpreting and responding to communication. Such a perspective on active listening places an emphasis on more than the spoken word to include actively listening through the senses and emotions. Clark (2004) draws attention to five key principles central to effective listening to children, including respect, openness and collaboration, honesty, patience and timing, and imagination. These principles are outlined in further detail below.

Principles central to effective listening

(Clark, 2004, pp. 3–4)

Respect

Children of all ages, backgrounds and abilities are important, unique and worth listening to.

Openness and Collaboration

Children use many different ways to communicate, requiring openness, receptiveness and willingness to learn from those who know them well.

Honesty

Honesty is needed about the extent to which we can act on children's views and to explain how other people's views may need to be taken into account.

Patience and Timing

Working with young children requires patience, especially if they have communication difficulties.

Imagination

Designing ways of listening that are enjoyable, varied and sensitive to children's strengths and abilities requires imagination.

Adapted from Listening as a way of life: Why and how we listen to young children

A pedagogy of listening

Consistent with an emphasis on active listening, the term *pedagogy of listening* (Rinaldi, 2006) highlights the idea that the early years practitioner or researcher working to access young children's views needs to be vigilant and perceptive of children's expressions, being particularly attentive to the multi-modal ways through which children communicate, giving rise to the term 'the hundred languages of children'. Similarly, Dalli and White (2016, p. 44) emphasise the importance of a relational pedagogy facilitating adults' learning to know the child and their particular 'communicative idiosyncrasies', including within their wider socio-cultural context. A pedagogy of listening builds on an understanding that children's language expression and comprehension is enhanced when adults are responsive and receptive to children's communicative endeavours and, therefore, privilege children's own voices (Johansson & White, 2011). It also rests on research that shows that responsive adults attend as much to gestures and bodily movements as to vocalisations in order to make communicative interpretations.

A number of important elements involved in a pedagogy of listening have been highlighted by Rinaldi (2005) and further emphasised by Clark (2011). Three key features of such an approach include: internal listening or self-reflection; multiple listening, or openness to other voices; and visible listening, which includes documentation and interpretation. Specifically, *internal listening* emphasises the importance of listening as a strategy for children – a reflective process for children to consider meanings, providing children with ongoing opportunities to process meanings and, through such attentive listening, to make discoveries and connections in order to make sense of their world. A key focus of internal listening, therefore, is to help children to find meaning in all that they experience. The feature of *multiple listening* draws attention to the opportunities that such an approach provides for practitioners and children to listen to each other and to themselves. Clark (2011, p. 20) further elaborates:

> This conveys the multifaceted nature of listening: it is not limited to one exchange between two individuals but is a complex web of interactions, continually moving from the micro to the macro level.

Finally, a focus on the element of *visible listening* places the emphasis on documenting using strategies such as note-taking, children's drawings, photographs and other visual methods. This enables practitioners and researchers to record children's expressions and responses to their experiences, and to create a trace or a visible artefact which, in turn, makes children's meaning visible to a range of individuals and groups, both within an early childhood setting and beyond.

An invitation to conversation

Engaging children in conversations occurs as a natural part of early childhood education. An essential feature of inviting and encouraging children to engage in conversation is being attentive to the environment in which conversations occur. A key aspect of developing such an environment in which children feel comfortable and at ease sharing their views is through a focus on building trusting relationships with the children participating in the research.

Johnson et al. (2014a) point out that if research is not conducted in a supportive, trustful environment, the data we gather from children may not accurately represent the views of the young children involved. Certain children may dominate the process and some children may feel uncomfortable if they do not have an established and trusting relationship with the early years practitioner or researcher. In *Steps for Engaging Young Children in Research Vol. 2* (Johnson et al., 2014b), useful strategies are outlined for helping researchers build trusting relationships with young children in order to enhance their opportunities for expression. Similarly, in Chapter 7, simple mindful activities appropriate for carrying out with young children in order to set the context and help children feel calm and relaxed are outlined and discussed. Many early childhood settings organise and design their learning environments in a way that invites and encourages children to engage actively with aspects of that environment and the people they share those environments with on a daily basis. Small, cosy spaces with lower-level room can noise ease stress that may inhibit conversations (Nilsen, 2017). Conversations may also flow more naturally and with ease when children are involved and absorbed in activities. In the extract below, the home setting provides a comfortable environment for an interview with a young child.

> Emerald's interview took place in her home. Her mother was present throughout the entire interview. Emerald was a kinetic chatterer. During our interview, Emerald tumbled on the sofa without missing a beat answering or telling her stories. She ran around the room, hid behind the curtains, and left the room to get props, such as hats and pictures, on many occasions, never leaving the context of her present story. She would keep talking in a louder voice when she left the room to let us know she was still with us, just getting something from her room.
>
> Extract from Irwin and Johnson (2005): *Interviewing Young Children: Explicating Our Practices and Dilemmas*

Planning and scheduling certain times of the day to invite children into conversation is also an essential feature of building an appropriate environment to engage children in conversation. Nilsen (2017, p. 176) draws attention to the concept of 'facilitated conversations' as, throughout the day, opportunities will arise to listen to children's conversations. Facilitated conversations can be planned during playtime conversations, during snack and mealtimes and during other everyday routines within early childhood settings. Opportunities such as these allow possibilities for children's social talk to be scaffolded by educators. Balancing lower-level and higher-level conversations during the day also assists in children's language and cognitive development. Below, strategies that are useful in scaffolding children's conversations in terms of moving them from concrete to abstract thinking are highlighted by Nilsen (2017).

> **Moving a conversation from concrete to abstract thinking**
>
> **(Nilsen, 2017)**
>
> **Level I:** Focuses on labelling and locating objects – *What is this?*
> **Level II:** Focuses on describing and recalling by filling in blanks in a sentence or urging remembering of a past event – *What did we use when we made this snack?*
> **Level III:** Focuses on summarising, comparing and inferring – *How do you think he felt when he saw the bus leave without him?*
> **Level IV:** Focuses on making predictions, problem solving and explanations – *What do you think they could do next?*

Listening to Young Children through Interviews and Focus Groups

There are many creative methods and means of carrying out effective interviews with young children. However, interviews with children in the early years require different skills and strategies to those required for interviews with older children or adults. Researchers keen to engage with children through one-to-one interviews without carefully considering the limitations of such an approach may actually inhibit children's ability to engage in spontaneous and meaningful conversations (Mukherji & Albon, 2018). Power dynamics between adults and young children are one of the major difficulties that faces researchers. Such power dynamics can be a barrier to the collection of high-quality evidence from young children. Other challenges include children's relatively short attention span and egocentrism, which may prompt them to respond to a question from a very particular perspective and in a manner that will be pleasing to an adult researcher.

Child-to-child interviews

Innovative strategies to overcome these challenges include inviting other children to be researchers themselves, by taking on the role of interviewing other children. This 'child-to-child' technique has been pioneered in international development as a tool for conveying information to children as well as for discovering their views (Clark, 2017). The thinking behind this method is that children, because of their 'inside knowledge', might be able to ask more relevant questions than adults. However, it should be noted that such an approach is more appropriate for use with older children. Older children can also work with younger children in order to help to elicit their views and one way of facilitating such an approach is to include children's older siblings as the interviewers. Such an approach is adopted in a study on active meaning-making with one- and two-year-olds, which was carried out with young children in Norway. In this study, early years practitioners explored how indoor play spaces in a kindergarten could become a more meaningful environment for young children (Clark, 2017).

The method of older children working with younger children can contribute to reducing some of the power differentials that may arise when adults engage in conversation with young children. Older children's interests, perceptions and understandings, at times, are more closely aligned to younger children's than those of adults, particularly in the case of an older sibling (Clark, 2017). A variation on this method of interviewing young children is to adopt a 'buddy partnership' approach to capturing children's meanings (Levy & Thompson, 2015, p. 137). Such a participatory approach involves pairing younger children with older children and encouraging each dyad to engage in conversations around the research topic under focus. Key to the success of such a participatory technique is the cultivation of a strong and unique relationship that can build between children throughout the duration of a project. In the Focus on Research below, the use of 'buddy partnership' as a technique to access the voices of young children was explored. The study was designed in order to respond to a request generated by a local authority in South Yorkshire, concerned about the achievement of boys in reading within parts of a particular city. In this study, 5- to 6-year-old boys were paired with 11- to 12-year-old boys, and each dyad was asked to contribute towards the creation of an information DVD that would help teachers and parents understand the factors that influenced children's engagement with reading.

FOCUS ON RESEARCH

A buddy partnership approach to interviewing young children

Levy & Thompson (2015)

Study aims

The study aim was to understand 5- to 6-year-old boys' attitudes towards reading, including factors that promoted/impeded engagement with reading.

- Video data revealed numerous examples of the 11- to 12-year-old boys using techniques such as *leading questions, gestures and prompts* to encourage the younger boys to talk about their perceptions of reading.

- Older children were able to use skilled questioning to enquire more deeply about the kind of books that younger children liked/disliked and offered prompts and suggestions to help younger children be more explicit, in a manner that would not have been possible within a child–adult research relationship.

Insights generated by this research approach emphasised that older children played a crucial role in the research, as their empathetic and playful approach meant that they communicated with the younger children in a context that was defined by the existence of shared understanding, enhanced by the closeness in age between these young and older boys, which would not have been possible within a child–adult research relationship (Levy & Thompson, 2015). The pairing of children of mixed ages promoted the creation of comfortable and relaxed research environments and the children spontaneously and naturally created informal research spaces within the rooms in which they were working. Older children demonstrated an instinctive understanding of the younger children's needs in this respect, and it is unlikely that adult researchers would have been able to manipulate the research environment in quite the same way. The project also revealed that, while the older boys were able to interact in a playful and relaxed manner with the younger children, they were also able to use their communication skills effectively to encourage a depth of dialogue with their partners. Variations on the 'buddy partnership' approach that have been used with children in early childhood settings include small friendship groups in which children are encouraged to engage in conversation around a particular topic with a small group of children and, especially, children with whom they have close friendships.

Child-led tours and walk-around interviews

The natural world of many children involves movement and activity, and to attempt to have children sit and focus can create unnecessary strain (Irwin & Johnson, 2005). Mobile methods (Griffin, Lahman & Opitz, 2014) such as child-led tours offer researchers a means to enhance their ability to interview children in a context that is natural and meaningful to the child. In a mobile interview, the researchers move along with the child in their natural environments and daily activities. This type of child-led interview mirrors a child's normal discussions with adults from their home life, where conversations may take place during shopping trips, on walks, and commuting to and from school. Child-led tours facilitate conversations with a child or group of children, with the child leading a 'tour' through a particular space of their choice, while the researcher annotates their experiences or assessments of the space (Johnson et al., 2014a). This kind of child-led mobile interview allows the researcher to learn from a child about places and features considered significant to them. It has been used effectively in both indoor and outdoor spaces, and in the evaluation of spaces for play (Nallari, 2014). In some cases, a still camera held by a child can improve the clarity of purpose of the activity, especially when the purpose is to learn about qualities of the physical environment or about specific places in a child's environment that have some particular meaning to them. Audio recording during a tour with an individual child, or a pair of children, is important if researchers wish to capture a child's spontaneous comments on their experiences of, and emotions about, familiar spaces while walking (Clark, 2011). The information that can come from these comments, generated during the child-led tour, can offer insights into a child's personal experience that do not typically emerge when using sit-down methods. In the Focus on Research below, children's perspectives on their outdoor learning spaces were explored, involving child-led tours conducted by the children in pairs.

> **FOCUS ON RESEARCH**
>
> **Child-led tours and young children's perspectives of outdoor learning spaces**
>
> **Merewether (2015)**
>
> - Multi-method approaches, including child-led tours and photography, used with 3- and 4-year-old children (four boys and four girls) explored their perspectives on the outdoor environment in their early childhood education setting.
> - In pairs, the children took the researcher on 'tours' of the outdoor space, pointing out and photographing 'interesting', 'special' or 'important' places.
> - Conversations during these tours were audio-recorded. In a follow-up visit, the photos were the focus of informal conversations with each pair. Each child identified three photos of the most important places photographed, which were added to a documentation book that progressively told the story of the research.

As highlighted in this extract, allowing the children to take an active and leading role in the research through the use of the child-led tours and the associated images and conversations generated through this approach provides an illustration of the effectiveness of multi-modal approaches to capturing children's meanings in the early years. Four key themes were identified through a focus on the children's photographs and conversations as follows: *Places for socialising; Places for pretending; Places for observing; and Places for moving.*

Similar work using child-led tours as part of a multi-method approach to capturing children's meanings was summarised by Merewether and

Fleet (2014). Potential difficulties and pitfalls that can arise when using a child-led tour approach, incorporating the use of cameras, are highlighted in the extracts in the Focus on Research below.

> **FOCUS ON RESEARCH**
>
> **Seeking children's perspectives: a respectful layered research approach**
>
> **Merewether and Fleet (2014)**
>
> **Study aims**
>
> This article draws on findings from a study (Merewether, 2012) that investigated 3- and 4-year-old children's perspectives about outdoor spaces in the Western Australian early childhood setting they attended.
>
> - As a familiarisation strategy, I invited pairs of children to show me, as an 'authentic novice' (Clark & Moss, 2005, p. 97), and to record with photos, the interesting/special important' places in the indoor setting. Although they took a few photos where the framing was out, or that were blurred (even though the cameras were self-focusing), overall, on this tour, the children proved themselves to be competent photographers who took deliberate, precise photos.
>
> - This first tour, however, revealed the importance of having conversations with the children about the photos they had taken. For instance, one photo appeared to me to be of a fluorescent light on the ceiling, but as the child pointed out, it was in fact a photo of me taken from a child's eye view: 'That's a photo of you and you're important'. Because I am standing underneath a light in the photo, I am silhouetted and difficult to see, but the light is prominent.
>
> - Another photo could have been interpreted as a photo of a flyscreen door; however, even though the children had been asked to take photos of important places indoors, the child told me this was a photo of the outdoors.
>
> - Electing to conduct indoor tours before conducting tours of outdoor areas turned out to be very advantageous. Not only did the indoor

tours provide an authentic context for children to become familiar with the equipment and practise their photography skills but these tours also provided a chance to discover potential challenges.

- For example, this is where I first encountered issues with the audio-recorders, and was also how I discovered that I needed to be explicit in asking pairs of children to take me on a tour 'together'. Otherwise, there was a tendency for each child in the pair to simultaneously conduct the tours individually.

- A rough map of the child-led tour that took place outdoors is presented below (Figure 5.1)

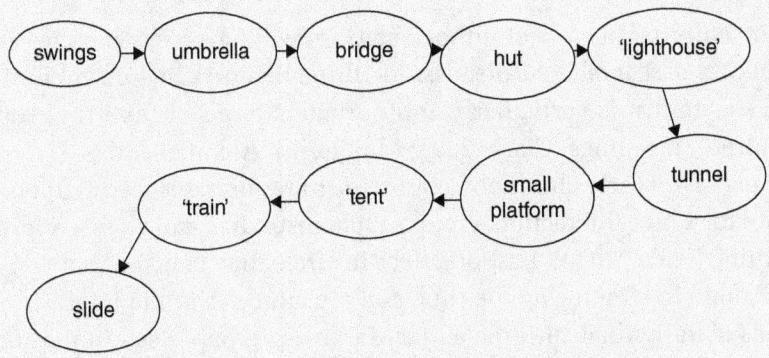

Figure 5.1 Map of child-led tour, which was conducted outdoors

Group child-led tours are extremely valuable but they have a different rationale and range of uses to individual child-led tours (Johnson et al., 2014a). With younger children, it may be very difficult to organise group-led tours, although young children working in pairs seems to work well. Johnson et al. (2014a) emphasise that group child-led tours may be suitable for small groups of children *over 5 years of age*. It also has a special value for children with additional needs as a means of enabling them to richly describe the barriers and challenges they face in their daily movements. The practitioner or researcher walks with a child and this enables a researcher to get closer to the lived experience of a child. A group tour is valuable for obtaining a range of different perspectives about a community, a local environment or an indoor institutional setting. As with the individual child-led tours, these older children feel encouraged when they are leading the tour. Depending on the research focus, the practitioner or researcher will invite the children to take them on a tour in order to point out and talk about places or place-related events that are relevant to a particular research exploration. In advance of a group child-led tour, it is important to provide opportunities for the children to discuss amongst themselves what route to take and where to go first in order to be able to discuss relevant issues. The process involves children being informed that, when they come to a place of interest on the tour, they should indicate to the group that they would like to stop and spend some time discussing this particular place.

Focus group interviews using a circle time format

Many children in early childhood settings will have regular experience of taking part in shared discussions through story-time or circle time and this format is particularly appropriate in terms of capturing young children's meanings (Clark, 2004; Mukherji & Albon, 2018).

Successful early childhood circle times are short, respectful opportunities for active interaction, group problem-solving, and well-scaffolded learning (Parks, 2014). Best practices in circle time demand that you are deliberate in structuring the time and are attentive to the interests and needs of individual children and children as a group. Respect the attention span of the children and plan circle times for young pre-schoolers that last no longer than 10 minutes. Focus group interviews with children in the early years, informed by the circle time format (Clark, 2005), can be less intimidating for young children than one-to-one interviews and can diffuse the balance of power between adult interviewer and child interviewees (Brooker, 2001; Carr, 2000). However, shy or less articulate young children may not have the confidence to contribute to these encounters in a group situation.

Particular strengths associated with focus group interviewing include the fact that children will often feel more comfortable when with other children that they know and like (Mukherji & Albon, 2018). Such a format can also encourage interaction between children and new ideas and meanings can be generated through interactions with different members of the group. In a group discussion, children can freely express their perspectives on an issue in an informal, relaxed manner that is closer to their everyday interactions with peers or friendly adults in early years settings (Johnson et al., 2014a). In such a format, children may feel less pressure to answer every question, especially those questions which individual children may not understand.

Storytelling and narrative approaches to listening to children

Narrative approaches to listening to children include a number of ways of helping children to communicate their ideas and responses relevant to a particular research topic. Storytelling is one of the ways through which children can be included in a research process and which adopts a format that many children will be familiar with in early childhood practice. As summarised by Burke (2015, p. 1):

> A story is composed of events that can be real, imaginary, or organized through forms such as pictures, words, songs or even dances. Relating the events of a story can also be termed a "narrative". Children often tell narratives along a time-line, describing self-identifying features, a sibling's birth, or the process of a day at school. Notably, these stories help children make sense of their world by engaging their feelings, exploring complicated feelings and emotions, or connecting them to childhood memories through their association with characters and illustrations in picture books.

A story may be drawn from a child's own life, or it can be based on a child's knowledge of a particular issue or event (Johnson et al., 2014a). Stories may be created by children individually, or children may construct stories with others. Storytelling techniques can take on various forms – less frequently, relying primarily on textual accounts or including graphic image. Children may engage in storytelling through providing biographies of other children or family members or, more widely, others in the community. Children may construct stories about an ideal life or idealised characters or may engage in storytelling that involves a focus on changes or events that have occurred (Johnson et al., 2014a). In the Focus on Research below, extracts from an article describing a research project on empowering children's voices through the narrative of drawings are presented.

FOCUS ON RESEARCH

Empowering children's voices through the narrative of drawings

Anne Burke (2015)

Memorial University

- As the researcher, I was particularly interested in looking at literacy practices developed through play pedagogy in school compared to how children constructed literacy in their out-of-school play at home. My research intent was to engage children, through narrative, in the types of texts and literacy events they use outside of the classroom. This is a very natural way for the children to share their stories about how literacy is constructed in their worlds.

- Focusing on the process involved in the construction of a story, and 'topic-centered narratives' in particular, I relate children's literacy moments as "snapshots of past events that focus around particular topics and themes and are fragments rather than extended narratives" (Jones, 2011, p. 112).

- Through observation of these literacy moments, we are able to analyze how a child creates meaning and constructs these moments as a story around a particular topic.

- We had created a unit on fantasy, using the story *The Paper Bag Princess*, and the children had been busy working on scenery for the castle in the block area, re-enacting different storylines through puppets.

- As part of the oral language retellings of story, Leslie wished to engage children in a discussion about stereotypes and gender. She knew that the children felt empowered by the protagonist in the story they were discussing, a heroine who stands up for herself, questioning stereotypical viewpoints of dress and image.

- Throughout the week we had seen this story narrative through a number of ways: as a puppet play where children explored what it meant to judge someone by their clothes, and how the character Ronald is 'just behaving badly'. We see how the children understand

- that the resolution means an end for some of the main characters, and in some cases we may have to lose something in order to gain something else.
- The play scenario, enacted by the children the day before, entitled "Ronald's apology", shows how children can also develop resolution in their own lives by exploring differing viewpoints of the characters, perspectives and ways to address acceptance and difference.
- After playmaking, Robert Munsch's popular tale, we gather together on the story mat to talk more about the book. I am curious to see how the children retell the story.
- Using their expressive language, the children become a part of the critical discussion about how the protagonist stands up for herself – using their own voices, they question stereotypical viewpoints, dress and image, and come to a critical understanding of *The Paper Bag Princess*.

Burke (2015) goes on to describe how some of the children were given the task of recreating the story through the drawing of a picture series, which sequenced the events of the story.

One of the children, Daneisha chose to draw Elizabeth the protagonist (see Figure 5.2 below) as a happy princess, now that she had told Ronald 'off for his rude behaviour.'

Sitting next to her at the writing and drawing centre, the researcher (here, 'R') asked her to retell the story through her drawing.

R: *I like your picture. It has many wonderful things about the story. Can you tell me about your picture?*
Daneisha: (excitedly, pointing with her tiny fingers) *See? There is the castle where she lives with her mom and dad. They are called the king and queen, you know, and there are trees here, but they are small because of the dragon burned all of them*
R: *I like how you drew Elizabeth* (smiling).
Daneisha: *You like her? Kieran said she was too tall* (laughing). *Her crown. Look! Her crown...* (circling the top of her crown with her whole hand) *Her head is in the sky.*
R: *Why do you think you drew her that big?*

Figure 5.2 Elizabeth, the protagonist, as illustrated by Daneisha

Daneisha: *That's the secret in my picture...* (She pauses and looks up at me and quietly says)
Do you really want to know why?
R: *Okay, tell me why?*
Daneisha: *Because... because... I think that is how Elizabeth feels now that she is not Ronald's friend* (in a really loud voice) *the bum* (laughing)!

Burke points out that Daneisha's narrative provided insight for her into how children know much more about life than adults sometimes expect and, furthermore, about how young children's narratives are central to their understanding of even a complex theme, such as stereotype and identity. Burke (2015, p. 9) summarises some of the key messages to be taken from this research process:

> The verbal retelling of the story showed how children explore the ideas of the plot, but can also extend the original ideas of the story. The collaborative play through painting, drawing, puppets, and role-play using the block areas, created a setting for the imaginary castle that enabled the children to feel the story as if it were alive. It reinforced narrative structure and allowed them to use their own words, drawing on their cultural understandings. Children used the narrative of their own lives and combined that with Robert

Munsch's beloved tale in order to explore differing viewpoints of the characters, perspectives, and attitudes of society. This was the first of many lessons, in which the children would learn the value of critical inquiry through narrative of self and story in a classroom.

Diaries are especially useful to explore children's use and perception of time. However, diaries may not be suitable for working with children in the early years, as the tasks involved may be too complex. A further difficulty might be ensuring confidentiality for diary extracts in both the school and home setting (Fargas-Malet, McSherry, Larkin & Robinson, 2010). Digital storytelling uses technological tools such as an interactive whiteboard, computer, mobile phone, or tablet (Lissenbee & Ford, 2018). These technological tools provide a foundation for offering digital storytelling experiences in a classroom and can be adapted for use in research with young children (Karakoyun & Kuzo, 2016).

Listening to children through play

Play can be considered as one of the most distinctive activities that children engage with and as one of the defining characteristics of childhood (Papadopoulou, 2012). Play, as well as learning, are natural components of children's everyday lives (Pramling Samuelsson & Asplund Carlsson, 2008). In the sections below, the possibilities for listening to children through a focus on their play activities are outlined and discussed.

Dramatic play as a strategy for listening to young children

Dramatic play is spontaneous, child-initiated and a part of children's everyday development (Nilsen, 2017). Socio-dramatic play is the interaction of two or more children in a play theme with each holding separate roles. Using their imagination, children create scenarios that enable them to consider and experience different possibilities. An insightful illustration of how play and, in particular, dramatic play, can effectively facilitate listening to and hearing young children's meanings is provided through reflecting on a study carried out by Papadopoulou (2012) on The Ecology of Role Play.

FOCUS ON RESEARCH

The ecology of role play: intentionality and cultural evolution (Papadopoulou, 2012)

Study aims

The aim of the study was to observe several role-play activities that were orchestrated and performed by the children themselves without external pressures or interference.

- The participants included 18 children, 10 girls and 8 boys, between the ages of 4 and 5 years at date of commencement, attending school for the whole day (from 7 am to 3 pm).

- The data presented here are taken from a larger study of children's school experiences that took place in the reception class of a Greek state primary school and lasted for four months.

- The methods used were participant and non-participant observation. Instances of children's pretend play were observed and recorded and notes were kept of the scenario, participants, negotiations, roles and narratives.

- When invited, the researcher participated in the play setting but refrained from suggesting or initiating any activities or modes of performing.

- In this way, play settings were initiated, directed, negotiated and performed only by the children themselves and thus might be admitted as reflecting only their intentions and perceptions.

- On some occasions, questions were asked after the end of the play session, concerning areas the researcher did not understand.

- Often the children were keen to explain why certain roles were carried out in certain ways and what the characteristics of different character roles should be.

Such clarifications proved useful during the stage of data analysis, offering the children's first-hand explanations of the structure and shared meanings.

The data analysis process involved the identification of emergent themes. The raw data, which included descriptive accounts of children's role play sessions, were read and re-read before general categories of meaning could be identified. The attempt was to discern what central themes engaged the children, notwithstanding different play scenarios, roles or participants. The four identified themes presented below refer to the qualities, characteristics, values, ideals and purposes that the children assigned to their invented character roles. Four key themes were identified: sheltered families, the battle between good and bad, disobedience and punishment, and the world of protectors and their protégés (Table 5.1).

Edmiston is a researcher who embraces play as a strategy that children and adults can participate in *together*, as opposed to play being seen as the preserve of young children to be observed at a distance by adults (Mukherji & Albon, 2018). By participating in children's play, Edmiston (2008) argues that researchers can share authority with children and, in so doing, raise and explore a range of issues that are important to them both.

Small world play interviews

Small world play involves children engaging with objects and artefacts to build a 'small world' in which they can use fantasy and imagination in order to create scenarios and develop scripts around their everyday experiences. Children use small-scale representations of real things like animals, people, cars, and train sets as play props (NCCA, 2009). This kind of play has the potential to promote child development across a number of domains. By providing young children with opportunities to express their feelings and thoughts and experiences through play, children's creative and imaginative skills are supported and reinforced. Small world play also offers the opportunity for children to build on their language skills, expanding their vocabulary and their understanding.

Other props, such as a puppet or a toy mobile phone, can help to put children at ease in order to help them take part in interviews. For example, toy mobile phones allow an interview to be conducted in the form of a role play (Johnson et al., 2014b). Through such an approach,

Table 5.1 Themes identified during role-play (Papadopoulou, 2012)

THEME	FEATURES OF THEME
Sheltered families	Children of both genders frequently engaged in this play theme. The 'family' always had a physical, enclosed space as its shelter. This was created by the children by lining furniture in a round shape to surround their playing space and isolate it from the remaining room.
The battle between good and bad	The scenarios of such play followed distinctive patterns. They were predicated on a struggle against the 'powers of evil' that meant no good to humanity and were trying to 'destroy the world'. These were the destructive forces that lived with the sole purpose of harming humans. They had super-powers and could do things that human beings could not. They could only be overcome by the 'super-powers of the good', an opposing team of super humans whose purpose was exactly the contrary: to save humanity from destruction.
Disobedience and punishment	This theme was explored in scenarios where the players enacted roles of naughty, disobedient and cheeky 'children'. They misbehaved, did not do as they were told and, in effect, they were punished. This could take place in a 'familial setting', where 'parents' advised, or instructed, their 'children' to behave in certain ways, but the 'children' remained disobedient. They intentionally chose not to follow 'parental' advice and consequently experienced negative consequences, such as getting 'cold', 'ill', 'lost', threatened by 'dangers', being 'stolen', having an 'accident' or being 'punished' and 'smacked'.
The world of protectors and their protégés	This meaning-category emerged frequently and consistently, as children constructed plots and narratives that reflected power differentials between characters. It included characterisations of people who were 'weak' or had to deal with situations that were beyond their capacity. They were unable to meet an overpowering challenge, their well-being was at risk, jeopardised by forces beyond their control, until a different character, one more powerful, knowledgeable, experienced and willing to protect them, appeared and saved the day.

children are supported to participate without feeling intimidated in the presence of the researcher. A further benefit of such an approach is that the process is primarily play based and children enjoy being part of it. This method can be especially useful in understanding children's perceptions of various environments, such as their perspectives on their early years learning environment.

Persona doll interviews

Related to small world play interviews, persona doll interviews have been used in educational settings to facilitate capturing children's interest and imagination through a primary focus on the 'person' of the doll. 'Persona dolls are specially created dolls (about the size of a toddler) used to tell stories that raise issues of equality, promote talk and discussion of personal thoughts and feelings...' (Nutbrown, 2011, p. 110). Having a doll take the place of an interviewer can sometimes help reduce the imbalance of power between interviewer and child (Johnson et al., 2014a). Persona dolls realistically represent children, their dilemmas and their feelings (Jesuvadian & Wright, 2011). Stories, which children narrate using the persona dolls, can be used as a starting point for discussion in a semi-structured interview. In the following section, the methods, data analysis and key findings from a study carried out to explore young children's experiences of and views on friendship are outlined. Particular emphasis is placed on the use of both small world play interviews and persona doll interviews to better understand their role in capturing young children's meanings.

FOCUS ON RESEARCH

A Pedagogy of Friendship: Young children's friendships and how schools can support them

Carter & Nutbrown (2016)

Study aims

The study aimed to listen to children to understand how they make meaning about their friendship experiences.

- A multi-method study was carried out using small world play interviews, drawings and persona doll scenarios to consider children's everyday experiences of friendship in school.

- The study took place in a school in the north of England and the small sample included seven children aged between 5 and 6 years of age.

(Continued)

- A range of child-appropriate research methods with individuals and groups were adopted: drawings, persona doll work and small world play interviews.

- The selected research methods created a range of opportunities for the children to express their friendship experiences.

- Children were invited to play with a set of miniature figures and playground equipment and to answer a set of semi-structured questions about different playground scenarios.

- The persona doll was called Zack. Zack was introduced to the children and talked to them about the friendship challenges he faced when moving house and starting school. Zack was looking for advice about how to join in a game that other children were playing.

Through a focus on Zack, the persona doll, children in the study were invited to give their advice on how Zack could overcome his difficulty in joining in activities, playing with other children and making new friends. Children's perspectives on how Zack could overcome these challenges identified unique aspects of their peer culture, including specific rules, routines, concerns and practices to which adults are often oblivious. Terms and expressions were devised by children to express rules in terms of how many children could join in a particular activity, such as that it is a *two-er* game or a *three-er* game.

The importance of a small object or toy was expressed by the children – being allowed to bring a pocket toy (a Lego figure, for example) to school was vital to them. Children indicated that these were a source of comfort at playtime if they were unsuccessful accessing play and friendship. These toys were kept in coat pockets and came out at playtime.

> Henry referred to his pocket toy as security if he found there was no-one to play with in the playground. Zack should say 'shall I take this to school so I can play with this at playtime?'... Zack should still try to make friends but if they say 'no' he still has something to play with.
>
> (Carter & Nutbrown, 2016, p. 405)

Having identified an understanding of children's perceptions of friendships, insights from the children and the literature were used to create the concept of a 'Pedagogy of Friendship'.

Three key themes were identified and are presented in Table 5.2 below.

Table 5.2 Summary: three features of a 'Pedagogy of Friendship'

FEATURE	THEME	DETAIL OF THEME
Feature 1	Practitioner knowledge relates to 'peer culture and friendship' findings	This feature emerged from what children expressed about their peer cultural practices. Having knowledge and awareness of children's peer cultural practices in relation to children's friendships will support practitioners to make appropriate practice decisions that are well informed by research in the field and in tune with children.
Feature 2	Valuing friendship relates to 'making and maintaining friendship' findings	The children told me how much friendship meant to them – having the belief and conviction to focus on children's friendships. This includes getting to know individual children well, knowing details about their personality, interests, previous social experience, home culture, childcare provision and family context. This will enhance children's social and emotional development and ultimately their holistic development.
Feature 3	Time and space for friendship relates to 'time and space for friendship' findings	The children were telling me they needed time and space to make and maintain their friendships. Practitioners can support children to develop agency and organise time and space in a school or setting in order to create the capacity for friendship. Practitioners need to allow the time for children to establish and maintain friendships.

6 Making children's meanings visible

In this chapter, the Reggio Emilia's conception of documentation as combining many forms of texts to make learning visible is elaborated on to inform our understanding of how to develop a more sophisticated level of visual literacy in children and in professionals working with young children. Drawing on material and principles developed in the Mosaic approach (Clark, 2017; Clark & Moss, 2001), the key focus of this chapter is highlighting illustrations of how combining text and image or video and image interact 'to create something more communicative than is possible with the use of a single medium' (Wien et al., 2011). The chapter also draws on some material from Steps for Engaging Children in Research (Johnson et al., 2014b). Using visual methods in research and early childhood education practice generates rich opportunities for young children to communicate their feelings and to share and display their knowledge and creativity.

Children's multimodal ways of creating meaning

Children have a unique and natural ability to communicate using multiple media and modes, such as textual, aural and visual representations and, in this sense, young children are 'meaning-makers par excellence' during the early years of child development (Wright, 2007, p. 37, as cited in Deguara, 2015). The authors highlight that these communication abilities develop and are supported in young children, prior to the acquisition of the skills of reading and writing.

Moreover, supporting these meaning-making abilities using multiple media and modes underpins and reinforces the development of literacy in later development. Children use a wealth of diverse multiple modes and materials to make meaning and typically move with ease between and across these different modes (Bock, 2016). Several studies have clearly illustrated children's multimodal ways of creating meaning (Deguara, 2015). A common thread across these studies is that children's experiences of engaging with a rich multiplicity of modes generates unique experiences and opportunities for children to engage in meaning-making. A range of techniques have been highlighted for listening to young children, which shift the balance away from an exclusive reliance on primarily the written or spoken word and onto visual and multi-sensory approaches, as emphasised in the Mosaic approach (Clark, 2017; Clark & Moss, 2001) and in Reggio Emilia pedagogical approaches. When children engage in drawing and image making, it enables them to communicate their feelings, share their views, ideas and perspectives, and demonstrate their creativity.

Reframing research with children through an engagement with visual artefacts

Reconceptualisations of children and childhood, as outlined in previous chapters, have contributed to the increased use of visual research methods with young children and to the development of effective and creative research methods and activities, through which children's meanings can be expressed and shared, if desirable and appropriate (Dockett, Einarsdóttir & Perry, 2017). Encouraging and supporting young children to make their ideas and working theories about the world visible to others creates possibilities for sharing children's meanings. thereby broadening our perspectives and our possibilities for greater responsiveness (Krechevsky et al., 2013). In the field of education, visual research has become more commonplace, particularly in research involving children (Semenec, 2017).

Listening to young children's ideas and views and facilitating their expression through drawings, photographs, film or video can generate deeper insights into children's lived experiences and their responses to those experiences. In contrast to more traditional approaches to doing research with children, research methods which involve children expressing their views and communicating through drawings and other means of visual expression also contribute to empowering children through participation in the production of knowledge (Thompson & Gauntlett-Gilbert, 2008). Beyond participating in research through expressing their views, children can be invited to contribute to the selection of creative research tools and activities by designing and developing the research instruments. In this way, they can participate in helping to select the method and the particular type of visual medium that they would like to use. In the Focus on Research below, Merewether and Fleet (2014) provide an account of research in which young children participated in the selection, design and development of visual tools and other appropriate tools for researching young children's meanings.

FOCUS ON RESEARCH

Seeking children's perspectives: a respectful layered research approach

(Merewether & Fleet, 2014)

Study aims

The present study investigated 3- and 4-year-old children's perspectives about outdoor spaces in the Western Australian early childhood setting they attended.

- Children vary in their abilities, experiences and preferences. A key feature of this study was providing children with a choice of ways in which they could participate to enable them to have opportunities to express their thoughts using ways in which they were comfortable.

- This was not always convenient for us as researchers, particularly when children exercised their right not to participate; however, we believe that limiting children's means of expression would have detracted from the integrity of the data by increasing the likelihood of responses provided to please the adult rather than representing genuine thinking.

Making children's meanings visible 129

- One strategy alone was not sufficient; a combination of strategies that offered possibilities for children and adults to work together was found to provide children with the most opportunities to express themselves.
- The study took place over eight weeks. Having gained parental consent, the site was visited each week for at least half a day, with some longer visits. Figure 6.1 below shows the focus of each weekly visit.

As can be seen from the different stages of the research process highlighted in Figure 6.1, children were included and informed about the study in multiple ways and on an ongoing basis. Children's willingness to participate in the study was also monitored on an ongoing basis, and indications of a lack of interest in a particular activity was considered

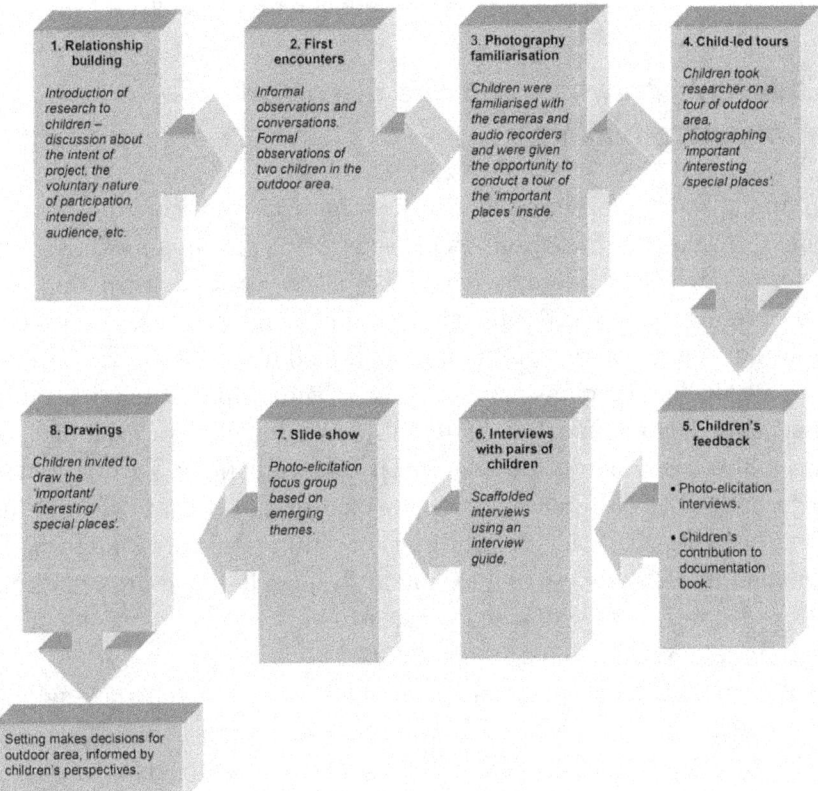

Figure 6.1 Focus of each weekly visit
Source: Merewether & Fleet, 2014

as a signal of a child's wish to withdraw. Children's participation in this study was also attentively and carefully scaffolded by means of developing a multi-layered approach to capturing their meanings. As summed up by the authors:

> ... it was not just the layering of strategies that was valuable in this study. Highly significant was the affordances the multimodal strategies provided for adult–children interactions, children–children interactions, and the possibility to make these visible. These strategies did not relegate the researcher to 'fly on the wall', nor did they relegate children to being voiceless objects of research. Rather, they provided a catalyst for dialogue amongst children and adults and thus developed relationships and the ability to communicate with each other, in a variety of ways.
>
> (Merewether & Fleet, 2014, p. 910)

Children's drawings and the discourse of meaning-making

Young children's meaning-making is a multifaceted, complex experience (Wright, 2007). Within the discourse of meaning-making, children's drawings can be understood as the process of constructing and interpreting signs in order to convey their thoughts, ideas, concepts or opinions (Duncan, 2013; Wright, 2007). Children's visual and artistic communication involves a combination of verbal and non-verbal text or assembled signs (Burke, 2015). In children's drawing, for example, the assembled signs could include visual representations, such as drawings, as well as children's commentary on the process of constructing their drawings. The rich possibilities for children's expression through the medium of drawing, and extended through the medium of telling, allow each of these symbolic domains to enrich and inform the other (Kendrick & McKay, 2009; Wright, 2007).

A number of factors have the potential to impact on the drawing process and the construction of children's meanings. These include the availability of resources and materials, the cultural context in which drawings take place and the extent to which drawings are created in collaboration with other children or adults (Einarsdóttir, Dockett & Perry, 2009). Historically, children's drawings were used to assess their development physically, in terms of their fine motor skills, and cognitively and emotionally, through a focus on how children represented the human figure at certain ages. However, more recently, the communicative power of children's drawings as a research tool to enhance our understanding of children's meaning-making has been highlighted (Tay-Lim & Lim, 2013).

Young children typically show interest and enjoyment in painting and drawing, which makes it a positive experience and one that is likely to allow them to feel at ease while communicating their ideas. Drawings are usually self-initiated and, therefore, using children's drawings lends itself to 'non-invasive, non-confrontational and participatory research' (Morrow & Richards, 1996, p. 100, cited in Roberts-Holmes, 2018). Below, key factors in the rationale for facilitating children's expression through drawings in research with children are briefly outlined.

Why use drawings in research with children?

Einarsdóttir, Dockett and Perry (2009)

Giving children control: Using drawings in research allows children to have some control over the nature of their engagement in data generation activities.

Non-confrontational basis for interactions: Children can draw without being forced to maintain eye contact; this can help to overcome the challenge of a power imbalance, where existing power structures can encourage children's responses that align with teacher expectations.

Familiar tools and materials: Drawing provides children with opportunities to communicate with familiar tools and materials and encourages children to engage in conversations in a meaningful way.

Taking time for children to respond: Using drawings in research encourages children to take time to respond to questions or engage in discussion as they take the time to draw, recognising that co-construction of meaning takes time and is a transformative process.

Combining verbal and non-verbal means of expression: Drawings in research also acknowledge that some children prefer to convey their perspectives and experiences through a combination of verbal and non-verbal means.

There are many different ways of including children's drawing in research, with much emphasis in contemporary research being placed on the associated process and journey to children's meanings, rather than on the content and end-product of children's drawings. In many cases, early years practitioners and researchers facilitate an extension of children's meanings through guided, gentle interviews and document the resulting narratives onto the visual representation or record it in a separate document. Children can be interviewed during the drawing process, during and after the drawing process or after an interval of time has elapsed following completion of the drawing (Einarsdóttir et al., 2009).

Draw-and-talk methods

Draw-and-talk methods offer many possibilities for guiding and scaffolding young children's meaning-making and for providing a more complete and comprehensive account of children's perceptions of the research issue at hand (Tay-Lim & Lim, 2013). Professionals working in the field of early childhood education are aware that young children enjoy drawing and talking with adults and peers around them. The nature and quality of the interactive process, between children and other children and between children and early years practitioners, has a central role in this methodology and is a key feature for the interpretation of the data. The important role of the practitioner in the co-construction of children's meanings is further explored below in a section on the role of co-construction in the drawing process.

Consulting children through drawings, either prompted or free drawings, can facilitate access to rich and meaningful knowledge about children and their thoughts and feelings in response to their experiences (Roberts-Holmes, 2018). However, drawings may be somewhat ambiguous or vague in form and content, so it is appropriate to give children the time and space to comment on and interpret their represented meanings. One way of better understanding children's intentions and achieving an accurate interpretation of children's drawings is discussing with the child what it is they are drawing *as they draw it* (Roberts-Holmes, 2018). This may be particularly appropriate with young children, who may not have yet developed formal writing skills (Coates & Coates, 2006). Draw-and-talk methods provide children with rich opportunities to represent reality and to create meaning when used as a research method. In the Focus on Research below, a study carried out by O'Rourke, O'Farrelly, Booth and Doyle (2017) invited children to talk about their first experiences of school in a disadvantaged community, using a draw-and-talk approach to represent their meanings. The potential benefits of positive early school experiences for children living with socio-economic disadvantage is emphasised by the authors, who draw attention to the need for greater insight into children's own perspectives on their experiences of school in the early years. Details from the study highlighted below are drawn from participants recruited as part of a wider Children's Thoughts about School Study, using a convenience sample of two designated disadvantaged schools. A multi-method approach was adopted to maximise the breadth of experiences captured (Darbyshire, McDougall & Schiller, 2005) and ensure the reliability of the data collected (Dockett & Perry, 2007).

FOCUS ON RESEARCH

'Little bit afraid 'til I found how it was': children's subjective early school experiences in a disadvantaged community in Ireland

O'Rourke, O'Farrelly, Booth and Doyle (2017)

Study aims

Understand and represent children's subjective experiences of the first months of formal schooling.

- Participants included 26 children (17 boys and 9 girls) aged 55.8–70.6 months.
- The research method highlighted here was a draw-and-talk approach in which children were provided with an A4 sheet of paper, crayons, and colouring pencils, and asked to draw a special picture of themselves in school.
- Children who wished to engage in conversation while drawing were asked general questions about their school experiences.
- Other children were invited to tell the researcher about their drawings, once they had completed their drawings.

Four key themes were identified following analysis of the drawings and accompanying children's narratives: *Me in school; What happens in school; Peers and friends;* and *My life around school.* Overall descriptions of school were mostly positive, representing it as a place of achievement, reward and connection, yet also one of difficulty and exclusion.

While much of the attention paid to children's drawings has been on the finished product and the labelling of that product, documenting children's narrative during the drawing process can help to record 'the journey of their construction of meaning' (Einarsdóttir, Dockett & Perry, 2009, p. 219). As can be seen in the Focus on Research above, emphasis is placed on the drawing process and children's accompanying narratives in order to listen attentively to children's voices. What children tell us, as well as the drawing itself, provide insight into their experiences.

Practitioners and other adults in the role of researcher play a central role through engaging with children to facilitate the co-construction of meanings in this way. Children's thoughts and ideas are expressed through these narratives and their meanings are co-constructed through guided interactions with practitioners/researchers, as illustrated in the study by O'Rourke et al. (2017), summarised above.

Drawings have been used in research with young children in less open-ended approaches, where children have been instructed or encouraged to focus on a particular memory or feeling associated with a particular experience they have had. Einarsdóttir, Dockett and Perry (2009) included children's drawings in research on their perspectives on starting school. In a study carried out in Australia, children in their first year of school were asked to reflect on what had changed for them over the year. Using a large piece of paper folded in half, children were asked to draw and/or write to complete the statements: 'When I started school I ...' and 'Now I ...' Comments were either written by children or scribed by the teacher, as illustrated in Figures 6.2 and 6.3.

Figure 6.2 Child's reflection on how he has changed during the first year of school

When I started school I was crying because it was scary and I made new friends and that made me happy. Now I am happy because I am used to school.

Figure 6.3 Child's reflection on how she has changed during the first year of school

When I started school I was sad because I didn't know anyone. Now I am happy because I know lots of people.

In the Focus on Research below, an extract is presented from a project in which children in two different environments, in Palestinian refugee camps in Lebanon and in the south-eastern part of Norway, were given the opportunity to express themselves through drawings. Once again, these children's drawings were generated in response to prompts, encouraging the children to draw something that made them happy and to draw something that made them sad. Conversations with the children once the drawings were complete provided further insight into the children's views. Comparisons were then made between the ways in which young children expressed themselves within the different cultural contexts.

> **FOCUS ON RESEARCH**
>
> **What makes me happy, and what makes me scared? An analysis of drawings made by Norwegian and Palestinian children**
>
> **Maajero and Sunde (2016)**
>
> **Study aims**
>
> To explore representations of happiness and fear in the drawings of children in Palestinian refugee camps in Lebanon and in the south-eastern part of Norway.
>
> - The number of participating children was 19 in Norway and 29 in Lebanon.[1]
> - Children were 5–6 years old.
> - Each child was asked to draw two pictures with the following instructions as guidance:
>
>   Draw what makes you happy
>   Draw what makes you scared
>
> ---
> [1] The reason for the difference in number between the two countries is that the number of children in the kindergarten groups was larger in the refugee camps than in the Norwegian kindergartens, and we did not want to exclude any children.

The researchers used similar materials and a similar format in both the Palestinian and Norwegian contexts. Children's drawings were made on large sheets of paper of the same size (A3) and of the same quality in both countries and also with the same kind of coloured pencils. A line was drawn down the middle of the sheet of paper, allowing the child to complete both the drawing of what made them happy and the drawing of what made them scared. In addition, the children were asked to briefly explain their drawings to the kindergarten teacher when they had finished their work and handed it in. Key findings in the study indicated that there are several similarities among the children's drawings of what made them happy: a bright sun, members of the family or friends and flowers and trees were often drawn. Representations of what made children scared were also similar across the different cultural contexts, with many children indicating animals as a source of fear. The Norwegian children were, however, scared of wild animals from remote areas that they would never meet in the Norwegian natural environments, such as lions, tigers and crocodiles. On the other hand, the Palestinian children were afraid of domestic animals in their own surroundings such as dogs and cats. Some of the children across the two cultural contexts were also afraid of imaginary characters, such as monsters, ghosts and dragons.

Free drawings and prompted drawings

The value and usefulness of exploring children's meanings through their visual representations is further highlighted by Duncan (2013) who emphasises that free drawings as a means of expression impose no boundaries on what can be included in representations.

Duncan (2013) draws attention to the fact that researchers may obtain different data when using prompted drawings and free drawings. Using the free drawing approach, children have control over all aspects of the process and can follow their own agendas, to a greater extent. Moreover, the free drawing activity can be framed as relaxed with no pressure on 'performing', which minimises the power imbalances that may exist between the child and adult (Duncan, 2013, p. 277). Researchers who use only children's prompted drawings may be accessing a constrained view of children's perspectives on play, for example, as these drawings tend to include only tangible objects such as sports equipment, toys or cartoons.

The importance of including both prompted drawings and free drawings in research with children is therefore recommended.

The benefits of allowing some time to elapse between drawing and talking with the child have also been emphasised. In allowing an interval between carrying out the drawing and having a conversation with the child about their drawing, the child is given greater opportunities to reflect on the topic and to express their point of view without being influenced by the interviewer, without time pressure and without being forced to talk about it (Einarsdóttir, Dockett & Perry, 2009). An important aspect of using drawings with children in research in a meaningful way is to avoid placing too much emphasis on the tangible outcome generated through the drawing process, and to focus to a greater extent on the relationship between children's narratives and their drawing process. Excessive focus on the final product can lead to a failure to capture the most crucial aspects of children's meaning-making.

The Together Old and Young (TOY) project began as a European-funded initiative in 2012 in response to the situation that, while people were living longer, many older people and young children were having less and less contact with each other. The aim of TOY is to bring young children and older adults together to share experiences, have fun, learn from each other and develop meaningful relationships. Intergenerational Learning (IGL) has been defined as 'the way people of all ages can learn together and from each other' (EMIL, 2014, p. 1, cited in Fitzpatrick, 2019). Through IGL, children have opportunities to form relationships with older people of mixed ages, abilities, cultures and experiences that may be quite different to the relationships typically experienced within the ECE service (Fitzpatrick, 2019). Current research in the area of IGL as a pedagogical approach within ECE, and carried out as part of a research project by Fitzpatrick, draws on the perspectives of ECE practitioners working within the context of IGL and further draws on the perspectives of young children and their experiences of IGL within these early childhood settings. Children's drawings and subsequent conversations with practitioners are one of the research methods through which children's perspectives are being included. As part of this IGL practice, children's regular visits to nursing homes and centres for older persons are facilitated by ECE practitioners, who document the children's experiences in a number of ways, many of which include children's drawings of their experiences and interactions, and photos of the people and the activities encountered during the visits. Early years practitioners working alongside the children also document the details of visits using textual and visual representations. These visual and textual documents facilitate ongoing reviewing and revisiting the children's experiences of their IGL visits and the particular interactions they have with the older people in the settings. In this way, the unique and unanticipated ways in which children process the meanings of their experiences can be identified and highlighted.

Off-task conversations in research using children's drawings

Research with children using drawings as a research tool to capture children's meanings has identified a variety of ways in which children's talk may be generated in response to their engagement in the drawing process (Coates & Coates, 2006). Children may talk related to the subject matter, as illustrated in the examples above where children engaged in narratives, either alone or with adults, around the content and associated topic of their drawings. However, children also typically engage in social talk when engaged with drawing in ECE settings, and these conversations are not always related to the topic or content of the child's drawing. Such conversation tends to focus to a greater extent on common issues of companionship. Coates and Coates (2006, p. 229) term these interactions as 'off-task' conversations where children talk about families, homes, class and friends. The authors go on to emphasise that these types of conversations have the potential to generate invaluable insights into children's backgrounds, children's concerns and feelings, and children's ways of thinking. Interaction with adults, such as researchers or early childhood educators, about the content of drawings also occur on a regular basis, not only helping to stimulate subject matter but also enabling the adult to model, reinforce and support the children's language (Coates & Coates, 2006).

Co-constructing meanings in children's drawings

Children's drawings can provide us with an evocative window into children's meanings. A significant and central feature of the expression of these meanings is how they are scaffolded through interactions with adults or older peers. Capturing young children's meanings is typically a collaborative process and meanings are often co-constructed and mediated through the early childhood practitioners' interactions with the child. Jordan (2004, cited in Tay-Lim & Lim, 2013, p. 70) highlights the importance of children and adults:

> ... developing inter-subjectivity as they each enter into a common space of meaning-making. The discussion is kept open-ended and the child's voice is given room for expression and exploration as the adult contributes respectfully by making links between the child's thoughts, affirming the child's ideas, and extending the child's views. As the adult facilitates the child's 'sense-making', she or he also acquires a shared understanding of the child's perspective. This approach allows for the fluidity of the child's ideas to emerge, to develop, and to be shaped and defined in the process.

Co-constructing meanings in research with young children moves us away from an exclusive adult-centred understanding and reinforces the notion of young children as influential and active agents, capable of contributing significantly to the joint interactive meaning-making activity. The types of questions that early childhood practitioners can use to scaffold and, thereby, contribute to extending children's thinking are also worth noting. An example of the types of questions that can elicit higher order thinking in older children (aged 6 years and over) are presented by Tay-Lim and Lim (2013, p. 76) with reference to a drawing by a 6-year-old child, presented in Figure 6.4.

Constructing theories

Questions that helped children to develop their own theories around what they had drawn and how they understood some of the associated concepts included:

- Why do you think we see stars only at night?
- Why do you think the astronauts need to dig out the rocks?

Forming hypotheses

Children can be helped to extend abstract thinking skills and build imagination by focusing on hypothetical situations such as:

- What happens/might happen if there is not water?

Figure 6.4 Child's drawing of space travel

Reasoning/logical thinking

Children can be supported to extend and expand their reasoning and logical thinking skills through questions such as:

- Why can't they take a car to the moon?

Analysing/evaluating/comparing

Probing questions related to children's drawings can also be used to build skills of analysis and comparison as illustrated in the following questions:

- Which do you think is the better way?
- Are they the same?

Elaborating/illustrating

Children can be scaffolded to expand on and elaborate on their ideas through questions such as:

- Can you tell me more about this gravity?
- A moon buggy? What is a moon buggy?

Problem-solving skills

Targeted questions can also scaffold children's thinking about problem-solving, as follows:

- What else do you think they can do...besides gluing...to join all the pieces together?

Analysing and interpreting children's drawings in research

Analysing, interpreting and sharing meanings generated in children's drawings can be a significant challenge for practitioners and researchers, although the complexity of this process may well depend on the research aims and objectives associated with children's drawings as a research tool, and the extent to which the practitioner/researcher wishes to engage with more technical principles, which underpin the analysis of children's drawings.

There are two distinct ways of approaching the analysis of children's drawings: one which is broadly projective, and another which focuses on content and not on interpretation (Merriman & Guerin, 2006). The focus here is largely on the content of children's drawings and the narratives generated through conversations with children about their drawings. Unlike other forms of data, there are few well-defined or widely accepted rules for the analysis of visual images and, in particular, children's drawings (Duncan, 2013). The context in which children's drawings are being explored will influence the way in which educators and researchers work to analyse, understand and interpret children's visual representations.

Children's input to this interpretative process is invaluable. In the following sections, a brief overview of different approaches to analysing and interpreting young children's drawings in research are outlined.

Annotating children's expressions on drawings

Many educators and researchers support children's expression of their meanings through documenting textual summaries of children's narratives using interviews and informal conversations, as we have seen in some of the examples above. Annotating children's expressions about their drawings is a simple and practical way of facilitating access to what the child is prioritising in their representation of a particular experience. In some contexts, these annotations alone will provide sufficient information that can be used to convey the key meanings that individual children attach to their visual representations.

Thematic analysis of children's drawings

A thematic analysis of children's drawings is appropriate when a number of drawings have been generated from children, focusing on a particular topic or research area. In the Focus on Research above, Maajero and Sunde (2016) used a thematic analysis in comparing similarities and differences in children's representation of what makes them happy and what makes them scared. A thematic analysis of the children's drawings indicated that the theme of nature and families was strongly associated with children's representations of happiness, while the theme of animals was identified in association with children's fears.

Framing analysis of children's drawings

Some researchers have used what is termed a 'framing analysis' to analyse and interpret children's drawings (Lämsa, Jokinen, Rönkä & Poikonen, 2017). Such an approach was used in a Finnish study, which sought to explore images of childhood (Lämsa et al., 2017). The study focus was how children, together with adults, represent childhood in the home and daycare settings in a one-week diary study. Children's pictorial representations and accompanying captions were used as a research method. The key analytical tool was framing, which was used to highlight what kinds of images are (re)produced and narrated. Two frames were identified in both the day-care and home settings. The first, portrayal of the child via culture and societal relations, prioritises the cultural context of childhood, which comprises its different environments and material and cultural resources, and reflects behavioural rules and expectations, as depicted in Figure 6.5.

The second framework generated a portrayal of the child via individuality, relationships and attachment, and describes childhood in the context of social relations and with reference to the child's personal features and skills, as depicted in Figure 6.6.

An analysis strategy such as that of the framing analysis outlined above provides an interesting and systematic method for interpreting and representing the meanings children wish to convey through their drawings. Such a strategy helps to provide a coherent means of accessing the different themes and issues which children represent in their drawings. However, the more complex and technical the analysis

Portrayal of the child via cultural products and societal relations

The child in childhood environments	The child of consumption and possession	The child of rules and expectations
Picture 1 (left) Here is the day-care centre's playground. It's been nice to make snowballs. Picture 2 (in the middle) WC Picture 3 (right) Small stones in the yard (after sanding the icy courtyard)	Picture 4 (left) Fireworks at the Christmas Street opening ceremony. Picture 5 (in the middle) Daddy had borrowed PlayStation 2! In the evening we played. Picture 6 (right) Cutting images from paper is a favourite thing to do. Cut and paste…	Picture 7 (left) 'In this picture is someone who forgot to put on his long johns. He had forgotten to put them on in the day care centre, and mother was cross'. Picture 8 (in the middle) 'It always goes wrong.' Self-critical fellow. Picture 9 (right) I asked what the child is doing in the picture. He answered: 'I'm making a bonfire with matches. Even though I am not allowed to touch matches.'

Figure 6.5 Sample framing analysis: Portrayal of the child via cultural products and social relations

Making children's meanings visible 145

Portrayal of the child via individuality, relationships and attachment			Framing of attributes
The child with relationships	The child performing social competence	The child with individual features and skills	The child as a learner
Picture 1 (left) Me and Heidi are having a snowball fight outside. Picture 2 (right) Our family is happy. Mummy and Daddy.	Picture 3 (left) Today that smaller girl Sara really saw a water monster in a puddle… I saw a brown hare with my dad on our way back home. Picture 4 (right) Funny picture of my sister Carita.	Picture 5 (left) I am at home and I am sick. Father stayed home to take care of me, and did not go to work. Picture 6 (in the middle) I'm at the cottage with my Daddy. But I miss my Mummy. Picture 7 (right) Lizard made of beads	Picture 8 'Here I am painting. And there also. With whom?' With Sari and that with Sari also.' (Sari is a kindergarten teacher student) (We noticed that the handedness of the child changed)

Figure 6.6 Sample framing analysis: portrayal of the child via individuality, relationships and attachment

becomes, the more adult-focused the interpretation is likely to become. There is a risk that in an over-analysis of children's visual representation we may obscure and move further way from the original objective of including children's drawings – to understand the phenomenon from the unique and different perspective of the child.

A number of points are worth considering when analysing children's drawings and these are broadly summarised below, adapted from Maxwell (2015) and Duncan (2013).

- Explore the initial impression of each picture and 'bracket' or subsume one's own value system, in order to resist any temptation to interpret. That is, to recognise and acknowledge that the researcher has a value and belief system, which can cloud and influence qualitative analysis.
- Systematically look for focal points, e.g. situations, people and objects and missing items (omissions).
- Synthesise what has been learnt from the individual components and assemble the information into a whole.
- Analysis and interpretation should not rely on extensive content or features possibly absent in young children's drawings, such as signs to anchor the image, human figures, colour or gaze.
- Take account of the entire drawing process and not just the tangible product.
- Adopt an approach that uses and privileges the meanings attributed to representations by the children themselves, rather than basing analysis solely on adult interpretations.
- Have a standardised process. This will ensure a systematic and consistent method of analysis with each drawing. In other words, using the same process with each drawing, with the same rigour.

Cameras and photographs in research with children

Over many decades, photographs have been used as research evidence, stimuli and prompts to generate further data and documentation of research processes (Rose, 2016; Einarsdóttir & Perry, 2017). Insightful examples of children's use of cameras and photographs in research have been generated through a focus on the Mosaic approach (Clark & Moss, 2001). These studies have inspired researchers to explore the multiple sites of meaning through which we can gain insight into young children's thoughts and feelings. Different ways in which photographs can be used in research with children include children taking photographs to create an image to represent their meaning, early childhood practitioners and researchers taking photos to document situations and events related to a research topic, and previously taken photos or images being used to prompt and stimulate conversations on a particular topic. Three different ways of using photographs in research with children are highlighted below by Holm (2008) and reinforced by Dockett et al. (2017). These are subject-produced images, researcher-produced images and pre-existing images.

> **Ways of using photographs in research with children**
>
> **Holm (2008)**
>
> **Subject produced images:** Researchers invite participants to photograph aspects of their lives and associated experiences and explore the images through conversations with participants.
>
> **Researcher-produced images:** Researchers document events or situations related to the research topic in focus.
>
> **Pre-existing images:** Existing, sometimes historic, photographs are used to explore a topic with participants.

Value of cameras and photographs with children

Much of the recent research involving young children and photography has relied on subject-produced images in approaches such as photo elicitation. Taking their own photographs provides children with the possibility of using a powerful visual language (Roberts-Holmes, 2018). Photographic methods allow children to exercise power during data gathering as they choose, and to take the photographs themselves, and the subsequent interviews and conversations with children will revolve around the images they have photographed, allowing them to direct the interview process (Martin & Buckley, 2018). Children using cameras to take their own photos of their ECEC setting is a relatively recent research technique. Children know that photographs are enjoyable and are valued by adults, so they will tend to have fun taking photos. Photographs are, thus, a powerful way for children to record aspects of their daily lives. Even very young children are quite capable of taking photographs of the events and situations that affect them. These photographs can then be printed out and further explored and discussed with the children.

Digital and disposable cameras

As pointed out by Clark (2017, p. 46) every piece of technology has certain 'affordances' that enable its users to carry out particular tasks. This also applies to equipment employed within a research context. These affordances will support research participants to communicate in certain ways. Advances in digital technology have been rapid over the past two decades. The reduction in the relative cost of digital cameras has led to their widespread use in schools and in early childhood settings. Some early childhood institutions (Roberts-Holmes, 2018) increasingly own digital cameras, computers and printing facilities. Children can see their results instantaneously on the camera itself and the subsequent computer printouts. This rapid process helps to focus children's attention on the photographs. If there is a delay of several days between taking the photos and seeing the results, the children's interest may have been lost and they may not be able to explain why they took the photos. Disposable single-use cameras are also successful with young children because they are less expensive than digital cameras. They are also small and light enough for the children to walk around with and put in their bags or their pockets to take with them. So, with disposable cameras, children may feel they have more control over the content of their photographs. Below extracts from an article on the value of using photographs with children in research highlight some of the benefits of using this research tool.

Value of using photographs with children

Research with children: methodological issues and innovative techniques

Fargas-Malet, McSherry, Larkin and Robinson (2010)

- Using photographs taken by the child or by the practitioner/researcher helps to build and maintain rapport between interviewer and child and may capture the children's attention more easily and for longer.
- It enables children to have control over choosing what they wish to talk about as their photos represent aspects of their own experiences and views.
- Children's own pictures can be used in an interview as an instrument to help children develop their answers to particular questions and, at the same time, to enable children to express facets of their lives in a unique way (Clark-Ibáñez, 2004).
- Children's own photographs are probably more likely to reflect what matters to them (Samuels, 2004).
- Photographs can also give structure to the interview, provide a focus, and act as a clear and tangible prompt or as a means for remembering.
- It represents an effective way of eliciting relevant detailed information and rich descriptions from the participants, leading to 'a far deeper understanding than a simple conversation' would (Newman et al., 2006, p. 301).
- Photographs can act as prompts to a child's personal story (Newman et al., 2006).

Photographs taken by young children can thus provide a platform of communication between adults and young children (Clark, 2005). Early research and development studies have included young children taking their own photographs of important places and people in their pre-school setting (Clark & Moss, 2001; Lancaster, 2003).

The 'London on your doorstep project' (Children's Society/Save the Children, 2001) used children's photographs as one tool to find out about their experiences of the wider environment. 'Outdoor spaces' was the focus of a study carried out to listen to young children (Clark & Moss, 2005) in which discussions based on photographs taken by 3- and 4-year-old children played an important role in deciding on changes to the play environment. The photographs served as a representation of children's experiences that might not be easily articulated in other ways. Other possibilities include adults taking photographs which they then use as prompts in order to explore children's views (Warming, 2005). A brief extract summarising some details of using photographs with children in research (Merewether & Fleet, 2014) is presented below.

FOCUS ON RESEARCH

Seeking children's perspectives: a respectful layered research approach

Merewether and Fleet (2014)

Study aims

The present study investigated 3- and 4-year-old children's perspectives about outdoor spaces in the Western Australian early childhood setting they attended.

- Photographs were taken by children on child-led tours of the early childhood setting.

- The researcher later spent some time with the individual children to explore the meanings they wished to represent through the photographs they had chosen to take.

- Following these conversations, children were asked to place a sticker on 'three photos of the most important places' and these were glued into the documentation book, as illustrated below in Figure 6.7.

Figure 6.7 Page from documentation book

Photo elicitation

Photo elicitation is a particular term used to refer to the use of photographs in the course of research interviews (Miller, 2016; Mukherji & Albon, 2018) as an aid or prompt to elicit responses. As discussed above, photographs can serve a purpose as a prompt rather than just being included as visual representations. Photo elicitation has been used in interviews with young children, either as an ice-breaker or as a focus for discussion (Mukherji & Albon, 2018). Photo elicitation has the potential to engage children in a natural way in a research project, to open up novel and interesting ways to participate in research, and to increase children's willingness to be involved (Dockett et al., 2017). In addition, it is an attractive and novel method for engaging young children in research.

In the Focus on Research below, extracts from an article on photo elicitation (Dockett et al., 2017) are presented.

FOCUS ON RESEARCH

Photo elicitation: reflecting on multiple sites of meaning

Dockett, Einarsdóttir and Perry (2017)

- This paper explores the method of photo elicitation and proposes the use of critical visual methodology as one means to interrogate the images involved.
- Issues of production, content, audience and interpretation are reflected on, as well as how these contribute to understandings of the visual element.
- The aim is to support critical reflection and conversation about what has been a widely adopted method in research with young children.
- The photo below was taken by a 5-year-old boy, Arnar, who participated in a project that had the dual purposes of exploring children's views of the preschool and enhancing educators' understandings of strategies that promoted listening to children's perspectives (Einarsdóttir, 2005).
- The project was conducted in one preschool in Reykjavik, Iceland.
- The participants were twenty-two 5- and 6-year-old preschool children – 12 girls and 10 boys. All of the children were of the same ethnic background and from similar socio-economic circumstances.

- Arnar was one of a group of children provided with digital cameras and invited to lead the researcher on a guided tour of their preschool environment.

- On the photo tour, Arnar pointed out what he thought was important in the preschool, what he liked and where in the playground he felt good. As he identified these, he took several photos. The researcher printed out the photos he had taken and, after a couple of days, returned to the preschool to talk with Arnar and his peers.

- During the individual discussions, Arnar was given a printed set of the photos he had taken. In his discussion, Arnar was asked about the photo of the playground he had taken. He corrected the researcher's description of the photo, indicating that he had instead taken a photo of his neighbourhood, with his home just visible in the background.

- The complexity of interpreting children's photographs and visual representations of children's meanings more broadly is clear when considering Arnar's photo of what appears to be the preschool playground.

- Discussion with the researcher indicates that this is not the case and that the background, rather than the foreground, of this photo is significant for Arnar.

Photobooks

Photobooks represent an extension of the activity of children or adults taking visual images with cameras of certain select aspects of the child's experience (Johnson et al., 2014a). A selection of relevant photographs can be presented in booklet format with textual commentary annotated by the child, or in collaboration with an adult, or alongside other visual material. Photobooks can be put together by children themselves or in collaboration with early childhood educators or researchers, depending on the context in which the photographs are being used. In Chapter 5, the method of using child-led tours was explored to support and enhance ways of listening to young children in research. Child-led tours involve a 'mobile conversation' (Johnson et al., 2014a, p. 77), whereby a child or a group of children guide the researcher(s) around spaces located within their everyday living environments (e.g. neighbourhood, places of work, school, etc.).

In a study of child well-being and ill-being in Peru (Ames, Rojas & Portugal, 2010, cited in Johnson et al., 2014b), the focus was on schooling environments, with the child-led tour and associated questions centring on children's perceptions of school, their likes and dislikes, and their experiences starting school. Data were collected and explored over two sessions. In the first session, the children were invited to guide the researcher around the school premises, with a view to creating a photo album for new students coming to the school. The children were asked to take photos of places and things that they considered would be most important for new students to know about, in order to help them settle into their new school. The researcher photographed the important places indicated by the children and subsequently asked children about their experiences. During the second session, the children discussed the photos and decided which ones to include in the photobook, along with their captions.

Findings from this study are further detailed in Chapter 7.

Photographs can, in these ways, become the focus for listening to young children in everyday situations and facilitating children's involvement in consultations (Clark, 2011). In the Focus on Research below, extracts are presented from a study of children between 3 and 4 years of age who were involved in taking photographs of aspects of their early childhood setting that they liked, in order to contribute to an understanding of developing services that are responsive to including the 'voice of the child'.

FOCUS ON RESEARCH

Photobooks: listening to young children study (1999–2000)

Clark and Moss (2001); Clark (2017)

- Photography facilitated access to children's meanings through visual representation and created opportunities to produce a finished product in which children could take pride.

- Twenty children participated (children aged under 3 years and aged 3 to 4 years).
- One set of photographs was made for each child to take home and a second set created to make an individual photobook with each child.
- These activities became a means of clarifying with children what they intended their photographs to be about and their feelings about results.
- Listening to children as they chose photographs they wished to include in their books was an important feature.

Some of the key areas that the younger children (under 3 years of age) highlighted in their photographs were friends, keyworkers, favourite play equipment, hidden spaces, scenes of days out, own artwork, trees and furniture. The older children, aged 3–4 years, used their photos to highlight key areas about younger children's lives in the early childhood setting, including: keyworkers with the children, mattresses, parents and visitors in the room, cots, changing areas, potties, towels, play equipment and washing areas.

Interpreting photographs in research with children

Interpreting photographs can present a number of challenges, as illustrated in the example above of Arnar's photograph in research carried out in Iceland on children's perspectives on aspects of their environment (Dockett et al., 2017). While Arnar's photo clearly depicted an image of the playground, it was only through further conversations with Arnar that it became apparent that the focus was on his neighbourhood and his house, which was visible in the background. Such challenges are common across a number of multimodal methods of expression, given the many meanings and interpretations that visual and other representations can generate. The benefits of the many participatory, multimodal methods that have been developed for research with children have been established, yet uncertainty remains about the role and purpose of the image within these. Dockett et al. (2017, p. 225) draw attention to a number of important questions about how we interpret meanings, as represented in children's photographs:

> For example, how are images to be analysed; does the image represent a child's 'reality'; is the image itself considered data, or is the major purpose of the image to stimulate discussion? Together, both photograph and discussion constitute the data within photo elicitation.

Many researchers do not wish to analyse the photos taken by children with too much emphasis on technical detail but rather rely on the qualitative conversations that accompany the image in order to capture the key meanings children wish to express. As noted above, the conversation with Arnar in the research project conducted by Dockett et al. (2017) helped to clarify some of the understandable misinterpretations and assumptions that can be made by practitioners and researchers in accessing young children's views and perspectives when engaging with the analysis and interpretation of photos and other visual images created by young children. Other researchers assert the view that the analytic tools used to incorporate photographs in research are often not outlined in sufficient detail (Byrne, Daykin & Coad, 2016; Rose, 2016). Rose (2016, cited in Dockett et al., 2017) outlines four sites of meaning-making in the interpretation of visual images: the site of image production; the site of the image itself; the site of circulation; and the viewing site of the audience. These sites highlight the processes involved in creating the photograph, the ways in which the photograph has been constructed, how the image is shared and how the audience views the photograph. Interpretation occurs at each of these sites according to Rose (2016).

Three modalities that influence the interpretation of images – technological modality, compositional modality, and social modality – are also central to the analysis. See Table 6.1 below, which presents more detail on these sites of meaning.

Table 6.1 Image sites and modalities

	Site of production	Site of the image	Site of circulation	Site of audience
Technological modality	How was the image made? What equipment was used – digital camera, disposable, or other?	What visual effects are used?	How is the image shared? Is there processing time between taking and viewing images?	How is the image displayed to the audience? Is the researcher part of the production and/or audience?
Compositional modality	What guidelines were provided around taking images? For example, what was the research theme or focus?	What is included in the image? What is omitted? What are the design elements? What is in the foreground and background? What is the focus?	In what form is the image circulated? Is the photo enlarged, cropped, or altered? What changes are made to the image in order to be circulated? For example, are faces pixelated or concealed?	What viewing perspectives are available? For example, child-eye level? Is there intertextuality? What draws or directs audience attention?
Social modality	Who made the image? Why was the image created? Would it have been generated without the research project? What are the photographer's intentions?	What visual meanings are included? What are the social identities of the maker, the owner and the subject of the image? What is the relationship between these people?	How is the image being viewed – in a magazine, on a noticeboard or on a computer? Who owns the image? What permissions are in place to share the image? Who controls the circulation of the image?	Who is the audience – professional, family, children or others? What relationships/connections exist between the audience and the photographer? What are the social identities of the audience? Who analyses the data? How does the audience shape the production of the image?

Adapted from Rose (2016, p. 25)

Map-making

Photographs and other visual representations created by young children can also be used in further activities, such as map-making and making photobooks, which allow children to further expand and elaborate on their perspectives on the issue being explored (Johnson et al., 2014b). Map-making may be particularly appropriate for use with older children beyond early childhood. However, the approach can be adapted for use with younger children. In the Listening to Young Children study (Clark, 2011), multimodal texts in the form of maps were created using children's photographs, drawings and writings. Walking around a particular space within an early years setting or outside the setting, prior to making the maps, has been found to support children's engagement with the map-making process. Maps can be made on large, circular pieces of paper, approximately 1 metre across. Map-making as a research tool is designed to provide a focus and stimulus for conversations with young children and can provide children with a way in which to think in detail about actual examples of their social experience. A key advantage to such an approach is that it can engage children effectively in thinking about concrete, everyday experiences, rather than responding to abstract questions (Johnson et al., 2014). For young children, it is recommended that conversations with children about the particular topic that is being explored through map-making precedes the map-making activity. An example of a topic that can be explored through map-making with young children is that of children's favourite play spaces. Conversations with the children about their favourite play spaces can help to scaffold their thinking on the topic. Children can then be invited to draw their play spaces and to place these spaces on the map. A play map showing places enjoyed by particular children can then be created. Engaging the children in this way can make the exploration more child-friendly and increase children's involvement in the process.

Magic carpet

The 'magic carpet' is a further possible research strategy that can be used to revisit and extend some of the visual representations in research with young children, and which has been used previously in the

Mosaic approach (Clark, 2017). For example, children's outings, explorations of an event, and visits to a particular place can be recorded and documented through photos, drawings and other visual representations of features of the experience. Early years practitioners and researchers can revisit and review these images and further explore the children's meanings though presentation in a cinematic format. This can be achieved, for example, by creating a presentation on a computer or tablet, and by sharing children's representations through a shared viewing of the images, if children are happy to participate and consent to this sharing of their material. The magic carpet effect can be created through creating a tent-like structure inside or outside the setting. Children can be invited to sit on rugs, cushions or mats and view the presentation in a warmly lit environment, resembling a cinema performance.

The journey to meaning in children's visual representations

The journey to meaning through children's visual representations can be a challenging process. Ethical issues are of paramount importance, with the need to ensure that permission has been obtained from all the relevant stakeholders being clearly understood and acted on. Stakeholders include the managers, the practitioners, the parents and the children themselves. Roberts-Holmes (2018) emphasises that, if researchers are taking away children's photographs for a research project, they need to make sure the children have a complete set of photographs as well. The author goes on to indicate that, for children, drawings may be personal creations in which intimate, and sometimes private, experiences and knowledge are shared with familiar people by the children. It is essential to clarify that the children do not feel uncomfortable with photos being made available to a wider audience.

Ethical issues such as confidentiality are of utmost importance, as any identifying information within a photograph should not be included in research without prior permission and only when comprehensive information has been provided about how the material will be used in the research report. It is also important that if children are taking photographs of one another, they are encouraged to ask other children if they are happy to have their photograph taken.

Practitioners and researchers as adults need to be aware that what a child may say in response to a question about a photograph or visual image may not always be accurate. Wright (2007) draws attention to a particular study where the researcher assumed the figure being represented in a child's drawing was the child, whereas in fact it was the child's mother.

When the adult questioned the child asking if the figure represented was her, the child nodded and, in subsequent telling of the event, referred to the character as 'me'. The ability to support children to engage with drawings and to encourage related narratives depends on the researcher's ability to establish empathic and trusting relationships in a safe context, based on mutual trust and a familiarity with the situations in which the children work. Gentle prompting to encourage children to extend their meanings and to reinforce a sense of confidence in the worth of their expressions of meanings are key features in the process of co-constructing meanings with children.

7 Mindful moments and performance of meanings

Mindfulness is commonly defined as 'paying attention in a particular way: on purpose, in the present moment, and non-judgmentally' (Kabat-Zinn, 1994, p. 4). In this chapter, the value of introducing mindful activities in order to support mindful moments in young children's everyday activities is explored, with a particular emphasis on how such activities can generate and enhance an ambience of focus and calm from which to engage in research with young children. The potential for such mindful activities to empower young children in their expression of feelings and meanings is also highlighted. In this way, we can consider using mindful practice as a tool in order to invite, encourage and engage children within a research process and to help create a safe and meaningful space in which children feel confident and calm in their thoughts and expression. The value of such an approach for facilitating researchers and professionals working with young children, to access their subjective expressions and meanings is also explored. The chapter begins with a focus on how we can use the power of stories to introduce the concept of mindfulness and how we can further encourage children to stop, listen, reflect on and understand their experiences. Activities such as mindful breathing and mindful hearing are explored in the context of enabling children to build powers of concentration and awareness, and possibly enhancing their ability to understand and express their views and meanings. The chapter moves to a focus on material that facilitates working with children to help them learn to engage in mindful and calming breathing activities, create colourful, calming bottles, and use drawings to capture and share their responses to their worlds. The chapter concludes with a consideration of a performance of children's meanings, engaging with theatre and music, and highlights simple exercises and games that can be useful in helping to access children's meanings.

Creating a mindful space for children's participation in research

In early years practice, the child as learner and the learning environment are closely connected (Hayes, O'Toole & Halpenny, 2017). Some of the key characteristics of positive learning environments are those that encourage and support children to learn at their own pace. Children need time and appropriate spaces in which imagination, creativity and the expression of their views and perspectives can emerge, and to be supported within an environment in which they feel secure and familiar with their surroundings. A safe and stimulating environment has been demonstrated as having considerable benefits for children (Hayes & O'Neill, 2019). For younger children, an 'experience expectable' environment in childcare classrooms is one in which teachers consistently provide positive and nurturing interactions within daily routines and activities to enhance children's learning (La Paro & Gloeckler, 2016, p. 157). Responsive and sensitive language, ongoing reassurance and encouragement provide young children with predictable signals, which enhance their sense of security and familiarity. Similar features of the environment operate to support and scaffold children's participation in research. Throughout previous chapters, valuable knowledge and guidelines have been drawn from *Steps for Engaging Young Children in Research* (Johnson, Hart & Colwell, 2014a). In the next section, a focus on Step 3 – building supportive trusting relationships – is prioritised through consideration of how mindful activities with young children can help to build an appropriate and safe setting and ambience, to enable more meaningful interactions with children and to enhance possibilities for capturing young children's meanings.

Building supportive and trusting relationships

Socio-cultural theories derived from the work of Vygotsky (1986) foreground the role of relationships, including pedagogical relationships with early years practitioners, in influencing the nature of children's learning and development (Hedges & Cooper, 2018). A focus on building trusting relationships facilitates the development of a safe, enjoyable environment in which children feel able to speak and share their views (Johnson, Hart & Colwell, 2014a). These authors go on to point out that if research is not carried out in a supportive, trustful environment, knowledge and information gathered may not accurately reflect the views of the young children involved. Prior research has also demonstrated that for children to open up and communicate with ease to adults during the research process they must feel that the adult is trustworthy, interested and supportive (Punch, 2015).

Knowledge of individual children's communications skills and levels of understanding are fundamental, alongside an awareness that there is likely to be great variation in these skills within any group of young children. Familiarity with the use of children's language, the nuances of their verbal expression and speech and the nature of their relationships all operate to build trusting and supportive relationships in the research process (Clark, 2017). Many of these features of the child-adult relationship and partnership in research can be established over time and throughout the research process, but it is often necessary, particularly when working with a group of children, for relationships and boundaries to be established prior to the start of the research and to be reinforced on an ongoing basis. Below, a number of fundamental issues are highlighted by Johnson et al. (2014) with reference to building positive and trusting relationships with children in the research process.

How to build positive relationships with children

Johnson, Hart and Colwell (2014a)

- Get to know every child's name and use it whenever possible – this provides a sense of belonging and shows that the researcher is interested in them. It can also help the children to remember each other's names.

- Allow some time for the child to lead discussions and activities – this shows that the researcher is interested in them and they have some power in the relationship.

- Get to know the child's family/friends/community – the researcher can discuss their lives with them. In doing this, the researcher is showing an interest in them and their experiences. The researcher may also discover a better understanding of children's lives, feelings and opinions.

- Praise the child often for their contributions and accomplishments.

- Respect the child and do not dismiss their opinions or cut across their conversations.

These guidelines are relevant regardless of whether the researcher works with the child on a daily basis or whether they are not so familiar with the child.

Supporting positive child-peer relationships and co-operation within groups

Relationships developed with children are of particular importance in facilitating children's participation and engagement in research (Waller & Bitou, 2011). Early years practitioners develop skills and knowledge from experience on how to foster and nurture positive interaction between children and adults and between children and their peers. When engaging in research with young children in groups, it is essential to make time to ensure that there are respectful and trusting relationships between children who can communicate with each other (Johnson et al., 2014). Early years practitioners use a range of adult–child interaction strategies, which can enhance the length and quality of children's interactions through 'sustained shared thinking' (CECDE, 2006, p. 6). This is where two or more individuals work together in an intellectual way to clarify an idea, solve a problem or evaluate an activity.

Such interactions are likely to occur when children interact on a one-to-one basis with adults or with other children. The importance of being able co-operate, negotiate and engage in turn-taking are all skills that children need in order to be able to work in groups. Early years practitioners promote and scaffold these skills in young children on a daily basis through their interactions in early years settings.

Benefits of mindfulness in the early years

Research on mindfulness, to date, has centred largely on adults rather than children and young people, so there is limited knowledge of the potential effects of mindfulness in the early years. However, increasingly, studies are focusing on younger age groups (Peacock, 2015).

The value of mindfulness practice in the early years for enhancing and reinforcing well-being and resilience in young children has been demonstrated (Meiklejohn et al., 2012). Moreover, young children's curiosity and openness to novel experiences may facilitate greater receptiveness to learning mindfulness (Peacock, 2015). However, the benefits of mindfulness for enhancing attention and focus in young children, and self-regulation skills, are worth exploring further with regard to potentially enhancing children's participation in the research process.

Enhancing attention and focus in young children

Key concepts emphasised and prioritised in contemporary early childhood education include many of the skills associated with what has been termed 'executive functions' – a set of cognitive skills associated with the development of the pre-frontal cortex in brain development during the early years (Baumeister, Schmeichel & Vohs, 2013). The pre-frontal cortex, which is known to be the slowest developing brain region, shows profound developmental changes right through to adulthood (Whitebread, 2013). Executive functioning, sometimes referred to as 'the air traffic control system of the brain' includes skills such as focusing attention, planning behaviours, inhibiting attention toward distractions and making decisions based on incoming information (Wood, Roach, Kearney & Zabek, 2018). Whereas studies with older children and adults have supported the benefits of mindfulness for enhancing skills of attention and focus, research with young children has been more limited. Mindfulness with young children, however, has been shown to have the potential to enhance some of the skills associated with executive functions, in particular, the skills of focusing attention. Specifically, a recent evaluation of the effectiveness, acceptability and feasibility of Mini-Mind, a 12-session Mindfulness Based Intervention created specifically for pre-schoolers, included a sample of 27 pre-schoolers, aged between 3 and 5 years of age (Wood, Roach, Kearney & Zabek, 2018). Mini-Mind aims to improve executive functioning skills in young children. Every session included brief yoga, mindful breathing and compassion components. In addition, each session used interactive and concrete activities to focus on developing attention and awareness toward one of the following experiences: taste, smell, sight, sound, touch, movement, emotions and loving-kindness. Although the majority of the effectiveness results did not reach statistical significance, the magnitude and direction of the results consistently demonstrated small-to-medium effects in favour of those children who received the intervention. Along with effectiveness, the acceptability and feasibility of Mini-Mind was evaluated. Overall, the curriculum was consistently rated as both highly acceptable to children and stakeholders and feasible to implement.

Enhancing self-regulation skills in young children

The development of fundamental executive function processes into metacognitive or self-regulatory behaviours and abilities amongst children aged 3–6 years has become established (Whitebread, 2013). The socio-emotional aspect of self-regulation refers, in general terms, to the ability to control and regulate emotional expressions (positive or negative) and to developing the skills to be able to interact with others in increasingly more complex ways in accordance with social rules. Researchers examining self-regulation in educational settings define the behavioural aspects of self-regulation as 'deliberately applying attentional flexibility, working memory, and inhibitory control to overt actions' (McClelland & Cameron, 2011, p. 32). Viglas and Perlman (2018) draw attention to a number of studies that have shown evidence of the positive impact of practising mindfulness on self-regulation (Black & Fernando, 2014; Flook, Goldberg, Pinger & Davidson, 2015).

Razza, Bergen-Cicco, and Raymond (2015) explored possibilities for enhancing children's self-regulation skills in a study involving 29 children between the ages of 3 and 5 years.

Three particular indices of self-regulation (i.e. attention, delay of gratification and inhibitory control) were targeted in the study. Significant effects were found across all three indices of self-regulation. More broadly, studies also indicate that children appear to show improvement in overall social and emotional competencies when exposed to relaxation and attention-training activities that help build links between feelings, thoughts and behaviours. In the Focus on Research below, a study exploring 9-year-old children's experiences of learning mindfulness to help develop their attentional skills is outlined.

FOCUS ON RESEARCH

Children's experiences of learning mindfulness to help develop their attentional skills

Carelse (2012)

Study Aims

The study set out to explore children's experiences of learning mindfulness to help develop their attentional skills.

- Six children aged 9 years took part in the study. The participant children included 4 boys and 2 girls.
- The research used drawings to facilitate the expression of children's experiences. Children were invited to draw, write and talk about their experiences of mindfulness.
- Drawings were used as a way of encouraging and facilitating the participants in expressing their experiences of mindfulness through a combination of drawing, writing and speaking.
- Children were provided with opportunities to draw or write about their experiences during the initial interview. Subsequently, at the final interview, these drawings were used to facilitate the children's

(Continued)

recollection and expression of their experiences of mindfulness, thereby enabling richer content to be gathered.

■ This range of media for self-expression was provided due to anticipation of potential challenges in verbally expressing the abstract and intangible experiences of mindfulness. Furthermore, by using drawings as prompts, the children had a record of their learning process.

Themes	Observations
Feeling calm, relaxed, happy and confident	The children's first and immediate experiences of mindfulness were all positive. Furthermore, at the initial and final interviews and in drawings, they expressed the view that the practices had a calming, positive and relaxing effect on them.
Awareness of body sensations and sounds	Awareness of body sensations included heart beating, muscles relaxing and being in an upright sitting position. Children also highlighted a detailed awareness of the external environment. Feeling more alert and energised and noticing sounds to a greater extent were also highlighted.
Memories and imaginary places	Most memories were about times when the children had felt happy and they depicted themselves doing something enjoyable. However, one child's drawing was of a recent event that had been upsetting.
Awareness of the attention itself	Some thoughts were simply observed and these were depicted in drawings. Others appeared to be related to practising specific techniques for sustaining the attention on the present moment.
	These experiences are interpreted as being representative of an awareness of thought processes related to self-regulation or meta-awareness.
Further findings	The research also explored any possible changes in the children's levels of mindfulness before and after the intervention. Any possible changes were not significant or measurable using the Child Acceptance and Mindfulness Measure (CAMM) questionnaire.

Qualitative differences in the kinds of pictures that the children drew as part of the study carried out by Carelse (2012) highlighted that in the later stages of the intervention the children appeared more detached from the content of their thoughts and also indicated ways in which they were using the mindfulness practices. Overall, the children described being better able to concentrate in class, feel calmer and improve relationships with friends and family.

Developmental considerations in using mindfulness with young children

Mindfulness with children in the early years requires close consideration of the features of such an approach that are suited and appropriate to the age of the children involved. While there are many similarities between practising mindfulness with children and with adults, a number of distinctions and differences are important to highlight. Key features to keep in mind include: the length of time over which a young child can attend to mindful activities; the use of simple and appropriate language to guide activities; ensuring methods, materials and activities are play-based and creative; and breath awareness and movement exercise (Peacock, 2015; Weare, 2013). Young children will benefit from shorter lengths of time in mindful activities. More specifically, young children may only be able to concentrate on a simple breathing exercise for a very short time, but as children become more familiar and comfortable with the activities, they can sustain attention and interest for longer periods.

More time is typically spent on actually doing the activities than on discussing the children's responses to and feelings about the activities (Weare, 2013). Explicitly discussing meta-cognitive ideas behind the practice of mindfulness will be beyond young children's cognitive abilities (Weare, 2013). Children in the early years and primary school years also benefit most from activities that allow for play and exploration and include a focus on the imagination. Breath awareness, movement exercises, yoga, body scans and visualisation have also been found to be particularly effective with young children (Mendelson et al., 2010; Peacock, 2015). Developmental considerations in using mindfulness with young children are summarised below, adapted from Peacock (2015).

Developmental considerations in using mindfulness with children

- *Keep exercises short*, particularly when first starting out. A breathing or listening exercise may only be 30 seconds to a minute long when you first start. Once the children are more familiar with the exercises, you may spend more time on them (2–5 minutes, depending on the children) (Thompson & Gauntlett-Gilbert, 2008; Weare, 2013).

- *Use simple language.* The use of props and simple analogies may help the children better understand the objective of a particular mindfulness-based activity (Thompson & Gauntlett-Gilbert, 2008; Zelazo & Lyons, 2012). One example of a simple analogy to help children better understand how to deal with wandering thoughts during a mindfulness exercise was developed by Thompson and Gauntlett-Gilbert (2008). In this analogy, they compare dealing with wandering thoughts to teaching an overly excited puppy to sit still. Getting angry when the puppy moves will not help the animal learn to sit still, much like how becoming angry with the self when attention wanders is not helpful. Instead, it is best to simply bring the puppy back to a seated position, much like gently bringing one's attention back to the point of focus (Thompson & Gauntlett-Gilbert, 2008).

- *Children in the primary school grades are imaginative* and learn well through activities that allow for play and exploration. Therefore, keep methods, materials and activities play-based and creative (Weare, 2013). Arts-based activities are a great idea, but remember that the intention of the activity is to promote present moment awareness.

- *Combining breath awareness with movement exercises*, such as stretching or hands-on activities, provide a means for expelling energy (Mendelson et al., 2010).

- *Specific mindfulness-based activities* that appear to be effective include yoga, body scans, breathing meditations and visualisation meditations (Mendelson et al., 2010; Napoli et al., 2005; Semple et al., 2010).

Adapted from Peacock (2015)

Calming and relaxing mindful activities with children

The following simple activities are suitable for helping young children to focus, to relax and to be calm while at the same time helping the practitioner/researcher to build rapport and trust in young children and to make them feel more comfortable about participating in research activities. The first of these activities encourages children to draw attention to their breath and helps them to begin to engage in mindful breathing.

Focus on mindful practice: three mindful breaths

Mindful breathing allows us to better align our breathing with our thoughts and associated feelings (Semple, Reid & Miller, 2005), thereby allowing possibilities for enhancing both the emotional and biological states of our bodies. Particularly when working with young children, it is essential to make sure that learning how to breathe mindfully is both an enjoyable and a relaxing activity. Mindful breathing enables children to calm themselves and to focus and relax so that a positive rapport can be developed before engaging with research.

Mindful breathing exercises are, therefore, useful activities for both early childhood practitioners who are familiar with the children they are working with, and for those researchers who have not yet built up a rapport of trust and confidence. As children develop through the early years, practising mindfulness with the guidance of a practitioner, parent or caregiver empowers children by showing that they are not alone in practising mindfulness but also by building and reinforcing skills and being able to use these skills as resources when needed. In the section below, a simple breathing activity, suitable for helping young children to engage in mindful breathing, is outlined.

FOCUS ON MINDFUL PRACTICE

Three mindful breaths

- Find a comfortable sitting position. Make sure you feel comfortable and can easily and normally breathe through your nose. You might like to try closing your eyes, or if you don't feel comfortable doing that, try doing what we call 'soft eyes', which means to just look down at the floor without really focusing on anything.

- Focus on breathing through your nose, noticing how the air feels cool coming in and may be slightly warmer as it leaves your body.

- You can also focus on your breath around your tummy – feeling it rise and fall as the air enters and leaves your body.

- Stay focused, as best you can, on your breath. Just notice the air as it enters and leaves your body. If your mind wanders, that's okay. Simply bring your attention back to the in-breath and out-breath, breathing in and breathing out. Tell yourself 'good job' for keeping your attention on your breathing.

- Now, begin to take three normal breaths, and try and focus just on the breath for all three.

- Now gently start to take notice of what is happening around you. Notice your body where it touches the floor. Notice what is in the room around you. Notice what sounds you can hear.

- Very gently, begin to move your fingers and toes, and slowly stretch your arms and legs.

At the end of this short focus on mindful breathing, ask the children open-ended questions such as 'What did you notice while you were doing this?' 'How was this sort of breathing compared with the way you normally breathe?'

Adapted from *I Just Want To Be ... Me – Mindfulness Activities for Young Children*, http://www.actonpurpose.com.au/Mindfulness-activities-for-young-children.pdf

Mindfulness jars

This activity provides children with a visual analogy of why using strategies to help us feel calm also helps us think more clearly. *The mind in a jar* activity can be referred to using a variety of terms such as *mindfulness jar, calming jar, glitter jar, jar of thoughts*. The key focus shared across all these terms is the aim of helping children to visualise their minds and thoughts by focusing on the colours and movement of the liquid, glitter and, if desired, objects, which are placed in a jar and then gently shaken for effect. An essential consideration in this activity is the necessity of being aware of child safety issues, and monitoring children very closely when they are creating and engaging with their jars is of paramount importance.

Mindfulness jars provide opportunities for children to choose the colours and materials they would like to include. These activities can be used for fun and pleasure alone but can also help children to think of a 'cloudy mind' and then think about a clear mind (Peacock, 2015, p. 46). This activity can also be used more broadly to help children relax and be calm at times when they may be experiencing more negative emotions. The present focus on these activities prioritises attention to building trusting relationships and creating calm environments in which young children feel comfortable to communicate and participate in a research process. In the section below, simple ideas are presented for engaging with children and facilitating their choices and creativity in making mindfulness jars.

Mindful jars

Mindful jars are a lovely way of working with children to make colourful jars, which they can fill with coloured liquids, glitter and other materials. This activity can teach children how strong emotions can take hold, and help them learn how to relax and have calming thoughts when these strong emotions feel overwhelming.

> Steps for creating mindful jars
>
> 1. Collect jam jars.
> 2. Fill the jar almost to the top with water.
> 3. Children can choose from different coloured dyes, glitters or sand to put in their jar. Choosing colours to match different emotions can also be fun for children.
> 4. Add glitter, sand, feathers or other chosen materials to the jar.
> 5. Ensure the lid is tightly sealed and use glue or tape to secure it further and to make the jar last longer.
> 6. Invite the children to shake their jars and then watch the contents fall slowly to the bottom of the jar.
>
> Invite children to imagine the glitter as their thoughts when they are angry or upset. Children can also be invited to imagine their minds full of whirling thoughts and then watch their thoughts slowly settle as they calm down. This activity helps children to learn about their emotions while also facilitating the practice of mindfulness, through focusing on the swirling glitter in the jar.
>
> Adapted from *25 Fun Mindful activities for Children and Teens*, https://positivepsychology.com/mindfulness-for-children-kids-activities/#mindfulness-activities-children

Mindful listening

Listening to ourselves and to others is an essential part of engaging effectively with research. Children in the early years may find it challenging to stay focused and listen to others for extended periods of time. This mindful listening activity helps children develop their listening skills, which requires them to use present moment awareness while, at the same time, helps them to slow down and to disengage from the hurried pace so typical in everyday routines. Simple mindful listening and breathing activities can enhance children's abilities to be able to focus and listen to what an early years practitioner or researcher is asking them to do. In the following section, a simple and fun mindful listening activity is outlined for enhancing children's listening and attentive skills.

> **Mindful listening**
>
> - Children sit quietly in the centre of a room with eyes closed.
> - If possible, open a window in the room.
> - Encourage the children to breathe deeply and slowly and to listen very carefully to the sounds that they hear, both within and outside the room.
> - Ask the children to spend a few moments thinking about the questions below.
>   - What is the loudest sound you hear?
>   - What is the quietest sound you hear?
>   - What other sounds do you hear?
> - Children sit with their eyes closed and try to identify as many different sounds in and outside the room as possible (e.g. sound of breathing, traffic outside, rain falling, birds, etc.).
> - Talk with the children about the different sounds that individual children have been able to identify.
>
> Adapted from Napoli (2005) and Peacock (2015)

Performance of meanings in the early years

Performance activities may include music, dramas, role plays, poems and puppets (Johnson, Hart & Colwell, 2016). More inclusive formats of performance may involve silent drama, mime and dance, which can also be very effective media for young children to convey feelings about places, people and things. Children with additional needs, non-verbal children and children whose first language is not shared with those of other children in the group may find such variations on performance less challenging. The growing recognition of the importance of the arts as a valuable and enriching component of early childhood education is a welcome and positive development (Brown, 2017).

In his chapter *An Introduction to Cross-Curricular Learning*, Jonathan Barnes outlines and discusses the different ways we can assess the skills and knowledge that children have acquired through their multiple learning experiences. One meaningful strategy for assessment, in his view, is what he terms 'performance of understanding' which he describes as:

> opportunities throughout the unit of work, for children to demonstrate the level and depth of their understanding ... The teacher will teach the required skills or knowledge and then give children a chance (independently or in groups) to use their new learning to solve a problem, create a product, presentation, collection, exhibition, performance or composition (Barnes, p. 277).

Performance and narrative can be incorporated into research approaches which aim to understand children's feelings about and responses to their experiences. However, beyond this, such methods are also effective for generating knowledge and insight into children's perceptions of interactions between other people and groups within societies. Johnson et al. (2016) point out that given the variety of contexts and situations in which performance and narrative can be used, allied to the fact that children are often familiar with and enjoy such methods, these strategies are potentially extremely valuable tools for a researcher.

Performance activities can include drama, music, role play, and storytelling through puppets. Multi-modal approaches to communication with young children, using textual, aural and visual formats, value creativity (Bock, 2016) and, thus, a variety of modes of expression are included. Providing varied and creative possibilities for communication and expression of ideas through a performance of meanings aligns well with the multi-modal dimension to young children's experiences and expression that has been foregrounded in previous chapters. Through performance and narrative approaches, children are encouraged to make meaning in innovative ways that engage them both affectively and cognitively. Creating spaces for this kind of exploration, both within and beyond the classroom, and through participatory research approaches with children, stimulates imagination, experimentation and learning; perhaps most significantly, it develops the child's sense of agency and voice (Bock, 2016; Kress, 2000).

In the following sections, strategies for enhancing young children's expression are outlined and discussed with a particular emphasis on music, drama, storytelling and role play. The chapter concludes with some further examples of simple activities that can be used to build rapport and help children to engage with the research process through a focus on their views and opinions.

Engaging with and through music in the early years

Young children enjoy singing, moving, dancing, creating their own compositions and engaging with musical instruments. Music can be used as part of mindfulness activities with young children, for example, when soothing music is played and children are invited to be still with their eyes closed. While listening to soothing music, children can be encouraged to focus on their feelings about what they hear. After such an activity, especially when such tools are used more often, young children may feel more emotionally, mentally and physically prepared to engage in the research process. Research suggests that early childhood practitioners play a central role in facilitating opportunities for children to engage with musical experiences.

Music can become part of the children's day, whether this involves singing songs and rhymes as part of care routines, or responding to, encouraging, talking about and joining in with children's spontaneous musical play (Young, 2005). More broadly, the arts are an important learning area for young children and are included in many education programmes, which provide a focus on meaning-making and communication (Garvis, 2012). The role of singing in the development of young children's sense of belonging in an early childhood setting for children aged from six months to two years has also been emphasised (Niland, 2015). In the Focus on Research below, as part of a music programme carried out in an Australian early learning centre, through a repertoire of songs, games and instruments, the children were introduced to music forms, including opera.

FOCUS ON RESEARCH

Pre-school children's encounters with *The Magic Flute*

Nyland, Acker, Ferris, and Deans (2011)

Study focus

The focus of this study, as an example of the centre's arts programme, was the formal music sessions the children participated in each week. A wide repertoire of songs, games and instruments were employed to introduce the children to various music forms, including opera. The centrepiece of the opera music was Mozart's *The Magic Flute*.

- The children's learning programme is designed and implemented by degree-qualified early childhood teachers and they also have specialist classes in dance, drama, visual art and music, offered by artists/teachers.

- In 2010, the children who were in the 4-year-old group were observed, in their music sessions, as part of an ongoing research project examining children's musical understandings and competence.

- Kylie, the music specialist, explained that the idea of presenting the opera to the children came from a combination of her interest in opera and in supporting those themes the centre was exploring in the general programme.

- Kylie decided to start her music sessions with the children by introducing them to the form of music she enjoys the most. The original plan was to present a number of the more familiar songs from the operas and sing some with the children and perhaps encourage musical play.

- This plan was totally subsumed by the children's interest in the one opera. 'The Magic Flute' therefore became an in-depth project pursued across the whole term.

- Over two months, eight music sessions were held with a group of fifteen 3- and 4-year-old children.

- This musical adventure was recorded through naturalistic observations, including videos, photographs and drawings to capture the children's experiences from different angles.
- The children discussed the music and characters, drew pictures of them in their home-room (Wright, 2007), introduced them into their dramatic play (de Vries, 2004) and dressed as princesses and Papageno (Figures 7.1 and 7.2).

Description of one music session – pacing, material used and concepts explored

Kylie greeted the children and invited them into a circle. The focus of this session included that of pitch and rhythm. Children were introduced to the idea that voice colour can contribute to different moods and emotions. The children were encouraged to feel their voices vibrate and experiment through vocalisation.

Another concept explored in the session was the role of audience and performer and the children had the opportunity to experience both roles.

Children were introduced, through games and activities, to different characters and songs from the opera.

Kylie streamed The Magic Flute, providing the children with the opportunity to be an audience and to engage with the characters in the story

Figure 7.1 Children's collaborative drawing of Papageno

(Continued)

Figure 7.2 Ruby's painting of Queen of the Night

and their varied vocals. The children watched intensely; some attempted to sing along. The viewing finished after 15 minutes.

After the music session, the room teacher invited the children to sit on the mat in the book corner. She told them that they were going to brainstorm; she asked questions and recorded the children's comments in a notebook.

Findings in *Pre-school children's encounters with The Magic Flute* provides an illustration of the children's engagement with Mozart's fairy tale. Most of the children displayed intense interest in this musical experience. The study carried out by Nyland, Acker, Ferris and Deans (2011) is based on the belief that children are competent communicators and music is one of the languages they use (O'Hagin, 2007). Such an approach to children's learning can tell us much about children's potential. As pointed out by Nyland et al. (2011), 'The Magic Flute' became a project and took on the structure of what Reggio Emilia scholars would call progettazione (Rinaldi, 1998), where educators provoke children to develop theories and strategies to test their hypotheses in collaboration with others (Edwards et al., 1998). As stated by Nyland et al. (2011),

> There is the interest shown in the topic, the interest is maintained by the different actors, the topic becomes an integral part of the

centre culture, the children and adults collaborate in the learning process, children verbally negotiate the meanings they take from the experience and express these understandings using many of the symbolic languages. Educators use questioning as a guide and a way of expanding interests, they present provocations and the children discover and learn and the educators learn about the children.

Drama as performance of meaning in early childhood

Drama as performance of meaning typically involves a structure and story prepared in advance, compared with role-play, which is a more free form of communication, designed to reveal how children feel about a particular situation or incident (Johnson et al., 2014a).

Children may re-enact a particular event through representing a sequence of actions. Additional resources and props such as face paint, masks and costume may also be used to heighten the dramatic content of vignettes or storytelling. Drama can also support children to create and present role-plays and dramatic representations of experiences in their lives. In research contexts where children are being invited to recall and describe events they have experienced, their views of and perspectives on these events can be innovatively portrayed through their design and performance of a short drama or series of vignettes. Props can be used if desired and such details can be negotiated with the children. Johnson et al. (2014) suggest that early years practitioners and researchers can deliver workshops in the initial stages, with participant children in small groups, in order to discuss the details with children and ensure that they are familiar with the procedures involved, and then move to discussion with all children. The time needed to prepare and rehearse will vary depending on the size and scale of the project. For example, designing and presenting dramas only for research (for recorders and facilitators) may be done within a day.

In the Focus on Research below, findings are presented from a wider PhD research project examining children's participation in Theatre for Early Years (TEY) as audience members, focusing on an interpretation of the pedagogy of the TEY event and situating it within the context of the children's wider cultural, relational and educational experiences. This article, however, focuses on a specific aspect of the children's experiences at Polka Theatre. Findings from the study indicate that the line between 'theatre as performance' and 'theatre as experience' is particularly loose for young children (Miles, 2018, p. 22); going to the theatre was always an event beyond simply performance, irrevocably tied to the context in which it occurred.

FOCUS ON RESEARCH

Bus journeys, sandwiches and play: young children and the theatre event

Miles (2018)

Study focus

Exploring young children's experiences of engaging with theatre in the early years.

- This article arises from empirical research with a group of children aged 3 and 4 years, who made repeated visits to watch TEY performances at Polka Theatre in London.

- Polka children's theatre stands out amongst the shop fronts on the main road running between Wimbledon and South Wimbledon (Figure 7.3).

- Polka programmes theatre devised for audiences of children and the adults who accompany them, being one of only a handful of theatres nationally who focus on young audiences.

- Of these young Polka audiences, a proportion are very young – 6 years old or under – visiting the building in order to experience what is often referred to in the UK as Theatre for Early Years (TEY) audiences.

- Between June 2014 and May 2015, I conducted empirical research into TEY reception at Polka Theatre, accompanying a small group of children aged 3 or 4 years to see seven of the TEY performances programmed there that year.

- The children all attended Eastwood Nursery School, a state-funded day nursery in nearby Roehampton.

Mindful moments and performance of meanings **183**

Figure 7.3 Exterior of Polka theatre

- I was interested in the children's reception of the TEY that we saw, both in the moment and afterwards, and was looking to trace a connection between the experiential and the pedagogical.
- After each performance, I worked with the children back at nursery, using a variety of methods to communicate about the theatre that we had watched.
- Examples of the methods that were used to communicate about the theatre they had seen included talk, object play, role play, playdough modelling, dance and drawing.
- The extended time spent with the children at nursery also meant I could draw on ethnography, remaining open to the different ways in which knowledge creation emerged during our time together (Figure 7.4).
- Parents and teachers were also involved in the research, both in reporting on their perceptions of the children's experiences and in sharing the personal or professional impact that the performances had on them (all parents and teachers visited Polka at least once during the research).

(Continued)

Figure 7.4 Clara dressed as Minnie Mouse and her drawing of this moment back at the nursery

- As well as informal interviews and day-to-day talk, parents had a research diary that they could use to note children's reactions at home.

Findings

Playing at Polka: Participation and agency in a social space	After our first visit to the theatre in June 2014, I asked research participant Elizabeth, aged 4, about her favourite part of the performance of *How Cold My Toes* by Travelling Light and she answered 'I liked it in the play area'. The written records and photographs I kept of our visits to Polka are full of references to the self-initiated play the children experienced at Polka either side of the performance. The pattern of our visits from nursery invariably involved 15 minutes or so of play in the foyer before the performance, followed by lunch and half an hour in Polka's outdoor play area.

Sandwiches at Polka: The wider theatre event and methodology	Pink (2009) emphasises the role that everyday sensory activities, such as walking or eating, may play in both the research relationship and in developing an understanding of affective and cognitive knowledge. Pink's thinking sheds new perspectives on the role that eating sandwiches together as a group played in this research. The room where we ate was light, with colourful decorations hanging from the ceiling and a long table with benches to allow everyone to sit together. Eating with the children was one mode of knowledge creation around the theatre event, where the atmosphere could be seen as reflective of a shared affective response to the performance we had seen.
Bus journeys to Polka: A shared sense of place	Our routine journeys to the theatre involved a walk of a few minutes down the hill from the nursery, past the blocks of flats where some of the children lived, to catch the 170 bus, from which we changed to the 93 to be dropped off at the doors of the theatre. I name the numbers so specifically because of the importance they took on for the children, some of whom shared an excitement in becoming knowledgeable about navigating our way to the theatre. The anticipation on our way to the theatre, the shared landmarks that we passed and the often drooping eyelids on the way back created shared knowledge of the theatre event. The design of the theatre was hugely significant in providing a landmark that the children could instantly recognise. As we stepped off the bus, the children would often point to the theatre just down the road from us, exclaiming their recognition. It was not only the land that we passed through on the bus that revealed itself as significant, but also the buses themselves. One of the participant children, Raj, was playing with some Playdough a week or so after our first visit to the theatre. I sat down with him and joined in. After a little while, I told him I was making 'the theatre'. He was keen to play along, but instead of making the theatre itself he made a rough cuboid which he told me was 'the bus'. As he pushed some figurines of people into his 'bus' he invited me: 'Let's get on the 93…let's get on the 170'.

(Continued)

> **The 'theatre event' for young children: Reconsidering hierarchies of experience**
>
> The findings discussed in this article reveal not only the importance of the journeys and spaces which are the contexts of theatre-going, but they also force a re-evaluation of an adult-centred sense of hierarchy in the theatrical event.
>
> As a theatre researcher who is aware of all that goes into creating TEY, it is inevitable that I saw the performance as the centre of our trips to Polka. In contrast, three-year-old Rayan's description to his mother of our first experience at Polka was worded as follows: 'I went on the bus. I saw a show man. We went with a few children. I ate apple on my way to the theatre. We come back to the school with my teachers'.
>
> Breaking the nursery routine to go to the theatre was always a significant event, even after it began to become familiar. From the bus journey, to playing in the theatre foyer, to eating our sandwiches after the performance, this was an experientially rich few hours in which performance played an important, but not exclusive, role.

Findings from the study *Bus journeys, sandwiches and play* outlined above provide insight into the many different, and often unexpected, types and categories of knowledge, which research with young children generates. As pointed out by Miles (2018, p. 35), the findings identified in the study, force 'a re-evaluation of an adult-centred sense of hierarchy in the theatrical event'. While adults might expect the theatre performances to be the pivotal focus of the children's responses, the associated journeys, spaces and rituals also tended to capture the children's attention and focus. Documenting young children's experiences of events and experiences allows us to stand back and re-evaluate children's lived experiences, to deconstruct adult assumptions around what matters in children's worlds and to replace these assumptions with a more balanced understanding of children's worlds. Consistent with this, Stephenson (2009) emphasises two key features that contribute significantly to a deeper understanding of children's perspectives. The first of these is allowing for a sustained and prolonged data collection period, which may be more practically achieved in research which is carried out by early years practitioners within and beyond their settings. The second feature highlighted was the intellectual process of stepping back from the research agenda, which allows other, less overt messages to be 'heard'.

Process drama and children's meanings

The use of drama as a pedagogical tool in early childhood is well established, with particular reference to children's frequent explorations in socio-dramatic/pretend play. The use of drama as a learning medium, referred to as process drama, is most appropriate when considering drama as a potential research method with young children (Brown, 2017).

Process drama is a medium in which early years practitioners and children collaborate to create an imaginary dramatic world and work within that world to explore a problem, a situation, or a story, not for an audience, but for the benefit of the children themselves. Key features of process drama, and its potential for application to researching a topic from the perspectives of children, are highlighted below.

Process drama as a medium for expression and exploration in the early years

Brown (2017)

- In process drama, children play a range of roles and engage in a variety of reflective out-of-role activities, requiring them to think critically beyond their own points of view and consider the topic from multiple perspectives.

- In process drama, young children, under the guidance of a teacher, work as a community. Collaborative problem solving, critical thinking, and negotiation are central to the process.

- In studying the rainforest, for example, kindergarten children can pretend to be rainforest experts who have been invited to travel to the rainforest and help the woodcutter, enacted by the teacher, understand the importance of the trees, perhaps suggesting alternative planting or harvesting work.

- Young children, in the role of community members, are challenged to share food from their gardens with outsiders who did not plant a garden.
- They have worked hard on their garden. Why should they share?
- The dramatic process allows children to respond intellectually, physically, and empathetically to an imagined situation created by the teacher or, often, by the children themselves.
- Through process drama, children do not simply absorb knowledge; they construct it, learning best when they are actively engaged, organizing knowledge and experiences in new ways towards a desired goal.
- Process drama is closely aligned with the way young children naturally learn through dramatic play (i.e. pretend play) in which they pretend to be someone else and/or someplace else.
- Using tenets from process drama, with teacher guidance, children as young as 3–8 years actively gain skills in dialogue, empathy, collaboration, and creative problem solving, by collectively pretending to be in an imaginary elsewhere.

Drama as a research method with young children can provide valuable opportunities to gain insight into aspects of children's lives. As noted in Chapter 5, child-led socio-dramatic play enables children to act out their own experiences and responses to those experiences. Children can also create and develop their own dramatic plot or story in order to convey their feelings about certain issues. Johnson et al. (2014) point out that, in these cases, it is likely the topic will come from the children themselves as the play develops and evolves, which, in turn, has the potential to provide children with valuable insight into particular issues that matter in their lives.

Storytelling dramas

Stories and role-play provide children with opportunities to expand on their perceptions of their experiences and many children find the process of storytelling a familiar and enjoyable mode of expression. Story dramas allow children to represent their ideas, feelings, and conflict resolution theories (Wright, Diener & Kemp, 2013), as well as relate to other children's stories (Curenton, 2006; Paley, 1990). Early years practitioners and researchers play a significant role in facilitating children's participation in storytelling, providing a safe environment for children to contribute ideas, become included as members of the group, and build relationships. Wright et al. (2008) provide some valuable, practical advice on supporting and scaffolding children's expression in the process of storytelling and drama activities. The first step involves building rapport with the child and inviting the child to take part in the storytelling activity. Once the child has agreed to participate, details such as ensuring the child is comfortably seated alongside the adult facilitator, and can clearly see what the adult is writing down as they narrate their story, are highlighted. Pacing the storytelling session appropriately is also essential, as the child may need time to decide on the particular story they wish to narrate. If a child hesitates or is slow to begin to tell their story, they can be encouraged using the following opening prompts.

> **Opening prompts**
>
> Prompts used if child does not start a story
>
> A lot of stories begin with, 'Once upon a time….' or 'Once there was a…'
> You can start your story however you want. Tell me what you want to say, and I will write it down.
>
> If a child still has difficulty beginning a story, the facilitator can say
>
> Do you want to think about it? Come tell me a story later.

As the child narrates their story, the facilitator records verbatim what the child says. At times, it may be helpful to read aloud some parts of the story to the child in order to remind them of what they have said and to encourage them to continue their story. Children may pause to reflect on what they want to say and to encourage them to continue they can be guided by the phrase 'So, then what happened?' A key feature of the storytelling process is to convey a sense of genuine interest and curiosity in what the child is narrating. Some further continuation prompts are provided below.

> **Continuation prompts**
>
> Re-read the last few sentences to the child, then ask *What happened next?*
> Summarise highlights of the story, then ask *Then what happened?*
> If a child is repeating the same action with the same characters, then the prompt increases in specificity. *What happened after (character) did (action)?*

According to Wright et al. (2008), children typically bring their stories to a natural ending using phrases such as 'That's all' or 'The end'. The facilitator should record this verbatim and then signal their understanding the story is coming to an end with the closing prompt 'Let me read it to you to make sure it is right', as children enjoy having their stories read back to them. This also provides the child with an opportunity to correct or amend any details they would like to change. The facilitator can then conclude the storytelling process with a further closing prompt such as 'Thank you for telling me that story'.

Most research on children's storytelling focuses on narrative structure and/or content of children's narratives and research-initiated story-stems, with the unit of analysis most often being the stories themselves (Bacigalupa & Wright, 2009; Wright, Diener & Kemp, 2013). Little research has examined the drama aspect of the storytelling process. In the study summarised in the Focus on Research below, storytelling dramas as a community building experience for pre-school children were explored, based on Vivian Paley's storytelling and story-acting process. Paley's storytelling process incorporates two interdependent activities, dictation and dramatisation, and is renowned for its impact on young children's psychosocial, language and narrative development (Cooper, 2005). This approach was adopted in order to explore storytelling dramas as a community building activity in an early childhood classroom.

FOCUS ON RESEARCH

Storytelling dramas as a community building activity in an early childhood classroom

Wright, Diener, and Kemp (2013)

Study aims

Exploring storytelling dramas as a community building activity.

- Videotaped data were collected in one preschool classroom with 22 children (13 boys, 9 girls, 3.9–5.3 years).
- Children with special needs had priority enrolment and there was great diversity in developmental levels within the classroom.
- Children varied substantially in speech and language skills, emotional regulation, attention, and social interaction skills.
- Included were 20 videotaped episodes, comprising 100 storytelling sessions, videotaped over a six-month period.
- Videotapes were analysed for patterns and themes representing community building within the context of one preschool classroom.
- The strategy allowed researchers to explore group dynamics in children's natural learning environment.

Four major themes emerged from the data of storytelling dramas: (1) *Individual Roles*, (2) *Group Membership*, (3) *Inclusion*, and (4) *Relationship Building*. Key roles identified within the theme of Individual Roles included children as storyteller, audience and actor – roles that provided children with rich opportunities for participation and contributing to the community. The theme of Group Membership emphasised the value of children's learning from one another's unique ideas and strengths, thereby promoting respect for others and building a sense of community. The theme of Inclusion highlighted the value of providing children with opportunities to learn about their individual abilities and those of their peers in the classroom. Similarly, children also learned to appreciate the differences and unique ideas of others while, at the same time, broadening their awareness of belonging to a group of children. Finally, the theme of Relationship Building identified how children share in meaningful experiences and can demonstrate an appreciation for each other's stories. Closer observations revealed the detail of actions and moments that connected children to one another (Wiener et al., 2013).

Multi-modal performance of meanings

Multiple modes and media platforms are used to facilitate children reading picture books, watching movies, playing video games, making videos, and sharing texts and images on social media (Wessel-Powell, Kargin & Wohlwend, 2016). These authors argue that these complex exchanges and communications have transformed young children's understanding of text and, in turn, our understanding of the term 'literacy'. Historically, literacy has meant giving meaning to and getting meaning from printed text. However, recent socio-cultural research has emphasised action and multi-modality (Kress, 2011) – the ways we make meaning through sensory modes such as visual image, movement, sound, and sound effects.

Multi-modal storytelling includes a focus on supporting children to think about and develop strong characters and to enhance children's ability to consider different modes and media in storytelling by performing plays, making films or manipulating puppets in dramatic performance practices.

Digital meaning-making in the early years

Digital media form a central part of children's experiences and offer rich opportunities for young children to construct and express meanings in a safe and scaffolded context. Digital media are also well aligned to an emphasis on multi-modal perspectives on children's experiences. Collaboration between UCL Institute of Education and Stockholm University, with a focus on gaining insight into creative ways of using digital technologies with young children, provided invaluable insights into theory, methods and practice surrounding digital technologies in Swedish pre-school education (Cowan, 2019). Potentials and challenges within the concept of 'digital languages' were explored through discussions, with leading academics working in the field of digital technologies, multi-modality and Reggio Emilia.

Possibilities for enhancing and deepening enquiries through digital technologies were highlighted but, in all cases, the potential use of technology was viewed through the lens of a strong foundational pedagogy, inspired by Reggio Emilia. As pointed out by Cowan (2019, p. 6),

> In this sense, the digital was another language among the 'hundred languages'; one form among many, with the connections between forms given particular thought and emphasis.

Further activities in research with young children

In their valuable resource, *Steps for Engaging Young Children in Research*, Johnson et al. (2014b) present and provide details on a range of strategies and activities for engaging young children in research, covering all aspects of research with children using a range of visual methodologies, storytelling and narrative methodologies, drama and performance approaches to engage and scaffold young children as participants in research. A brief overview of some additional simple activities and exercises which can be used in research with children is outlined in this section.

Wellbeing exercise

The overall aim of this method is to explore what children consider to be a good or bad life for children of the same age and sex, living in their community, including an examination of sources of risk and protective processes. The method has been adapted for use with groups of young children. The researcher acts as group facilitator, creating a shared set of drawings representing 'good' and 'bad' lives for children in their communities, based on instructions and commentary provided by the children. This generates a set of children's indicators of wellbeing and ill-being, as well as capturing processes of consensus and disagreement within the group. A detailed description of the procedures to be followed in applying this method is included in *Steps for Engaging Young Children in Research* (Vol. 2). In the Focus on Research below, findings are presented from a study carried out with children in Peru in 2011, exploring their perspectives on their understanding of concepts of wellbeing and ill-being in their everyday lives.

> **FOCUS ON RESEARCH**
>
> **Children's views on wellbeing in Peru**
>
> **Ames, Rojas and Portugal (2010)**
>
> Children's participation in the wellbeing exercise and related research activities generated useful insights into what they believe constrains or supports their agency and wellbeing.
>
> Children aged 5–6 years, strongly associated 'ill-being' with lack of parental protection, which they explained in terms of parental death, absence and prolonged illness, and violence within the home.
>
> The lack of parents or having violent parents was synonymous with being unprotected: 'nobody shows concern for him', 'he doesn't know if he'll have anything to eat', 'he won't have a place to live'. Children determined that lack of care was made visible through children's physical appearance, as looking unkempt and dirty, appearing hungry and sad.
>
> Wellbeing, on the other hand, was associated with protection and with having adequate material and social resources: parental care and their support of children's schooling, family assets like cars, agricultural fields and animals (the latter two associated with rural areas), and children's possession of toys and time and space for play were all emphasised as important to their sense of wellbeing.

Happy day/sad day

This is a simple activity designed to invite children to draw a 'happy day' and a 'sad day' with a view to identifying and further discussing their perspectives on sources of happiness and sadness. Individual conversations or discussions with children in pairs are facilitated by early years practitioners/researchers. These narratives can further generate information about individual children's experiences (e.g. identifying likes/dislikes, worries and hopes, roles and responsibilities, time-use). Further details on this method are outlined below.

> **Happy/sad day**
>
> **Johnson, Hart and Colwell (2014b)**
>
> This method elicits information from children about the events or situations that make them happy or sad. It can be carried out as part of an individual interview with young children.
>
> - Children are asked to draw two pictures; one representing a day in which a child felt happy, and another in which a child felt sad.
> - The researcher discusses the drawings with the child, prompting as needed: *Tell me what the happy day was like for this child; What happened?; Who was with her/him?; What do you think the child will remember most about this day?*
> - The exercise is repeated for 'the sad day', and the researcher asks what would improve the situation for the boy/girl experiencing the sad day.

Who's important to me

This activity also provides a helpful illustration of how early years practitioners/researchers can use simple and enjoyable activities to elicit valuable information from young children, with a view to understanding how children prioritise certain people in their everyday lives. Key features of this activity are outlined further below.

> **Who's important to me?**
>
> **Johnson, Hart and Colwell (2014b)**
>
> This method gathers information about children's interpersonal relationships, who children feel closest to and why.
>
> - The method has been adapted for use with young children in groups so that they draw pictures representing all the people in their lives that matter most to them.
> - The researcher then lists individually the people identified as priorities by children.

> In the next phase, a large sheet of paper with a symbol representing a child in the middle is placed where everyone in the group can see. The children instruct the researcher where the names of the people (e.g. mother, brother, neighbour, teacher) should be placed on the paper – the closer to the child, the more important the relationship.
>
> - The researcher facilitates a discussion with prompts such as: *Who have you drawn?; Why?; Who else is important?; Who do you go to when you have a problem? Tell me a time when this happened; Who else do you know in your neighbourhood?*

Johnson et al. (2014b) draw attention to the fact that although individual interviews with the children can be useful for building rapport and familiarity, these one-on-one interviews may not be the preferred formats for communication. It is, therefore, important to combine this more traditional interview technique with approaches that include drawing, play, photography, and child-led tours.

Capturing meanings and moving forward with new understandings

This chapter draws together key concepts and principles outlined in the preceding chapters with regard to researching young children's meanings and developing strategies to access, record and interpret children's perspectives and experiences. Particular emphasis is placed on early years practitioners as being well positioned to mediate effective research strategies with young children. The close, reciprocal relationships that educators build with the young children they work with can contribute very positively to more accurately accessing, interpreting and capturing the meanings expressed by young children. With a focus on capturing children's meanings and documenting everyday moments in early childhood, this chapter provides a synthesis of the multiple imaginative ways in which we can capture young children's meanings through the use of multi-modal research methods.

Getting close to children's thinking

UNICEF (2014, p. 15) states that 'children drive change; children are experts on their own lives. They can contribute valuable knowledge to validate and enrich the evidence base if only they have a chance to be heard.' In order to nurture and facilitate this potential for children to drive change, it is necessary for adults to explore ways of getting closer to children's thinking and to find effective means through which the co-construction of children's meanings can be achieved. Quality practice and research in early childhood education implies an emphasis on and interest in children's theories about the world they inhabit. Moreover, such practice helps to ensure that children's theories about the world are valued and considered on their own, rather than being compared with adult ways of understanding and, thereby, modified accordingly (Areljung & Kelly-Ware, 2017). In order to capture and share children's meanings and to provide opportunities for extending children's thinking and learning, early childhood practitioners listen to and help children to build on their theories (Sommer, Pramling Samuelsson & Hundeide, 2013).

A key challenge in doing research with children is that young children's thinking is typically less accessible than that of their adult counterparts. A particular feature of children's thinking in the early years is that it tends to draw on the concrete world in order to formulate ideas and the expression of these ideas (Carpendale et al., 2018), while much of adult thinking is abstract. However, making language visible through documenting children's work and their expressions is a powerful means through which children's thinking can be made more accessible (Salmon, 2008). Visible thinking can be described as any kind of observable representation that documents and supports the development of an individual's or group's thoughts and questions (Ritchhart, Palmer, Church & Tishman, 2006). Thinking becomes more visible when practitioners document children's progress by recalling events and evidence of children's thinking. A variety of media can be used to document children's thinking, such as recording and transcribing conversations with children, accompanied by photographs, drawings and other multi-modal representations. Creatively collating multi-modal representations of a child's meanings allows practitioners to explore and further connect children's ideas and expressions with their own observations on children's learning and development. These strategies may facilitate not only access to children's ideas and feelings but also allow greater insight into young children's thinking processes (Salmon, 2008). Documentation in this way also promotes and supports a culture of thinking in young children (Ritchhart, 2002; Salmon, 2008), as it enables children to become aware of their own thought processes. Practitioners, children and their families benefit from engaging with documentation that highlights and provides greater clarity around ideas and modes of thought that children draw on to express their views. Effective documentation of children's meanings further enables adult educators and researchers to avoid making assumptions about children's ideas and perspectives – assumptions that may not do justice to the richness and complexity of young children's meanings.

Reification – giving concrete form to an abstract understanding

Wenger (1998) refers to 'reification' as 'the process of giving form to our experience by producing objects that congeal this experience into 'thingness' (Wenger, 1998, p. 58). Claxton and Carr (2004) further develop this concept with particular reference to documentation in the context of early childhood education. Capturing learning moments, documenting children's development through the use of multi-modal methods such as drawings, textual accounts, photo images – all of these activities are considered as reification – are 'a tangible reminder and a public testament to learners, teachers and families that such actions are, at least occasionally, within this child's compass' (Claxton & Carr, 2004, p. 94).

Documenting everyday moments in early childhood

Documenting children's everyday moments in early childhood settings and beyond these settings is key to enhancing and updating our understanding and further developing an appreciation of the everyday detail of children's learning, development and children's feelings and responses to the world they inhabit. Through such documentation, practitioners, and adults more broadly, understand the learning opportunities and the associated environments that are involved in what children know and what children do (Rogoff, Dahl & Callanan, 2018). An important aspect of this focus is gaining insight into the *lived experience of the child*, defined as:

> What a child sees, hears, thinks and experiences on a daily basis that impacts on their personal development and welfare whether that be physically or emotionally. As practitioners we need to actively hear what the child has to say or communicate, observe

what they do in different contexts, hear what family members, significant adults/carers and professionals have said about the child, and to think about history and context. Ultimately, we need to put ourselves in that child's shoes and think 'what is life like for this child right now?'

(Cambridgeshire and Peterborough Safeguarding Children Partnership Board (CPSCPB), 2020, p. 3)

As a tool of observation and interpretation, the practice of documenting is part of the daily life in early childhood education (Kroeger & Cardy, 2006) and generates knowledge of children's lived experiences in context. Early years practitioners, as part of their daily routines, observe, record, interact and scaffold children's learning, documenting children's meanings in the natural context of their daily routines and rituals. Typically, children build natural and trusting relationships with practitioners and their behaviour is not notably affected by the presence of practitioners as researchers. The importance of understanding children's lives in context and within their cultural contexts is thus emphasised, as outlined in the following extract:

> It is crucial to examine (rather than assume) generality of findings across populations and situations; to interpret findings based on knowledge of children's lives rather than researchers' intuitions; and to study children's development in the ecologies in which it occurs. We call for research on how children everywhere learn to navigate across and participate in the distinct cultural settings of their everyday lives.
>
> (Rogoff, Dahl & Callanan, 2018, p. 6)

A particular method of documenting children's everyday moments is that of learning stories. Learning stories are a form of documentation in which the early childhood education practitioner develops a story, which is generally articulated as a letter to the child and illustrated with photos of the selected situation (Carr & Lee, 2019; Knauf, 2019). The learning stories method was originally developed in New Zealand and is still used in New Zealand today as a key assessment for children of pre-school age (Carr & Lee, 2019). Children's participation in documenting their everyday moments is reinforced through the narrative feature of learning stories and the direct way in which individual children are addressed and communicated with within this documentation format (Knauf, 2017). Children's self-reflexivity is also further facilitated though such an approach.

Educators and researchers as the instrument of understanding the child

Responsive educators are highly engaged with children, attuned to their cues and needs, and able to respond in individualised ways that foster social, behavioural and academic development (Hamre, 2014). Adults facilitating young children's participation in research need to create opportunities as well as adopt appropriate skills to engage effectively with young children. The role of early years practitioners in making this a reality through co-constructing children's meanings has become increasingly important. Bath (2013) suggests that conceptualisations of listening are best understood if they are embedded within an ethics of care, which brings adults and children together in contexts and practices where the rights of the child are respected. However, the contexts in which listening to young children typically occurs, and the power differential of the participants involved, may often be problematic. Ensuring young children's participation in research through sensitive, appropriate, rights-based approaches is essential in order to promote and advocate on behalf of children (Blanchet-Cohen & Elliot, 2011). Greater appreciation of the valuable role that early childhood practitioners can play in facilitating and carrying out meaningful research with young children further highlights the distinctive and significant role that practitioner/researchers play as an instrument of understanding children's meanings in early childhood.

Specifically, with reference to methodological issues in research with young children, the development of the techniques of the Mosaic approach (Clark, 2017; Clark & Moss, 2001) draw on diverse, visual and active ways of gaining children's perspectives. As its name suggests, the Mosaic approach implies the use of multiple rather than single methods (Bath, 2013). In the Focus on Research below, an illustration of how early childhood practitioners can collaborate and work alongside researchers in order to mediate and act as an instrument of understanding of children's meanings, through adopting the Mosaic approach, is summarised. Children's subjective perceptions and associated constructions of care, both as caregivers and as care-receivers, were explored in a pre-school classroom in the US. Early childhood practitioners facilitated the presence of a researcher in the classroom, introducing the researcher as a *scientist* to the children, as this was a term previously explored with children in their curriculum. In this way, children were encouraged and supported to feel comfortable asking the researcher any questions that they were interested in exploring. A total of 15 children, aged 3–5 years, took part in the study.

FOCUS ON RESEARCH

Mosaic of care: Preschool children's caring expressions and enactments

McCormick (2018)

Study aims

Explore young children's constructions of care by capturing expressions, enactments, and interpretations of care as they occurred in an ECCE preschool setting.

- Across a period of 6 weeks, the researcher spent 3 days per week (3 hours per visit) in the Sunflower room gathering data, a total of approximately 54 hours.

- The data sources involved in this study merged both visual modes (observation, photo/video documentation, child-generated artifacts like artwork and books) and verbal/voice modes (child conferences and informal conversations) to capture a diversity of children's enactments and expressions of care.

- Each data source held equal weight in representing children's construction of care.

- Notes gathered through observation provided entry points for informal conversations with the children.

The careful planning and collaboration between early years practitioners and researcher is emphasised in the study above. A focus on multi-modal methods, adopted and implemented over an extended period of time, contributed to ensuring access to these children's views, generating rich and insightful understanding of young children's constructions of care.

Drawing together the data gathered across these multi-modal methods, which included transcripts from video and audio recordings, visual artefacts (i.e. photographs, child-generated art, and reflection books), and observation notes, young children's experiences of care, as they converged and diverged across the texts, were analysed (McCormick, 2018). Five key themes were identified and are briefly summarised as follows:

Minimising the discomfort or pain of others

Children's enactments of the desire to minimise discomfort or pain of others were illustrated through children engaging in acts of kindness in response to the distress or upset of another child, such as making a card to comfort a child whose father was away for a short time. Children's fantasy play also revealed instances of providing comfort and care to children in the varied roles that they adopted.

Support relationships

Children expressed their views on and enacted clear examples of co-operatively engaging with other children in order to help friends to achieve a goal, which was not possible to achieve alone. The sense of belonging to a community was also evident in the data informing this theme.

Promote positive emotion

Across the varied modes of data collected, children's satisfaction and pleasure in providing care was demonstrated. One child was observed to check on and monitor the wellbeing of a younger child on a regular basis, and this enactment of caregiving provided both the older and younger child with feelings of satisfaction. Observations of children taking on the role of firefighters demonstrated children's feelings of pride in 'rescuing' and 'healing' those who needed care.

Enhance healthy and safe habits

Healthy and safe self-care habits, for example choosing to eat healthy foods, washing hands to ensure hygiene, and maintaining positive sleep routines, were observed and discussed with the children, and clearly understood as a priority of care.

Ensure the longevity and sustainability of their shared resources

The preservation and care of shared resources, in order to ensure that these resources would be available for future use, were evident as priorities for children as discussions generated through a focus on the photos and observation data recorded. Through their activities and associated conversations, children's awareness of more global sustainable practices such as avoidance of waste were also emphasised.

Enacting children's citizenship and voicing children's agency

The concept of children's citizenship presents an opportunity for considering the extent to which it incorporates an emphasis on children as active meaning-makers. Bacon and Frankel (2014, p. 21) further argue that:

> ... in order to effectively respect children as meaning-makers, there needs to be some recognition that citizenship values are not simply a product of structure, a pre-defined status, shaped and managed by those in power, but also a product of agency. One important aspect of children's participation and involvement in society is the contribution they make to defining and negotiating norms and values.

A key component of ensuring children's citizenship is promoting young children's participation in the decision-making processes on matters directly affecting their learning and development, where this is deemed to be appropriate and desirable with reference to children's wellbeing. All children are born with civil, political, social and economic rights, which facilitate children's participation in matters significant within their everyday lives (Sierra-Cedilloa et al., 2019). The principle of children's participation is enshrined in Article 12 of the United Nation's Convention on the Rights of the Child (UNCRC, 1989). However, the UNCRC qualifies, to some extent, the right of the child to express their views, when it emphasises 'the views of the child being given due weight in accordance with the age and maturity of the child' (Article 12, United Nations, 1989). Murray (2016) points out that the younger children are, therefore, the less likely they will be considered as capable of forming and expressing their own views. Significantly, children's repertoires of participation are typically influenced by ethnicity, social class and ability/disability (Wood, 2014), with race, sex and perceived physical attractiveness often influencing the maintenance of boundaries between social groups.

Acknowledging children as meaning-makers also requires taking account of the interplay between structure and agency (Bacon & Frankel, 2014). Hammersley (2016) emphasizes the pointlessness of adopting a model for children's agency and autonomy without taking into consideration the complex contexts and structures that potentially enable or impede such agency.

Other authors draw attention to the social, cultural and political contexts in which children's agency develops (Abebe, 2019) and the importance of understanding that children's agency is supported as they take part in social practices, cultural contexts, and in social interactions (Kjørholt 2005; Lee 2001). Creating an environment that invites children to participate, together with and alongside adults (Taft 2015) acknowledges the respective roles and positions of children and adults as well as how they are connected (Wyness 2012).

Kellett (2011) notes, researchers working with children and young people have placed a greater emphasis on active citizenship for children rather than citizenship as a preparation for the responsibilities of adulthood.

In Chapter 1, the importance of participation including an emphasis on enhancing *information, understanding, voice, and influence* was highlighted – key participation rights drawn from UNCRC, Article 12 (Mayne et al., 2018). Insight into the various levels of information that can be provided to children, the understanding that may result from this information, the scope given to children to express their views and the degree to which their voices ultimately exert influence in research contexts must all be considered. Each of these four elements plays a unique role in upholding and enhancing children's rights in research and emphasises the need for consideration.

The hierarchical model of participation developed by Mayne et al. (2018) enriches our understanding of what constitutes meaningful participation in research for young children, providing insight into how children's agency can be nurtured and scaffolded. Central to this model is the notion that participation is more than 'taking part'; it is a cumulative, planned and resourced process leading to improvement and change that is understood by children' (Groundwater-Smith, Dockett & Bottrell, 2015, p. 33). In the Focus on Research below, in a study by Gray and Winter (2011), children's participation is designed in such a way as to fulfil criteria at an advanced level, according to the model developed by Mayne et al. (2018). Specifically, this study involved 3- and 4-year-old children who contributed to many aspects of a research project, including choosing the research questions, data collection methods and how the findings would be disseminated.

FOCUS ON RESEARCH

Hearing voices: participatory research with preschool children with and without disabilities

Gray and Winter (2011)

Study aims

Extend current thinking on participatory research by engaging young children with and without a known disability in all aspects of a research project.

- Matched according to age and gender, six dyads of children chose the research questions, selected the research methods, gathered the data and disseminated their findings.

- The study comprised 36 children (18 boys and 18 girls) aged between 3 years and 5 months and 4 years and 10 months.

- Children with disabilities included eight children on the autistic spectrum, four with attention deficit disorder, three with a visual impairment, two with Down's syndrome and one with cerebral palsy.

- A qualitative multi-method approach (small group discussions, observations and staff interviews) facilitated the exploration of children's subjective experiences of their ECE setting.

A number of unique features of this study are highlighted by Gray and Winter (2011). First of all, a range of creative and innovative research methods at the consent stage of the process were implemented. These methods were informed and guided by the Mosaic approach developed by Clark and Moss (2001) and Moss, Clark and Kjørholt (2005). Creative, appropriate methods were developed and tailored to meet the needs of all children, including those children lacking the verbal skills to express their consent. Importantly, children themselves were given the opportunity to select the methods through which they wished to participate in the study. These methods included the use of an artefact, Molly (a rag doll), thumbs up and down stickers, smiley faces, drawings, disposable cameras and tape recorders. Children were also involved in a very active manner in designing the type and content of questions that they felt should be included in the study. This was achieved through using Molly, as a prompt to help the children think and talk about the type of questions they would like to ask. Children were informed that Molly would be starting at their school in September and were asked what question(s) they thought she might ask them about school before she started. All of these simple strategies, developed to involve the children centrally in the design of the study and the inclusion of creative tools that facilitated children's natural engagement and involvement, provide excellent examples of how children's participation can be crafted in meaningful and appropriate ways.

The question that emerged as being most important from the children's interactions with Molly was *What do we like most and what do we like least about our school?* Once this question was agreed on, the children were encouraged to work in pairs to discuss the methods they would use to identify and document their likes and dislikes. There was considerable variation in the different approaches that each pair selected, with the most popular choices being: tape recording interviews with staff and children, attaching thumbs up and thumbs down signs to most- and least-liked objects, taking pictures using the disposable cameras and doing paintings. Findings from these activities and engagement with children showed that, although they had individual preferences, there was considerable agreement in the areas/aspects in their pre-school that they liked.

- The most common preferences highlighted included *having friends, the staff, visits to places outside the setting, baking, dressing up, painting, working with play dough, playing with blocks, looking at books, playing outside, playing in the sand tray, card making.*

- The most common dislikes were fewer in number and included: *bins* – which were described as smelly and dirty, *teachers making you stop playing to do something else, water and sand trays*, although the latter was also a favourite for some children.

- An examination of their individual preferences showed that five of the eight children with autism preferred *jigsaws* to other objects. In contrast, and as might be anticipated, jigsaws were least preferred by children with a visual impairment, who also disliked *drawing, writing and beads*.

Using creative and innovative ways to present the research problem to the children, for example using a doll to facilitate understanding, provided children with enough contextual information to enable them to form a significant level of understanding, which in turn empowered them to discuss options and make decisions about how they would carry out selected elements of the research. The children's opportunities for influence were scaffolded by providing them with a forum (at their pre-school graduation) to dramatise their findings for family members in the audience. School leaders then made decisions about what changes would be made as a result of the children's research.

Universal definitions of citizenship typically do not include young children in the status of citizenship, based on the view that children do not, as yet, have competences such as rationality and independence – abilities which are associated with citizenship (Larkins, 2014). However, very young children are in the process of learning and of evaluating their beliefs about what makes life worthwhile, even while they are very dependent on their families and others around them for input and guidance (Coady, 2008). Rights based policy and practice for early childhood connects directly with the concept of respect of young children's role in realising their rights. A shift in the young child's status within policy and practice is signalled by the move away from policy that is based on adult perceptions of 'children's needs' and towards policy that is based on respect for children's rights and that recognises that children themselves have a role to play in defining their needs (Woodhead, 2008).

In an effort to address the exclusion of young children's participation in research that can inform policy decisions and policy initiatives with the potential to impact directly on their lives, the Young Children as Researchers (YCAR) study (Murray, 2012) set out to conceptualise the different ways that young children (aged between 4 and 8 years) can be considered as researchers. YCAR established that professional researchers regard decision-making based on evidence as important research behaviour. Key findings from the YCAR study highlighted how young children participating in YCAR showed how they based decisions on evidence quite naturally, by combining sensory information with reasoning to identify a rationale for choice. Moreover, when YCAR children engaged in making decisions based on evidence, they often displayed their agency. Not only did YCAR children act as researchers, basing decisions on evidence to construct and apply understanding but they also acted as co-researchers for the YCAR study itself, gathering, analysing and interpreting evidence. Thus it can be argued that children aged 4 to 8 years participating in the YCAR study behaved as researchers, and demonstrated sufficient 'age and maturity' to show themselves 'capable of forming their views' in 'matters affecting them' (OHCHR, 1989).

In the Focus on Research below, an ethnographic study carried out in the US with children aged 3–5 years explored the concept of citizenship through the lens of young children in order to identify some of the ways in which these young children enact citizenship in their everyday lives within early childhood settings.

FOCUS ON RESEARCH

Young children's everyday civics

Payne (2018)

Study aims

The aims of the study were to explore the concept of citizenship through the lens of young children in order to identify some of the ways in which these young children enact citizenship.

- The data included here represent a fundamental argument in the study: civic education needs to reframe how it sees civic action to include and take seriously young children's meaning-making of their world.

- The Civic Action and Young Children study was a year-long, video-cued multi-vocal ethnography (Tobin, Adair & Arzubiaga, 2013; Tobin, Wu & Davidson, 1991) of three classrooms at Cielo Head Start center located in a large south western city.

- The center served over 300 3-, 4-, and 5-year old children. The student population was 65% Latino, 33% African American, and 2% White.

- As a Head Start Center, the school's socio-economic makeup is low income with nearly 100% of students receiving free lunch. This article draws on data from one general-education classroom that had 19 students, whose demographics mirrored the school makeup.

- Data collection for this study included participant observation photographic artifacts, filming of short scenes and full days (per video-cued ethnography), interviews, and work sample collection.

- Shifting our view of civic education from an adult lens to one that focuses on the everyday actions of young children in support of their community requires that we shift our very ideas about what it means to be civic.

- We also observed how their everyday relationships and interactions highlighted a different vision of being civic and more caring and relational idea of the common good.
- Etzioni (2015) explains that communitarians define community by two characteristics: (a) by a 'web of affect-laden relationships' (p. 7) and (b) some commitment to shared values, norms, meanings, history, and identity.

Study conclusions

Young children work together in everyday ways to construct, reinforce, and experiment with the very notion of community. They are developing their 'web of affect-laden relationships' within a classroom community that is a civic space for varied members of the public to come together.

Young children's notion of the common good, of caring for one another, of being civic, has heart.

Young children are relationally invested in the common good of their classroom civic spaces.

These relationships are interwoven with children developing and negotiating a set of shared values, norms, meanings, history, and identity.

If we attend to what young children are showing us, what it looks like when they are navigating new relationships, constructing a new community, then we can expand our notions of civic education.

While children have traditionally been excluded from definitions of citizenship, more recent and current perspectives emphasise the potential for children's inclusion through a model of citizenship which emphasises connectedness, interdependence and community (Devine, 2002; Payne, 2018). The importance of promoting young children's agency in early childhood education, and more broadly across all educational institutions, is foregrounded in such studies. Agency is not a static concept but dynamic and unfolding through the actions of the participants, and reinforced and supported through that participation.

Transformative potential of research: revisiting and moving forward with new understandings of children's meanings

The transformative potential of research is to enable change within the research context and to empower those who participate within it. Research has the potential to contribute to transformation in the everyday practices of life in the home and in family contexts, outside of home contexts, such as in services for young children and their families, and in broader societal and global contexts that pose challenges and risks for young children (Farrell et al., 2016).

Possibilities for transformation lie in conceptual understandings of research *with* children rather than on or about children (Kellet, 2005), where children are seen as holding rights as active participants and competent interpreters of their own worlds – as persons with the right to be seen and heard within their sites of experience on issues that affect them (Christensen & James, 2008; Mayall, 2003; Tisdall, 2012).

Langhout and Thomas (2010) draw attention to the significance of embracing the role of children as social actors and co-researchers. Specifically, they make the case that participatory action research with children does not involve imposing the same set of conceptual or methodological principles from research with older youth or with adults. The potential for research to be transformative and to generate new understandings of children's experiences requires the development of a different skill set and competencies to inform research expertise, research projects and research products. Early years practitioners are well placed, in terms of the skill set and competencies and the practical experience of applying these skills in their work with young children, to collaborate in and nurture the potential for such transformation to occur.

Participatory action research with young children foregrounds significant issues and questions relating to power, knowledge and participation and challenges the knowledge-making process that favours power (Clark, 2010; Langhout & Thomas, 2010; Reason & Bradbury, 2006). Redrawing the boundaries between adults' and children's roles in the research process provides possibilities for research to generate new questions and raise challenges to the status quo, rather than offering easy solutions to adult-defined problems. In this way, action research with young children can provide a means of going beyond simply revealing power differences to developing more democratic forms of knowledge building. As summarised by Langhout & Thomas (2010, p. 61):

> Research that affects children can be further reinvigorated by reconceptualizing the research process as an intervention in and of itself, where children learn skills through guided participation and active engagement. In other words, research and intervention are not separate steps, but rather are the components of praxis, or an embodied theory, with an agenda of creating conditions that facilitate individual and group empowerment, as well as social change.

In the Focus on Research below, a child-centred model for involving children in the evaluation of their own pre-school settings is outlined, in a study carried out in an early childhood setting in China. Observations of teaching and learning observations of teaching and learning in six rural kindergartens in three counties was undertaken, plus group interviews of all the teachers and approximately 15–20 family members (often grandparents and parents). The authors were contracted to evaluate the effectiveness of Early Childhood Care and Development (ECCD) programs funded by Plan China in poor rural communities in China. This ECCD project aimed to provide early care and development for children under 6 years of age.

The focus was on advancing the quality of care by parents and guardians of children under 6 years of age, through building a community-based early care and development service system. In order to understand how the kindergartens were experienced by children, it was also necessary to gain insights into what policy people supported, what resources were provided to children by the teachers and what the families thought about early learning in their community.

The study incorporated a five-step process in order to effectively access the children's views on their early childhood settings with a particular focus on: *Building an initial relationship with children; Power relations; Using a range of tools to conceptualise the research process; Giving time to children to reflect* and *Interviews as dialogue and conversation.*

FOCUS ON RESEARCH

A child-centred evaluation model: Gaining the children's perspective in evaluation studies in China

Fleer and Li (2016)

Study aims

To explore a child-centred evaluation model for evaluation of their pre-school settings.

- The central method of evaluation focused on gaining the perspective of children through inviting children to draw what they liked or did not like about their pre-school.

- In groups of five to six, children took photographs during a community walk with the researchers of what they liked or did not like about their community.

- Video interviews were conducted with small groups of children after their community walk.

- Total data included 252 children's drawings, 1000 photographs, 20 hours of video interviews/30 hours video observations, and document analysis of relevant kindergarten materials from six kindergartens in three villages over a two-week period.

Including a focus on the children's views and adopting a multi-modal approach to accessing these young children's views facilitated the evaluation of early education and development services, which incorporated a unique perspective on how the services are experienced and understood.

What were the findings from the children's participation in the study?

Children's drawings depicted a wide range of features, many of which appeared to be related to nature and the outdoors, including: butterflies, moon, fish, birds, flowers and trees, turnip, clouds, duck, and water pool. This focus on nature and the outdoors was also reflected in children's photographs, including: flowers and trees, chickens, vegetables in the garden, slides in the garden, trucks, and bricks and stones. Children also highlighted a preference for toys, which they had photographed in shops, and expressed their pleasure at being able to play on the slides in the kindergarten. These findings were then translated into possible actions for Plan China. Specifically, the drawings and related comments by children were reviewed and discussed, by comparison and in contrast with textbooks, which were found to be the central content of the curriculum in the kindergarten. Based on the findings from children who participated in the evaluation, recommendations were made for educators to use local materials such as wood, cardboard, bricks and stones, flowers and vegetables in order to design their play environment, with a view to supporting children's development in ways that reflect their interests.

Findings in the study outlined above demonstrate the value and importance of including young children's perspectives in research that focuses on aspects of children's everyday lives. Evidence such as that generated in the study by Fleer and Li (2016) draws attention to the need for research-for-transformation of the settings in which children live (Farrell et al., 2016).

Blurring the boundaries and reducing the power imbalance between young children and adults in the research process enables the production of robust data and effective research methodology that facilitates accessing children's views on what is meaningful to them in their early childhood settings. Such approaches have the potential to support policy directions for early childhood education and to transform children's living and learning environments in ways that children themselves wish such changes to take place.

Further evidence of the significant contributions that young children can make to developing policy and shaping substantial policy initiatives is evidenced in a consultation with young children, aged 3–5 years, in Ireland to contribute to a whole-of-Government strategy for babies, young children and their families. The *'First 5* Strategy', launched by the Department of Children and Youth Affairs (DCYA) in 2018, is the first national strategy for children in early childhood in Ireland, and builds on the many positive developments for young children in recent years. The strategy sets out how to develop a system of integrated, cross-sectoral and high-quality supports and services – in order to develop and support an effective early childhood system – that will help all babies and young children in Ireland to have positive early experiences. The strategy explains why this system should be developed, what it should look like and, most importantly, the necessary actions that need to be taken. A key component of the development of the First 5 Strategy was a consultation with children aged 3–5 years. This consultation was based on the principle that childhood is a social construction and that children should be considered as competent social actors active in the construction of their lives and agency (Coyne, Mallon & Chubb, 2018). Some of the details of this consultation are outlined in the Focus on Research below.

FOCUS ON RESEARCH

First 5 report on the National Consultation with Young Children

Coyne, Mallon and Chubb (2018)

Aims of consultation

The objective of the consultation was to give young children (aged 3–5 years) the opportunity to express their views on issues that affect their lives directly. The purpose was to gain an understanding about young children's likes, dislikes and wishes about living in Ireland to inform policy decisions concerning early childhood services and wider provision for young children and families.

- The consultation was with a random sample of children in Ireland who were attending pre-school in ECE settings and junior infant classes in primary school. The sites participated in the consultation during the week of 14–18 December 2015.

- Six pre-school and six primary school settings participated in the consultation process and the educators at these settings managed the parental consent process on behalf of the consultation team. To facilitate each consultation team to conduct up to two consultations each day (i.e. with pre-school and primary school children), each pair of pre-school and primary school settings were in close proximity.

- This consultation used a participatory arts-based mosaic approach as this approach has been successfully used to research young children's experiences and views.

Capturing meanings and moving forward **217**

- Since there is not one single method that suits all children and all circumstances, it is important to use a variety of methods to gain insight into children's experiences. Methods were tailored to the individual child's strengths and preferences as well as to the focus of the research. Being flexible is a key issue so the researcher should adjust to the modes of communication preferred by the children rather than those in which the researcher feels most confident.

- The questions were tailored to the developmental stage of very young children aged 3–5 years and these were:
  - What do you like about living in this area?
  - What do you not like about living in this area?
  - If you had a magic wand, what would you wish for or change?

- The data were obtained using puppets, group interviews and drawings, as these tools have been shown to facilitate successful data collection and obtain rich insights from children aged 3–5 years. Eleven themes were identified that captured what pre-school children liked about living in their area.

Home and family	Having a family and a home were very important to children and they derived a lot of joy and comfort from their families. In relation to their family, many children expressed their feelings of love towards parents and siblings. Children also included details of their bedrooms, surroundings, trampoline, shoes, blankets, as well as the experience of being at home. They also mentioned pets (dogs, cats, fish) and names of their pets.
Doing things, going places and playing with parents, siblings and grandparents	Pre-school children enjoyed many forms of interaction with members of their family. In particular, they mentioned spending time together, going places and playing at things they liked. Going to places with their grandparents was also pleasant for the children.
Playing	Playing was a very important activity for the young children. Playing with friends or pets was very popular, as was playing with specific toys that they were fond of, such as cars, trains, engines, rockets, balloons and dolls.
Nature and playing outdoors	Children expressed their love of nature and playing outdoors. Seeing rainbows, planes in the sky, trees and butterflies were all part of this appreciation. The natural environment also offered them stimulating opportunities to play, climb, squelch in the mud, or build snowmen.

(Continued)

Going to the park/ playground and playing	The pre-school children relished the chance to play in the park or playground. Many of them were keen to mention that there was a green space in their local area. With regard to playgrounds, children very much enjoyed certain facilities such as slides, see-saws, roundabouts, sand and swings. Some children particularly liked the green colour of the playground.
Leisure activities	Children enjoyed the experience of going out to the cinema to see certain films and getting treats but also expressed an interest in watching movies or cartoons at home on their television. Other leisure activities enjoyed by the children included swimming, reading, baking, painting and making things. Facilities such as swimming pools were greatly appreciated by the children, as many were enthusiastic about partaking in this activity. Reading was also popular amongst the children. Finally, the children clearly enjoyed engaging in creative activities.
Having hygiene care	Another theme that emerged in relation to what the children liked was hygiene care. This theme refers to children's fondness of certain hygiene routines such as brushing their teeth and having their hair washed.
Animals	Children also expressed the view that they animals. In particular, they liked the experience of going to the zoo and seeing interesting things such as crocodiles and penguins. Common animals such as dogs, rabbits and hedgehogs were also popular.
Eating and getting treats	Eating was something the children distinctly liked. Certain types of food were favoured by the children, many of which were vegetables. Eating sweets and treats such as biscuits, jellies and lollipops was also something children enjoyed.
Being at pre-school	Being at pre-school was spoken about favourably by some of the children. Pre-school was considered fun by these young children, and they particularly liked getting to play with certain toys and games.
Christmas	The children were very enthusiastic about Christmas, which is not surprising since data collection occurred in December. Specific aspects of Christmas that the children were fond of included receiving cards and presents, characters related to Christmas such as Santa and Rudolph, and having a tree in their house.

Findings based on this national consultation with young children, aged 3–5 years, are a testament to the ability and competence that these young children demonstrate, in terms of being able to clearly articulate their views and perspectives when provided with meaningful opportunities and facilitated through the use of appropriate research tools. Insight into the detail of young children's thoughts and feelings can only be achieved through engagement and consultation with these children, within the context of their everyday lives. The insights generated through this process of engagement with young children demonstrated their expertise as research participants and, more importantly, their expertise in the experience of being children. Attending to the detail of children's perspectives and views allows us to stand back from what has been socially constructed (by adults) as understandings of children and childhood, and to move forward with new understandings of the lived experience of children with the potential to contribute to transforming these experiences (Harcourt, 2011).

Sharing the power with children

Meaningful participation for young children in research is achievable through different formats and fora, some providing greater emphasis on children's participation throughout the research process, while others, depending on the context and the research topic and objective, may allow more limited participation modes. As outlined in previous chapters, children's competence in research can be enhanced through providing them with democratic opportunities for participation, and methodologies that scaffold the expression of meanings in appropriate and creative ways. The profound value and importance of such participation and the potential for such participation to influence early childhood practice and policy is emphasised by Trevarthen (2011, p. 173) as follows:

> The policies and administration of early education and support for social development constantly need re-defining, or re-inspiring, by taking into account the perspective of a young child. They must acknowledge the intuitive abilities and values, and growing initiatives that are present in the child from birth and that

motivate learning. Innate impulses of human imagination, with strong aesthetic and moral feelings, make sharing of experience and building of meaningful memories possible for a young person. They also determine the suffering that follows if they are not respected.

Pedagogical documentation provides opportunities for sharing power with and between early years practitioners and the settings in which they work, the children they work alongside and the families of these children. Enabling children to share in the power of generating, giving and receiving information and knowledge helps to address the challenge of ensuring that we support children to develop and attain meaningful intellectual and social skills (Trevarthen, 2011).

Capturing young children's beliefs and experiences of learning can contribute significantly to our understanding of the nature of this learning process in the early years and of children's first experiences of learning in more formal educational contexts. In the Focus on Research below, young children's own views on their learning were captured in a study carried out in a school in Western Australia.

FOCUS ON RESEARCH

Sharing power with children: repositioning children as agentic learners

Ruscoe, Barblett and Barratt-Pugh (2018)

Study aims

Examine the perceptions of children on how they learn in the first year of school.

- Seventeen children (5–6 years of age) participated.
- Children were invited to draw a picture of themselves in the act of learning, and prompted to explain their drawing using the question: 'How do you learn?'

- Children's explanations were recorded during the drawing process.
- A thematic coding process was used to organise key words and phrases into common themes evident in the children's explanations of themselves in the act of learning.
- Four prominent themes for discussion emerged: affective traits of the learner; the child's role as a learner; the identity and place of the educator; and the learning environment.

Themes	Findings
Affective traits of learner	Learning was described as a happy experience offering exciting opportunities for children. All but one of the 17 children in the study depicted positive images of themselves in their drawing, using embellishments such as smiling faces and rosy cheeks. Friendships were also mentioned consistently in relation to being happy and learning.
Child's role as learner	The desire of children to be active in their learning was strongly evident in the study. Sixteen children provided evidence, either verbally or through the nature of their engagement in the task, that they saw themselves as capable, independent and/or knowledgeable. Following the rules was also an important part of being a learner. Children also explained that, to learn, the child's role was to work hard, believe that they can do things, and/or have a go.
The identity and place of the educator	The identity of the educator was shared between home and school. More children stated that they learnt from their family than from their teacher. However, the teacher was mentioned far more frequently but not necessarily with regard to learning. Three children who associated learning with teachers emphasised academic content such as literacy and numeracy. The children viewed the teacher as a respected person in the room. This was evidenced in the children's desire for their teacher's personal feedback and approval.
The learning environment	All but two children drew themselves in a school environment. Fourteen children drew their classroom and seven of them drew themselves sitting at a desk doing pencil and paper work. Only three students associated an outdoor environment with learning, all of whom were boys. Experiences in the outdoor environment are attributed to different characteristics such as 'fun', 'real', 'imagination' and 'exciting', and suggest that entertaining the idea of outdoor learning may offer some intrinsic benefits for children.

Ruscoe et al. (2018) draw attention to the fact that, in order to avoid adult assumptions about the source of the children's enjoyment in the present study, the children's comments needed to be contextualised within the thick descriptions of their broader explanations. This was exemplified in the views of one child, who drew herself sitting at a desk writing – a representation which, alone, might have conveyed the sense that her primary source of enjoyment in learning was in sitting at her desk. However, when invited to talk further about the speech bubble that she attached to her drawing stating 'I love this day', the child explained that she was happy because she was 'learning new stuff'. Ruscoe et al. (2018) point out that the frequent challenge and novelty the child experienced may be the source of her motivation for learning, rather than the physicality of learning at a desk.

Findings from this study provide testament to the idea that sharing the power with children in the research process has the potential to generate pedagogical alternatives, informed by first-hand accounts of learning from a child's perspective, rather than the approximations of adults (Ruscoe et al., 2018). Findings also highlight the fact that young children perceive learning as a holistic experience, rather than primarily as an academic experience, reinforcing the concept that academic learning alone runs contrary to the holistic nature of learners in early childhood (Barblett et al., 2016). The reciprocal and collaborative nature of the child–educator relationship, contributing significantly to how wellbeing is achieved for children, is also underlined in the study findings, acknowledging children's role as active contributors to the effectiveness of the learning environment. As pointed out by the study authors, adult perceptions of learning, as a notion that is too abstract for young children, limit studies exploring what children believe is the best way to learn and tend to seek the perspectives of older children, most frequently in response to specific programmes (Harcourt & Mazzoni, 2012). Sharing the power with young children in the research process thus facilitates the cultivation of child-responsive early childhood education, essential for the wellbeing and development of a young mind (Trevarthen, 2011).

Synthesising perspectives to generate a more equitable reality of childhood

The adult's image of children is a key element to how we relate to them. Relational pedagogy has interactions and communications at its heart and acknowledges sociocultural contexts (Hedges & Cooper, 2018; Papatheodorou, 2009). As emphasised throughout previous chapters, early years practitioners engage with young children in ways that are fluid, dynamic and responsive. This ensures that children's learning intentions are respected and are neither overshadowed nor overtaken by practitioners' intentions to be shaped into academic outcomes (Goouch, 2009). Children and educators are reconceptualised as being competent, having agency and enjoying collaboration, and as leading figures and co-authors of learning (Oliveira-Formosinho & Formosinho, 2016). This co-construction of learning journeys is a primary feature of the work that early years practitioners accomplish on a daily basis with young children. An essential characteristic of this accomplishment is the ability to reposition the child and the adults' role in daily practice, thereby being open to a view of the world and knowledge that is more receptive to the unpredictable – to negotiation and participation (De Sousa, 2019).

Empowering and scaffolding young children's participation in research on matters that affect their lives, in a manner that is respectful of both children and adults' rights, can help us to move closer to the generation of democratic knowledge that includes both adults' and young children's perspectives (Clark, 2011). Generalisations about children are rather problematic, as they are not a homogenous group (Pufall & Unsworth, 2004). It cannot be assumed that all children desire responsibility for decision-making or that participation confers benefits on all children, irrespective of situation (Coyne, 2006; Stegenga & Ward-Smith, 2008; Zwaanswijk et al., 2007). However, it is equally important to acknowledge young children as competent, intuitive and eager partners in the making and communication of meaning. Multi-modal, innovative research methods, appropriate and inviting to the natural creativity and co-operation of young children, make it possible to share power with young children in the research process. Pedagogical documentation is a mode of making visible and developing the plural identities of children. Beyond this, pedagogical documentation is a mode of developing a professional identity committed to a childhood participatory pedagogy (De Sousa, 2019). Fochi (2019, p. 340) foregrounds the construct of 'welcoming the child's universe', which involves the adult/practitioner/researcher assuming a welcoming attitude with children. This, in turn, facilitates reducing the gap between the child and the adult world, thereby changing the hierarchy of relationships and the possibilities for educational trajectories. Specifically, this involves overcoming a transmissive vision of knowledge and sharing the power with children to create and express meanings.

Creative, welcoming and innovative research methods with children in the early years have empowered children to demonstrate their expertise as research participants and, more importantly, their expertise in the experience of being children. Harcourt (2011) draws our attention to the fact that such research and the associated findings generate critical points for reflection on how life might be observed and experienced by children more generally. In order to achieve greater coherence between the child and the adult perspective, it is necessary to be open to the challenge of de-constructing conceptions about the role of the adult in the day-to-day pedagogical development, and then reconstructing it, by highlighting the importance of the relationship between adults and children (Fochi, 2019).

Harcourt (2011, p. 341) sums up key elements in achieving this coherence:

> In terms of the adult standpoint it is important, at times, to stand back from what has been socially constructed (by adults) as understandings of children and childhood. We may need to re-evaluate this positioning and reflect upon the existence of a complementary construct, that of the lived experience of children and childhood. Further examination of this construct may provide an opportunity for children and adults to work together and to give value to different perspectives on the same notion. It would also provide the time and the space for a coming together – for an exchange and debate of ideas – and provide reciprocal learning that would be of great benefit to both adults and children. In this way, we may develop a greater symmetry between the two viewpoints and give rise to a more equitable reality of childhood.

References

Abebe, A. (2019). Reconceptualising children's agency as continuum and interdependence. *Social Sciences*, MDPI, Open Access Journal, Vol. 8(3), 1–16.

Akin, R. (2011). Beyond the Linguistic: Reflecting on Video Data Gathered and Interpreted with Children. *Contemporary Issues in Early Childhood*, 12(4), 399–402. DOI: 10.2304/ciec. 2011.12.4.399

Alanen, L. (2001). Explorations in generational analysis. In L. Alanen and B. Mayall (Eds.), *Conceptualizing child-adult relations,* (pp. 11–22). Routledge Falmer

Alcock, S. (2000). Pedagogical documentation: Beyond observations. Occasional paper. No. 7. Institute for early childhood studies. Victoria University of Wellington, New Zealand.

Alderson, P. (2008). Children as researchers: Participation rights and research methods. In P. Christensen & A. James (Eds.), *Research with children: Perspectives and practices* (2nd ed., pp. 276–290). Routledge.

Alduncin, N., Huffman, L. C., Feldman, H. M., & Loe, I. M. (2014). Executive function is associated with social competence in preschool-aged children born preterm or full term. *Early Human Development*, 90(6), 299–306.

Ames, P., Rojas, V. and Portugal, T. (2010). *Methodological Note 1 - Methods for research with children: Lessons learned, challenges and proposals from the experience of Young Lives in Peru, Lima*: Grade; Niños del Milenio. [Online, in Spanish] available at http://www.ninosdelmilenio.org/wp-content/uploads/2012/10/nm1.pdf

Areljung, S. & Kelly-Ware, J. (2017). Navigating the risky terrain of children's working theories, *Early Years*, 37(4), 370–385. DOI: 10.1080/09575146.2016.1191441

Astington, J. W. (2003). Sometimes necessary, never sufficient: False-belief understanding and social competence. In B. Repacholi & V. Slaughter (Eds.), *Individual differences in theory of mind: Implications for typical and atypical development* (pp. 13–38). Psychology Press.

Atwater, J. B., Carta, J. J., Schwartz, I. S., & McConnell, S. R. (1994). Blending developmentally appropriate practice and early childhood special education: Redefining best practice to meet the needs of all children. In B. L. Mallory, & R. S. New (Eds.), *Diversity and developmentally appropriate practices: Challenges for early childhood education* (pp. 185–201). Teachers College Press.

Bacigalupa, C. & Wright, C. (2009). "And then a huge giant grabbed me!" Aggression in children's stories. *Early Childhood Research and Practice*, 11(2), 1–14.

Bacon, K. & Frankel, S. (2014). Rethinking Children's Citizenship: Negotiating structure, shaping meanings. *International Journal of Children's Rights*. Vol 22(1) 1–14. DOI: 10.1163/15718182-55680003

Bae, B. (2009). Children's right to participate – challenges in everyday interactions. *European Early Childhood Education Research Journal*. 17 (3): 391–406. DOI: 10.1080/13502930903101594.

Baker, L. (2006). Observation: A complex research method. *Library Trends*. 55 (1), 171–189.

Banaji, M. R., & Gelman, S. A. (2013). *Navigating the social world: What infants, children, and other species can teach us*. Oxford University Press.

Barblett, L., Knaus, M., & Barratt-Pugh, C. (2016). The pushes and pulls of pedagogy in the early years: Competing knowledges and the erosion of play-based learning. *Australasian Journal of Early Childhood*, 41(4), 36–43.

Barnes, J. (2015). An introduction to cross-curricular learning. In P. Driscoll, A. Lambirth & J. Roden, (Eds.), *The Creative primary curriculum* (2nd ed., pp. 260–279). Sage Publications.

Baron-Cohen, S. (1991). Precursors to a theory of mind: Understanding attention in others. In Whiten, Andrew (Ed.), *Natural theories of mind: Evolution, development, and simulation of everyday mindreading*, pp. 233–251. Basil Blackwell.

Bateman, A. (2017). Hearing children's voices through a conversation analysis approach. *International Journal of Early Years Education*, 25(3), 241–256. DOI: 10.1080/09669760.2017.1344624.

Bath, C. (2013). Conceptualising listening to young children as an ethic of care in early childhood education and care. *Children & Society*, 27, 361–371.

Baumeister R.F., Schmeichel B.J., Vohs K.D. (2013). Self-Regulation and the executive function: The self as controlling agent. In Kruglanski A. & Higgins E.T. (Eds). Self-regulation and the executive function: The self as controlling agent. *Social psychology: Handbook of basic principles*. (2nd ed., pp. 516–539.) Guilford.

Bell, N. (2008). Ethics in child research: rights, reason and responsibilities. *Children's Geographies*, [online], 6(1), 7–20.

Benford, R. D., & Snow, D. A. (2000). Framing processes and social movements: An overview and assessment. *Annual Review of Sociology*, 26, 611–639.

Black, D., & Fernando, R. (2014). Mindfulness training and classroom behavior among lower-income and ethnic minority elementary school children.

Journal of Child and Family Studies, 23(7), 1242–1246. DOI: 10.1007/s10826-013-9784-4.

Blanchet-Cohen, N. & Elliot, E. (2011). Young children and educators engagement and learning outdoors: A basis for rights-based programming. *Early Education and Development*. 22(5) 757–777. DOI: 10.1080/10409289.2011.596460.

Bock, Z. (2016). Multimodality, creativity and children's meaning making: Drawings, writings, imaginings. *Stellenbosch Papers in Linguistics Plus*, 49, 1–21. DOI: 10.5842/49-0-669

Bogels, S., Hoogstaf, B., Van Dun, L., De Schutter, S., & Restifo, K. (2008). Mindfulness training for adolescents with externalizing disorders and their parents. *Behavioural and Cognitive Psychotherapy*, 36(2), 193–209. DOI: 10.1017/S1352465808004190

Breathnach, H., Danby, S. & O'Gorman, L. (2018). Becoming a member of the classroom: supporting children's participation as informants in research. *European Early Childhood Education Research Journal*. Vol 26(3), 393–406.

Bronfenbrenner, U. (1986). Ecology of the family as a context for human development: Research perspectives. *Developmental Psychology*, 22, 723–742.

Brooker, L. (2001). Interviewing children. In MacNaughton, G., Rolfe S.A., and Siraj-Blatchford, I. (Eds.), *Doing early childhood research: International perspectives on theory and practice* (pp. 162–177). Open University Press.

Brooks, E. & Murray. J. (2016). Ready, steady, learn: School readiness and children's voices in english early childhood settings. Education 3–13: *International Journal of Primary, Elementary and Early Years Education* 46 (2), 143–156.

Brooks, M. (2009). Drawing, visualisation and young children's exploration of "Big Ideas", *International Journal of Science Education*. 31(3), pp. 319–341.

Broström, S. (2012). Children's participation in research. *International Journal of Early Years Education*, 20(3), 1–13. DOI:10.1080/09669760.2012.715407

Brown, V. (2017). Drama as a valuable learning medium in early childhood. *Arts education policy review*. 118(3), 164–171.

Bruzzesse, J.M., and C.B. Fisher. (2003). Assessing and enhancing the research consent capacity of children and youth. *Applied Developmental Science* 7(1), 13–26.

Burke, A. (2015). *Empowering children's voices through the narrative of drawings*. Unpublished PhD thesis, Memorial University of Newfoundand.

Burman, E. (1994). *Deconstructing developmental psychology*. Routledge.

Buysse, V., Sparkman, K., & Wesley, P. (2003). Communities of practice: Connecting what we know with what we do. *Council for Exceptional Children*, 69, 263–277.

Byrne, E., N. Daykin, and Coad, J. (2016). Participatory Photography in Qualitative Research: A Methodological Review. *Visual Methodologies* 4(2), 1–12.

Carelse, B. (2012). *Children's experiences of learning mindfulness to help develop their attentional skills*. PhD. University of East London.

Carpendale, J., Lewis, C. & Muller, U. (2018). *The development of children's thinking: Its social and communicative foundations.* Sage Publications.

Carr, M. (2000). Seeking children's perspectives about their learning. In A. Smith, N. Taylor, & M. Gollop (Eds.), *Children's voices: Research, policy and practice.* Pearson Education.

Carr, M. & Lee, W. (2019). *Learning Stories in Practice.* Sage Publications.

Carter, C., & Nutbrown, C. (2016). A pedagogy of friendship: Young children's friendships and how schools can support them. *International Journal of Early Years Education,* 24(4), 395–413.

Center on the Developing Child at Harvard University (2011). Building the brain's "air traffic control" system: How early experiences shape the development of executive function. Working paper No. 11. Retrieved from https://www.developingchild.harvard.edu

Centre for Early Childhood Development and Education (CECDE) (2006). *Síolta, The National Quality Framework for Early Childhood Education.* Dublin: CECDE

Chak, A. (2007). Teachers' and parents' conceptions of children's curiosity and exploration. *International Journal of Early Years Education,* 15(2), 141–159. DOI:10.1080/09669760701288690

Christensen, P., & James, A. (2008). *Research with children: Perspectives and practices* (2nd ed.). Routledge.

Clark, A. (2001). Ways of seeing: Using the Mosaic Approach to listen to young children's perspectives. In A. Clark, A.T. Kjørholt, & P. Moss (Eds.). *Beyond listening: Children's perspectives on early childhood services,* (pp. 29–50). The Policy Press.

Clark, A. (2004). *Listening as a way of life: Why and how we listen to young children.* National Children's Bureau for DfES.

Clark, A. (2005). Listening to and involving young children: A review of research and practice. *Early Child Development and Care,* 175(6) 489–505.

Clark, A. (2008). *Early childhood spaces: Involving young children and practitioners in the design process.* Working Paper 43. The Hague: Bernard van leer Foundation.

Clark, A. (2010). Young children as protagonists and the role of participatory, visual methods in engaging multiple perspectives. *American Journal Community Psychol,* 46, 115–123.

Clark, A. (2011). Breaking methodological boundaries? Exploring visual, participatory methods with adults and young children. *European Early Childhood Education Research Journal,* 19 (3), 321–330. DOI: 10.1080/1350293x.2011.597964

Clark, A. (2017). *Listening to Young Children.* Jessica Kingsley Publishers.

Clark, A., Kjorholt, A., & Moss, P. (Eds.). (2005). *Beyond listening: Children's perspectives on early childhood services.* Policy Press.

Clark, A., & Moss, P. (2001). *Listening to children: The mosaic approach.* London: National Children's Bureau.

Clark, A., & Moss, P. (2005). *Spaces to play: More listening to young children using the mosaic approach.* London: National Children's Bureau.

Clark-Ibáñez, M. (2004). Framing the social world with photo-elicitation interviews. *American Behavioral Scientist* 47, 1507–1527.

Claxton, Guy & Carr, Margaret. (2004). A framework for teaching learning: The dynamics of disposition. *Early Years.* 24, 87–97. DOI: 10.1080/09575140320001790898.

Coady, M. (2008). Beings and becomings: historical and philosophical considerations of the child as citizen. In Glenda Mac Naughton, Patrick Hughes and Kylie Smith, (Eds). *Young children as active citizens: Principles, policies and pedagogies.* (pp. 2–14). Cambridge Scholars Publishing.

Coates, E. (2002). I forgot the sky! Children's stories contained within their drawings, *International Journal of Early Years Education,* 10(1) pp. 21–35.

Coates, E. & Coates, A. (2006). Young children talking and drawing, *International Journal of Early Years Education,* 14(3), 221–241. DOI: 10.1080/09669760600879961

Coleyshaw, L., Whitmarsh, J., Jopling, M., & Hadfield, M. (2010). Listening to children's perspectives: Improving the quality of provision in early years settings. *Department for Education,* 5, 33–46.

Collaborative for Academic, Social, and Emotional Learning. (2012). *2013 CASEL guide: Effective social and emotional learning programs: Preschool and elementary school edition.* Chicago, IL: Author.

Colliver, y. (2017). From listening to understanding: interpreting young children's perspectives, *European Early Childhood Education Research Journal,* 25(6), 854–865. DOI: 10.1080/1350293X.2017.1380882.

Conroy, H., & Harcourt, D. (2009). Informed agreement to participate: Beginning the partnership with children in research. *Early Child Development and Care,* 179(2), 157–165. DOI: 10. 1080/03004430802666973.

Cook, T., & Hess, E. (2007). What the camera sees and from whose perspective: Fun methodologies for engaging children in enlightening adults. *Childhood,* 14(1), 29–45.

Corsaro, W. A. (1997). *The sociology of childhood.* Pine Forge Press.

Cowan, K. (2019). Digital meaning making: Reggio Emilia-inspired practice in Swedish preschools. *Media Education Research Journal,* 8(2), 11–29.

Coyne, I., Chubb, E., & Mallon, D. (2018). *First 5: A national consultation with young children on a whole-of-government strategy for babies, young children and their families.* Dublin: Government of Ireland.

Coyne I. (2006). Consultation with children in hospital: children, parents' and nurses' perspectives. *Journal of Clinical Nursing.* 15(1), 61–71.

Cruddas, L. (2007). Engaged Voices – Dialogic Interaction and the Construction of Shared Social Meanings. *Educational Action Research.* 15(3), 479–488.

Curenton, S. (2006). Oral storytelling: A cultural art that promotes school readiness. *Young Children,* 61(5), 78–87.

Dahlberg, G., Moss, P., & Pence, A. R. (2007). *Beyond quality in early childhood education and care: Postmodern perspectives.* Falmer Press.

Dalli, C., White, E. J., Rockel, J., & Duhn, I. (2011). *Quality early childhood education for under-two-year-olds: What should it look like? A literature review.* Wellington, New Zealand: Ministry of Education.

Darbyshire, P., C. McDougall, and W. Schiller (2005). Multiple Methods in Qualitative Research with Children: More Insight or Just More. *Qualitative Research,* 5(4), 417–436

DCSF. (2018). *Mark making matters: Young children making meaning in all areas of learning and development.* The National Strategies/Early Years. London: DCSF.

De Sousa, J. (2019). Pedagogical documentation: the search for children's voice and agency, *European Early Childhood Education Research Journal,* 27(3), 371–384. DOI: 10.1080/1350293X.2019.1600807

De Vries, P. (2004). The extra-musical effects of music lessons on pre-schoolers. *Australian Journal of Early Childhood,* 29, 6–10.

Devine D. (2002). Children's citizenship and the structuring of adult / child relations in the primary school. *Childhood,* 9(3), 303–320.

Dockett, S. Einarsdottir, J. & Perry, B. (2017). Photo elicitation: reflecting on multiple sites of meaning, *International Journal of Early Years Education,* 25(3), 225–240. DOI: 10.1080/09669760.2017.1329713

Dockett, S., and B. Perry. (2007). Children's transition to school: Changing expectations. In A.W. Dunlop and H. Fabian, (Eds.), *Informing transitions in the early years,* (pp. 151–168). Open University Press.

Dockett, S. & Perry, B. (2011). Researching with young children: Seeking assent. *Child Indicators Research,* 4(2), 231–247. DOI: 10.1007/s12187010-9084-0.

Dockett, S., Perry, B., & Kearney, E. (2013). Promoting children's informed assent in research participation. *International Journal of Qualitative Studies in Education (QSE),* 26(7), 802– 828. DOI: 10.1080/09518398.2012.666289.

Duncan, P. (2013). *Drawing as a method for accessing young children's perspectives in research.* PhD thesis: University of Stirling.

Dunphy, E. (2008). *Supporting Early Learning and Development through Formative Assessment. Research Paper.* Dublin: National Council for Curriculum and Assessment.

Edminston, B. (2008). *Forming ethical identities in early childhood play.* Routledge/Taylor & Francis Group.

Edwards, C. Gandini, L., & Forman, G. (Eds.). (1998). *The hundred languages of children: The Reggio Emilia approach—Advanced reflections* (2nd ed.). Ablex.

Edwards, D., and Alldred, P. (2001). Children and school-based research: "Informed consent" or "educated consent". *British Educational Research Journal,* 27(3), 347–365.

Einarsdóttir, J. (2003). When the bell rings we have to go inside. Preschool children's views on the primary school. *European Early Childhood Educational Research Journal. Transitions. Themed Monograph Series,* 1, 35–50.

Einarsdóttir, J. (2007). Research with children: Methodological and ethical challenges. *European Early Childhood Education Research Journal,* 15(2), 197–211.

Einarsdottir, J. (2011). Icelandic children's early education transition experiences. *Early Education and Development,* 22(5), 737–756.

Elkind, D. (2007). *The power of play: Learning what comes naturally.* Da Capo Press.

Einarsdóttir, J. Dockett, S. & Perry, B. (2009). Making meaning: children's perspectives expressed through drawings. *Early Child Development and Care,* 179(2), 217–232. DOI: 10.1080/03004430802666999.

Elliott, R., C. T. Fischer, and D. L. Rennie. (1999). Evolving Guidelines for Publication of Qualitative Research Studies in Psychology and Related Fields. *British Journal of Clinical Psychology,* 38, 215–229.

Ericsson, S. & Boyd, S. (2017). Children's ongoing and relational negotiation of informed assent in child– researcher, child–child and child–parent interaction. *Childhood.* 24(3), 300–315.

Etzioni, A. (2015). Common good. In M. T. Gibbons, E. Ellis, & K. Ferguson (Eds.), *The encyclopedia of political thought* (pp. 1–7). Wiley Blackwell Publishing.

Fargas-Malet, M, McSherry, D., Larkin, E., & Robinson, C. (2010). Research with children: Methodological issues and innovative techniques. *Journal of Early Childhood Research* 8(2), 175–192.

Farrell, A., Kagan, S., & Tisdall, M. (2016). Early childhood research: An expanding field. In A. Farrell, S. Kagan & M. Tisdall (Eds.). *The Sage handbook of early childhood research* (pp. 1–12). Sage Publications.

Farrell, A., Kagan, S. & Tisdall, K., (Eds.) (2016). *The Sage handbook of early childhood research.* Sage Publications.

Fawcett, M. & Watson, D., (2016). *Learning Through Child Observation.* Jessica Kingsley Publishers.

Ferraris, M., (2013). *Documentality: Why it is necessary to leave traces.* Translated by R. Davies. Fordham University Press.

Fitzpatrick, A. (2019). Towards a pedagogy of intergenerational learning. In M. Kernan & G. Cortellesi (Eds.), *Intergenerational learning in practice. Together Old and Young.* (pp. 40–54). Routledge.

Fleer, M., (2016). The Vygotsky project in education – The theoretical foundations for analysing the relations between the personal, institutional and societal conditions for studying development. In D. S., Gedera & Williams, P. J. (Eds.), *Activity theory in education: Research and practice.* (pp. 1–15). Sense Publishers.

Fleer, M. & Li, L. (2016) A child-centred evaluation model: gaining the children's perspective in evaluation studies in China, *European Early Childhood Education Research Journal,* 24(3), 342–356. DOI: 10.1080/1350293X.2016.1163934

Fleet, A., Patterson, C., & Robertson, J. (Eds.). (2017). *Pedagogical documentation in early years practice: Seeing through multiple perspectives.* Sage Publications.

Flewitt, R. (2005). Conducting research with young children: some ethical considerations, *Early Child Development and Care*, 175(6), 553–566.

Flook, L., Goldberg, S. B., Pinger, L., & Davidson, R. J. (2015). Promoting prosocial behavior and self-regulatory skills in preschool children through a mindfulness-based kindness curriculum. *Developmental Psychology*, 51(1), 44–51. DOI: 10. 1037/a0038256.

Flottman, R., McKernan. A., & Tayler, C. (2011). *Victorian early years learning and development framework – Evidence paper practice principle 2: Partnerships with professionals*. Melbourne Graduate School of Education, Department of Education and Early Childhood Development.

Fochi, P. (2019). Pedagogical documentation as a strategy to develop praxeological knowledge: the case of the observatory of childhood culture – OBECI, *European Early Childhood Education Research Journal*, 27(3), 334–345. DOI: 10.1080/1350293X.2019.1600803.

Ford, K., Sankey, J., & Crisp, J. (2007). Development of children's assent documents using a child-centred approach. *Journal of Child Health Care*, 11(1), 19–28.

Forman, G., & Hall, E. (2005). Wondering with children: The importance of observation in early education. *Early Childhood Research and Practice*, 7(2).

Gallacher, L. A., & M. Gallagher. (2008). Methodological Immaturity in Childhood Research? Thinking Through Participatory Methods. *Childhood*. 15 (4), 499–516. DOI: 10.1177/ 0907568208091672.

Garvis, S. (2012). Exploring current arts practice in kindergartens and preparatory classrooms. *Australasian Journal of Early Childhood*. 37 (4), 86–93.

Gelman, S A. (2009). Learning from Others: Children's Construction of Concepts. *Annual Review of Psychology*. 60(1), 115–140.

Gergely G & Csibra G., (2005). The social construction of the cultural mind: Imitative learning as a mechanism of human pedagogy. *Interaction Studies*. 6(3), 463–481.

Giardiello, P. (2011). The roots and legacies of four key women pioneers in early childhood education: A theoretical and philosophical discussion. unpublished doctoral thesis, University of Sheffield.

Giardiello, P., McNulty, J. & Anderson, B. (2013) Observation, Assessment and Planning Practices in a Children's Centre. *Child Care in Practice*, 19(2), 118–137, DOI: 10.1080/13575279.2012.743871.

Giudici, C., Rinaldi, C., & Krechevsky, M. (Eds.). (2001). *Making learning visible: Children as individual and group learners*. Reggio Emilia, Italy: Project Zero; Reggio Children.

Gloeckler, L., & La Paro, K. M. (2015). Toddlers and child care: A time for discussion, dialogue and change. *Zero to Three*, 36(2), 45–52.

Goodfellow, J. (2009). *The early years learning framework: Getting started.* Deakin West, ACT: Early Childhood Australia. Available at: http://www.earlychildhoodaustralia.org.au/nqsplp/wp-content/uploads/2012/05/RIP0904_EYLFsample.pdf

Goodfellow, J., & Hedges, H. (2007). Practitioner research "centre stage": Contexts, contributions and challenges. In L. Keesing-Styles & H. Hedges (Eds.), *Theorising early childhood practice: Emerging dialogues*. (pp. 187–210). Pademelon Press.

Goouch, K. (2009). Forging and fostering relationships in play: Whose zone is it anyway? In T. Papatheodorou & J. Moyles (Eds.), *Learning together in the early years: Exploring relational pedagogy* (pp. 139–151). Routledge.

Gorman, G.E. and Clayton, P. (2005). *Qualitative research for the information professional: a practical handbook*, Facet.

Government of Ireland (2018). *First Five: A Whole-of-Government Strategy for Babies, Young Children and their Families 2019-2028*. Dublin. Department of Children and Youth Affairs.

Graham, A., Powell, M., & Taylor, N. (2015). Ethical research involving children: Encouraging reflexive engagement in research with children and young people. *Children and Society*, 29(5), 331–343.

Gray, C. & Winter, E. (2011). Hearing voices: participatory research with preschool children with and without disabilities, *European Early Childhood Education Research Journal*, 19(3), 309–320. DOI: 10.1080/1350293X.2011.597963

Greenberg, M. T., & Harris, A. R. (2012). Nurturing mindfulness in children and youth: Current state of research. *Child Development Perspectives*, 6, 161–166. DOI: 10.1111/j.17508606.2011.00215.x

Greene, S., and M. Hill. 2005. In S. Greene and D. Hogan (Eds.) *Researching children's experience: Methods and methodological issues*. (pp. 1–21). Sage Publications.

Greig, A., Taylor, J., & McKay, T. (2013). *Doing research with children* (3rd ed.). Sage Publications.

Griffin, K. M., Lahman, M., & Opitz, M. F. (2014). Shoulder-to-shoulder research with children: Methodological and ethical considerations. *Journal of Early Childhood Research*, 14(1), 18–27.

Groundwater-Smith, S., S. Dockett, and D. Bottrell. (2015). *Participatory research with children and young people*. Sage Publications

Guillemin, M., and S. Drew. (2010). Questions of Process in Participant-Generated Visual Methodologies. *Visual Studies*. 25(2), 175–188. DOI: 10.1080/1472586X.2010.502676.

Haiman, P. E. (1999). Developing a sense of wonder in young children. *Brown University Child and Adolescent Behavior Letter*, 46(6), 52–53.

Hallahan, K. (1999). Seven models of framing: Implications for public relations. *Journal of Public Relations Research*, 11(3), 205–242.

Hammersley, M. (2016). Childhood studies: A sustainable paradigm? *Childhood*, 24 (1), 113–127.

Hamre, B. (2014). Teachers' daily interactions with children: An essential ingredient in effective early childhood programs. *Child Development Perspectives*. 8(4), 223–230.

Harcourt, D. (2008). Young children's constructs of quality. *Paper presented at the Annual Conference, European Early Childhood Education Research Association*, September 3–6, 2008, Stavanger, Norway, University of Stavanger.

Harcourt, D. (2009). *Standpoints on quality: Young children as competent research participants*. Australian Research Alliance for Children & Youth.

Harcourt, D. (2011). An encounter with children: seeking meaning and understanding about childhood. *European Early Childhood Education Research Journal*, 19(3), 331–343. DOI: 10.1080/1350293X.2011.597965

Harcourt, D., J. Einarsdottir, (Eds.) (2011). Special Issue: Children's Perspectives and Participation in Research. *European Early Childhood Education Research Journal* 19(3).

Harcourt, D. & Gray, C. (2013). Action in children's participatory research. *International Journal of Early Years Education*, 21(4), 265–267. DOI: 10.1080/09669760.2013.868239

Harcourt, D., & Einarsdottir, J. (Eds.). (2011). Introducing children's perspectives and participation in research, *European Early Childhood Education Research Journal*, 19(3), 301–307.

Harcourt, D., & Hägglund, S. (2013). Turning the UNCRC upside down: A bottom-up perspective on children's rights. *International Journal of Early Years Education*, 21(4), 286–299.

Harcourt, D., & Mazzoni, V. (2012). Standpoints on quality: Listening to children in Verona, Italy. *Australasian Journal of Early Childhood*, 37(2), 19–26.

Harcourt, D., Perry, B., & Waller, T. (Eds.). (2011). *Researching young Children's perspectives: Ethics dilemmas of educational research with children*. Routledge.

Hardman, C. (1973). Can there be an anthropology of children? *Journal of the Anthropology Society of Oxford*, 4(1), 85–99.

Hart, R. (1998). The developing capacities of children to participate. In V. Johnson et al. (Eds.), *Stepping forward: Children and young people's participation in the development process* (pp. 27–31). IT Publication.

Hart, R. (1992). *Children's participation: From tokenism to citizenship. UNICEF Innocenti Essays, No. 4, Florence*, Italy: International Child Development Centre of UNICEF.

Hayes, N. & O'Neill, S. (2019). Little changes, big results: the impact of simple changes to early years learning environments, *Early Years*, 39(1), 64–79. DOI: 10.1080/09575146.2017.1342223

Hayes, N., O'Toole, L. & Halpenny, A.M. (2017). *Introducing Bronfenbrenner: A Guide for Practitioners and students in Early Years Education*. Routledge.

Hayes, N. (2013). *Early years practice: Getting it right from the start*. Gill & McMillan.

Hayes, N., O'Toole, L., & Halpenny, A. M. (2019). *Introducing Bronfenbrenner: A guide for practitioners and students in early years education*. Routledge.

Hedges, H. & Cooper, M., (2018). Relational play-based pedagogy: Theorising a core practice in early childhood education, *Teachers and Teaching*, 24(4), 369–383.

Hill, M. (2005). Ethical considerations in researching children's experiences, In S. Greene & D. Hogan (Eds.) *Researching children's experience* (pp. 61–86). Sage Publications.

Holm, G. (2008). Photography as a Performance. *Forum: Qualitative Social Research Sozialforschung* 9(2).

Hurley, J.C., and M.K. Underwood. (2002). Children's understanding of their research rights before and after debriefing: Informed assent, confidentiality, and stopping participation. *Child Development*, 73(1), 132–143.

Irwin, L. G., & Johnson, J. (2005). Interviewing children: Explicating our practices and dilemmas. *Qualitative Health Research*, 15, 821–831.

James, A. (2007). Giving voice to children's voices: practices and problems, pitfalls and potentials. *American Anthropologist*, 109 (2), 261–272.

James, A. & Prout, A. (1990). *Constructing and reconstructing childhood: contemporary issues in sociological study of childhood*. Falmer Press.

James, A., & Prout, A. (Eds.). (1997). *Constructing and reconstructing childhood*. Falmer.

Jay, J., Knaus, M., & Hesterman, S. (2014). High quality early childhood education in the early years of school. *Every Child*, 20(3), 22–23.

Jenks, C. (2005). *Childhood*. 2nd ed. Routledge.

Jesuvadian, M. K., & Wright, S. (2011). Doll tales: Foregrounding children's voices in research. *Early Child Development and Care*, 181(3), 277–285.

Joerdens, S. H. (2014). Belonging means you can go in: Children's perspectives and experiences of membership of kindergarten. *Australasian Journal of Early Childhood*, 39(1), 12–21.

Johansson, E., & White, J. (Eds.). (2011). *Educational research with our youngest: Voices of infants and toddlers*. Springer Science & Business Media.

Johnson, V., Hart, R., & Colwell, J. (Eds.). (2014a). *Steps for engaging young children in research: The guide*, Vol. 1. The Hague: Bernard van Leer Foundation. Available at: https://bernardvanleer.org/publications-reports/steps-engaging-young-children-research-volume-1-guide/. Accessed 1 Feb 2015.

Johnson, V., Hart, R., & Colwell, J. (Eds.). (2014b). *Steps for engaging young children in research: The researcher toolkit*, Vol. 2. The Hague: Bernard van Leer Foundation. Available at: http://www.bernardvanleer.org/files/Steps-to-Engaging-Young-Children-in-Research-vol-2.pdf. Accessed 1 Feb 2015.

Johnson, V., Hart, R., & Colwell, J. (2016). International innovative methods for engaging young children in research. In R. Evans, L. Holt, & T. Skelton (Eds.), *Methodological approaches. Geographies of children and young people* (Vol. 2). Springer.

Jones, A. (2011). Seeing the messiness of academic practice: Exploring the work of academics through narrative. *International Journal for Academic Development*, 16(2), 109–118.

Jordan, B. (2004). Scaffolding learning and co-constructing understandings. In A. Anning, J. Cullen, & M. Fleer (Eds.), *Early childhood education: Society and culture*. (pp. 31–42) Sage Publications.

Kabat-Zinn, J. (1994). *Wherever you go, there you are: Mindfulness meditation in everyday life*. New York, NY: Hyperion

Karakoyun, F., & Kuzu, A. (2016). The investigation of preservice teachers' and primary school students' views about online digital storytelling. *European Journal of Contemporary Education*, 15(1), 51–64.

Kellett, M. (2005). *How to develop children as researchers*. Sage Publications.

Kellett, M. (2011). *Researching with and for Children and Young People*. Centre for Children and Young People Background Briefing Series, no.5. Lismore: Centre for Children and Young People, Southern Cross University.

Kendrick, M. & McKay, R. (2009). Researching Literacy with Young Children's Drawings, In M. Narey, (Ed.). *Making meaning: Constructing multimodal perspectives of language, literacy, and learning through arts-based early childhood education*. (pp. 53–70). Springer.

Kjørholt, A. T. (2005). *Childhood as a Social and Symbolic Space: Discourses on children as social participants in society*. Ph.D. thesis, Norwegian University of Science and Technology (NTNU), Trontheim, Norway.

Knauf, H. (2017). Learning stories: An empirical analysis of their use in Germany. *Early Childhood Education Journal*, 46(4), 427–434.

Knauf, H. (2019). Learning stories, pedagogical work and early childhood education: A perspective from German preschools, *Education Inquiry*. 11(2), 94–109. DOI: 10.1080/20004508.2019.1591845.

Knowles, C., & Sweetman, P. (2004). *Picturing the social landscape: Visual methods in the sociological imagination*. Routledge.

Krechevsky, M., Mardell, B., Rivard, M., & Wilson, D. (2013). *Visible learners: Promoting Reggio-inspired approaches in all schools*. Jossey-Bass.

Krechevsky, M., Rivard, M., & Burton, F. R. (2009). Accountability in three realms: Making learning visible inside and outside the classroom. *Theory Into Practice*, 49(1), 64–71.

Kress, G. (2000). Design and transformation. In B. Cope and M. Kalantzis (Eds.) *Multiliteracies: Literacy learning and the design of social futures*. (pp. 153–161). Routledge.

Kress, G. (2011). Discourse analysis and education: A multimodal social semiotic approach. In R. Rogers (Ed.), *Introduction to critical discourse analysis in education* (2nd ed., pp. 205–226). Routledge.

Kress, G., & van Leeuwen, T. (2006). *Reading images*. Routledge.

Kroeger, J., & T. Cardy. (2006). Documentation: A hard-to-reach place. *Early Childhood Education Journal*. 33 (6), 389–398.

La Paro, K. & Gloeckler, L. (2016). The context of child care for toddlers: The experience expectable environment. *Early Childhood Education Journal*. 44(2), 147–153. DOI 10.1007/s10643-015-0699-0.

Lancaster, P. (2003). *Listening to young children*. Open University Press.

Lämsä, T., Jokinen, K., Rönkä, A. & Poikonen, P. (2017). Childhood reproduced: images of childhood represented in children's daily lives in home and day-care settings, *Journal of Family Studies*, 23(2), 161–179. DOI: 10.1080/13229400.2015.1106334.

Langhout, R. & Thomas, E. (2010). Imagining participatory action research in collaboration with children: An introduction. *American Journal of Community Psychology*, 46(1-2), 60–66.

Lansdown, G. (2010). The realisation of children's participation rights: Critical reflections. In B. Percy-Smith & N. Thomas (Eds.), *A handbook of children and young people's participation: Perspectives from theory and practice* (pp. 11–23). Routledge.

Larkins, C. (2014). Enacting children's citizenship: developing understandings of how children enact themselves as citizens through actions and acts of citizenship. *Childhood*, 21(1) 7–21.

Lee, N. (2001). *Childhood and Society: Growing Up in an Age of Uncertainty*. Open University Press.

Levy, R., & Thompson, P. (2015). Creating buddy partnerships with 5- and 11- year old boys: A methodological approach to conducting participatory research with young children. *Journal of Early Childhood Research*, 13(2), 137–149.

Lisenbee, P. S., & Ford, C. M. (2018). Engaging students in traditional and digital storytelling to make connections between pedagogy and children's experiences. *Early Childhood Education Journal*, 46(1), 129–139.

Lubeck, S. (1994). The politics of developmentally appropriate practice: Exploring issues of culture, class and curriculum. In B. Mallory & R. New (Eds.), *Diversity and developmentally appropriate practices: Challenges for early childhood curriculum* (pp. 17–43). New York: Teachers College Press.

Lucas, C., Bridgers, S., Griffiths, T., Gopnick, A. (2014). When children are better (or at least more open-minded) learners than adults: Developmental differences in learning the forms of causal relationships. *Cognition*, 121(2), 284–299. DOI: 10.1016/j.cognition.2013.12.010

Lundy, L. (2007). "Voice" is not enough: Conceptualising Article 12 of the United Nations Conventions on the Rights of the Child. *British Educational Research Journal*, 33(6), 927–942.

Lundy, L., McEvoy, L., & Byrne, B. (2011). Working with young children as co-researchers: An approach informed by the United Nations Convention on the Rights of the Child. *Early Education and Development*, 22(5), 714–736. DOI: 10.1080/10409289.2011.596463.

Maagerø, E. & Sunde, T. (2016). What makes me happy, and what makes me scared? An analysis of drawings made by Norwegian and Palestinian children, *European Early Childhood Education Research Journal*, 24(2), 287–304. DOI: 10.1080/1350293X.2016.1143267

MacNaughton, G., Rolfe, S. A., & Siraj-Blatchford, I. (2001). *Doing early childhood research* Allen & Unwin.

MacNaughton, G. M., Smith, K., & Davis, K. (2007). Researching with children: The challenges and possibilities for building 'child friendly' research. In J. A. Hatch (Ed.), *Early childhood qualitative research* (pp. 167–205). Routledge.

Malaguzzi, L. (1994). Your image of the child: Where teaching begins. *Early Childhood Educational Exchange*, 96, 52–61.

Mannion, G. (2007). Going spatial, going relational: Why 'listening to children' and children's participation needs reframing. *Discourse*, 28(3), 405–420.

Marshall, N. & Shibazaki, K. (2011). Two studies of musical style sensitivity with children in early years, *Music Education Research*. 13(2), 227–240 DOI: 10.1080/14613808.2011.577771.

Martin, S. & Buckley, L. (2018). Including children's voices in a multiple stakeholder study on a community-wide approach to improving quality in early years setting. *Early Child Development and Care*. 190(9), 1411–1424 DOI: 10.1080/03004430.2018.1538135.

Mashford-Scott, A., & Church, A. (2011). Promoting children's agency in early childhood education. *Novitas – ROYAL (Research on Youth and Language)*, 5(1), 15–38.

Mason, J., & Danby, S. J. (2011). Children as experts in their lives: Child inclusive research. *Child Indicators Research*, 4, 185–189.

Maxwell, T. (2013). What can year-5 children's drawings tell us about their primary school experiences? *Pastoral Care in Education* 33, (2), 83–95. DOI: 10.1080/02643944.2015.1034758

Mayall, B. (2000) Conversations with children: working with generational issues, In: P. Christensen & A. James (Eds). *Research with children.* (pp. 120–135). Falmer Press.

Mayall, B. (2002). *Towards a sociology for childhood: Thinking from children's lives*. Open University Press.

Mayall, B. (2003). Sociology Can Further Children's Rights. *Education Journal* (72), 7.

Mayall, B. (Ed.). (1994). *Children's childhoods: Observed and experienced*. Falmer Press.

Mayne, F., Howitt, C. & Rennie, L. (2016). Meaningful informed consent with young children: looking forward through an interactive narrative approach, *Early Child Development and Care*, 186(5), 673–687. DOI: 10.1080/03004430.2015.1051975

Mayne, F., Howitt, C. & Rennie, L. (2018). A hierarchical model of children's research participation rights based on information, understanding, voice, and influence, *European Early Childhood Education Research Journal*, 26(5), 644–656. DOI: 10.1080/1350293X.2018.1522480

Mayne, F., & Howitt, C. (2014). Reporting of ethics in early childhood journals: A meta-analysis of 10 journals from 2009 to 2012. *Australasian Journal of Early Childhood*, 39(2), 71–79.

Mayne, F., & Howitt, C.. (2015). How far have we come in respecting young children in our research? A meta-analysis of early childhood research practice from 2009 to 2012. *Australasian Journal of Early Childhood.*, 40(4), 30–38.

McClelland, M. M., & Cameron, C. E. (2012). Self-Regulation in early childhood: Improving conceptual clarity and developing ecologically valid measures. *Child Development Perspectives*, 6(2), 136–142.

McCormick, K. (2018). Mosaic of care: Preschool children's caring expressions and enactments. *Journal of Early Childhood Research*. 16(4), 378–392. DOI: 10.1177/1476718X18809388

McIntosh, C., & Stephens, C. (2011). A storybook method for exploring young children's views of illness causality in relation to the familial context. *Early Child Development and Care*, 182(1), 23–33. DOI: 10.1080/03004430.2010.534161.

Meiklejohn, J., Philips, C., Freedman, M. L., Griffin, M. L., Biegel, G., Roach, A., Saltzman, A. (2012). Integrating mindfulness training into K-12 education: Fostering the resilience of teachers and students. *Mindfulness*, 3(4), 291–307. DOI: 10.1007/s12671-012-0094-5

Meltzoff, A. N. (2007). "Like Me": A foundation for social cognition. *Developmental Science*, 10, 126–134.

Mendelson, T., Greenberg, M., Dariotis, J., Gould, L., Rhoades, B., & Leaf, P. (2010). Feasibility and preliminary outcomes of a school-based mindfulness intervention for urban youth. *Journal of Abnormal Child Psychology*, 38, 985–994. DOI: 10.1007/s10802-010-9418-x

Merewether, J. (2012). *The outdoors as a pedagogical space: Children's perspectives.* Unpublished Master of Early Childhood dissertation, Macquarie University, Sydney.

Merewether, J. (2015). Young children's perspectives of outdoor learning spaces: What matters? *Australasian Journal of Early Childhood*, 40(1), 99–108.

Merriman, B. & Guerin, S. (2006). Using children's drawings as data in child-centred research. *The Irish Journal of Psychology*. 27(1-2), 48–57.

Miles, E. (2018) Bus journeys, sandwiches and play: young children and the theatre event, *Research in Drama Education: The Journal of Applied Theatre and Performance*, 23(1), 20–39. DOI: 10.1080/13569783.2017.1396889

Miller, K. (2016). Learning about children's school preparation through photographs: the use of photo elicitation interviews with low-income families. *Journal of Early Childhood Research*. 14 (3), 261–279.

Moore, T., M. McArthur & Noble-Carr, D. (2008). Little voices and big ideas: Lessons learned from children about research. *International Journal of Qualitative Methods* 7(2), 77–91.

Morrow, V. & Richards, M. (1996), The Ethics of Social Research with Children: An Overview, *Children & Society*, 10, 90–105.

Moyles, J., & Papatheodorou, T. (2009). Endpiece. In T. Papatheodorou & J. Moyles (Eds.), *Learning together in the early years: Exploring relational pedagogy* (p. 228). Routledge.

Mukherji, P., & Albon, D. (2018). *Research methods in early childhood: An introductory guide* (3rd ed.). Sage Publications.

Murray, J. (2012). Young Children's Explorations: Young Children's Research? *Early Child Development and Care*. 182 (9), 1209–1225.

Murray, J. (2016). Young children are researchers: Children aged four to eight years engage in important research behaviour when they base decisions on evidence, *European Early Childhood Education Research Journal*, 24(5), 705–720. DOI: 10.1080/1350293X.2016.1213565.

Murray, J. (2017). *Building Knowledge in Early Education: Young Children are Researchers*. Routledge.

Nallari, A. (2009). *Ways of accessing preschool children's experience of the physical environment: A comparison of research methods*. Unpublished manuscript. PhD Program in Environmental Psychology, Graduate Center of the City University of New York.

Napoli, M., Krech, P., & Holley, L. (2005). Mindfulness training for elementary school students: The attention academy. *Journal of Applied School Psychology*, 21(1), 99–125.

National Council for Curriculum and Assessment (NCCA). (2009). *Aistear: The early childhood curriculum framework*. Dublin: NCCA.

Newman, M., Woodcock, A. and Dunham, P. (2006). Playtime in the borderlands: children's representations of school, gender and bullying through photographs and interviews. *Children's Geographies*, 4(3): 289–302.

Niland, A. (2015) 'Row, row, row your boat': singing, identity and belonging in a nursery, *International Journal of Early Years Education*, 23(1), 4–16. DOI: 10.1080/09669760.2014.992866.

Nilsen, B. (2017). *Week by week: Plans for documenting Children's development*. Cengage Learning.

Nutbrown, C. (2011). *Key concepts in early childhood education* (2nd ed.). Sage Publications.

Nyland, B. A, Ferrisa, J. & Deans, J. (2011). Pre-school children's encounters with The Magic Flute. *International Journal of Early Years Education* 19(3), 207–217.

O'Hagin, B. (2007). Musical learning and the Reggio Emilia approach. In *Listen to their voices: Research and practice in early childhood music education*, ed. K. Smithrim and R. Uptitis, 196–110. Toronto: Canadian Music Educators' Association.

O'Kane, C. (2000). The development of participatory techniques. Facilitating children's views about decisions which affect them, in: P. Christensen & A. James (Eds) *Research with children* (pp. 136–159). Falmer Press.

Office of the High Commissioner for Human Rights (OHCHR). (1989). *The United Nations Convention on the Rights of the Child*. http://www.ohchr.org/en/professionalinterest/pages/crc.aspx.

Oliveira-Formosinho, Júlia. (2012). Participatory educational environments: A challenge to educators pedagogic imagination. *Keynote presented at the 22nd EECERA Conference*, Oporto, Portugal.

O'Rourke, C., O'Farrelly, C., Booth, A., & Doyle, O. (2017). Little bit afraid 'til I found how it was: Children's subjective early school experiences in a disadvantaged community in Ireland, *European Early Childhood Education Research Journal*, 25(2), 206–223. DOI: 10.1080/1350293X.2017.1288386

Pálmadóttir, H. & Einarsdottir, J. (2015). Video observations of children's perspectives on their lived experiences: Challenges in the relations between the researcher and children. *European Early Childhood Education Research Journal*, 24(5), 721–733. DOI: 10.1080/1350293X.2015.1062662.

Paley, V. G. (1990). *The boy who would be a helicopter: The use of storytelling in the classroom.* Harvard University Press.

Papatheodorou, T. (2009). Exploring relational pedagogy. In T. Papatheodorou & J. Moyles (Eds.), *Learning together in the early years: Exploring relational pedagogy* (pp. 3–17). Routledge.

Papatheodorou, T., & Luff, P. (2011). *Child observation for learning and research.* Pearson Education.

Parkes, L. (2014). Circle time: Making large group activities work. *Texas Child Care Quarterly*, 38(2).

Parson, M. & Stephenson, M. (2003). Giving children a voice: research rights and responsibilities, paper presented at the *European Early Childhood Research Conference*, August 2003, Glasgow.

Payne, K. (2018). Young Children's Everyday Civics, *The Social Studies*, 109(2), 57–63. DOI: 10.1080/00377996.2018.1446897

Peacock, J. (2015). *Mindfulness practices and children's emotional and mental well-being: Activities to build and strengthen everyday resilience. Adapted for primary school teachers.* Unpublished PhD thesis.

Perry, B. (2000). Attunement: Reading the Rhythms of the Child. *Early Childhood Today*, 15(2), 20.

Piaget, J. (1951). *Play, dreams and imagination in childhood.* Heinemann in association with the New Education Fellowship.

Piaget, J. (1952). *The origins of intelligence in children.* Norton.

Pink, S. (2009). *Doing Sensory Ethnography.* Sage Publications.

Piper, H., and J. Frankham. (2007). Seeing Voices and Hearing Pictures: Image as Discourse and the Framing of Image-Based Research. *Discourse* 28(3), 373–387. DOI: 10.1080/01596300701458954

Pramling Samuelsson, I., & Asplund Carlsson, M. (2008). The playing learning child: Towards a pedagogy of early childhood. *Scandinavian Journal of Educational Research*, 52(6), 623–641.

Premack, D., & Woodruff, G. (1978). Does the chimpanzee have a theory of mind? *Behavioral and Brain Sciences*, 1(4), 515–526. http://dx.doi.org/10.101.

Prout, A., & James, A. (1997). A new paradigm for the sociology of childhood? Provenance, promise and problems. In J. Allison & P. Alan (Eds.), *Constructing and reconstructing childhood* (2nd ed., pp. 7–33). Falmer Press.

Pufall, P. Unsworth, R. (Eds.) (2004). *Rethinking Childhood.* New Brunswick: Rutgers University Press.

Punch, S. (2015). Children as research subjects: The ethical issues. *Bangladesh Journal of Bioethics*, 6(1), 6–10.

Razza, R. A., Bergen-Cico, D., & Raymond, K. (2015). Enhancing preschoolers' self-regulation via mindful yoga. *Journal of Child & Family Studies*, 24, 372–385.

Reason, P., & H. Bradbury, (Eds.) (2008). *The SAGE Handbook of Action Research: Participative Inquiry and Practice.* (2nd Ed.) Sage Publications.

Rempel, K. (2012). Mindfulness for children and youth: A review of the literature with an argument for school-based implementation. *Canadian Journal of Counselling and Psychotherapy*, 46(3), 201–220.

Rinaldi, C. (1998). Projected curriculum constructed through documentation-Progettazione: An interview with Lella Gandini. In C. Edwards, L. Gandini, and G. Forman (Eds.). *The hundred languages of children: The Reggio Emilia approach-advanced reflections*, (pp. 113–125). Ablex.

Rinaldi, C. (2003). The Teacher as Researcher. *Innovations*, 10(2).

Rinaldi, C. (2004). The relationship between documentation and assessment. *Innovations in Early Education The International Reggio Exchange*, 11(1), 1–4.

Rinaldi, C. (2006). *In dialogue with Reggio Emilia: Listening, researching and learning.* Routledge

Rinaldi, C. (2004). The relationship between documentation and assessment. *Innovations in Early Education The International Reggio Exchange*, 11(1), 1–4.

Rintakorpi, K. (2016). Documenting with early childhood education teachers: pedagogical documentation as a tool for developing early childhood pedagogy and practises, *Early Years*, 36(4), 399–412. DOI: 10.1080/09575146.2016.1145628.

Rintakorpi, K., Lipponen, L. & Reunamo, J. (2014). Documenting with parents and toddlers: a Finnish case study. *Early Years*, 34(2), 188–197. DOI: 10.1080/09575146.2014.903233.

Ritchhart, R. (2002). *Intellectual character: What it is, why it matters, and how to get it.* Jossey-Bass.

Ritchhart, R., Palmer, P., Church, M., & Tishman, S. (2006). *Thinking Routines: Establishing Patterns of Thinking in the Classroom. Paper prepared for AERA Conference*

Robbins, J. (2003). The more he looked inside the more Piglet wasn't there: What adopting a socio-cultural perspective can help us see. *Australian Journal of Early Childhood*, 28(2), 1–7.

Roberts-Holmes, G. (2018). *Doing Your Early Years Research Project: A Step by Step Guide.* Sage Publications.

Robson, S. (2006). *Developing thinking and understanding in young children.* Routledge.

Rogers, S., & Evans, J. (2008). *Inside role-play in early childhood education: Researching young children's perspectives.* Routledge.

Rogoff, B. (2003). *The cultural nature of human development.* Oxford University Press.

Rogoff, B. & Dahl, A.& Callanan, M. (2018). The importance of understanding children's lived experience. *Developmental Review.* 50, 5–15. DOI: 10.1016/j.dr.2018.05.006.

Roosevelt, D. (2007). Keeping real children at the center of teacher education: Child study and the local construction of knowledge in teaching. In D. Carroll, H. Featherstone, J. Featherstone, S. Feiman-Nemser, & D. Roosevelt (Eds.), *Transforming teacher education: Reflections from the field* (pp. 113–138). Harvard University Press.

Rose, G. (2016). *Visual Methodologies: An introduction to the researching with visual materials*. 4th ed. Sage Publications.

Ruscoe, A., Barblett, L , Barratt-Pugh, C. (2018). Sharing Power with Children: Repositioning Children as Agentic Learners. *Australasian Journal of Early Childhood* 43(3), 63–71.

Salamon, A., & Harrison, L. (2015). Early childhood educators' conceptions of infants' capabilities: The nexus between beliefs and practice. *Early Years*, 35(3), 273–288.

Salmon, A. (2008). Promoting a culture of thinking in the young child. *Early Childhood Education Journal* 35 (5), 457–461

Salmon, A. (2010). Engaging children in thinking routines. *Childhood Education* 86(3), 132–137.

Samuels, J. (2004). Breaking the ethnographer's frames: reflections on the use of photo elicitation in understanding Sri Lankan monastic culture. *American Behavioral Scientist* 47, 1528–1550.

Sancar, F. H., & Severcan, Y. C. (2010). In search of agency: Participation in a youth organisation in Turkey. In B. Percy-Smith & N. Thomas (Eds.), *A handbook of children and young people's participation: Perspectives from theory and practice* (pp. 277–286). Routledge.

Schiller, W. & Einarsdottir, J. (2009) Special Issue: Listening to young children's voices in research – changing perspectives/changing relationships, *Early Child Development and Care*, 179(2), 125–130. DOI: 10.1080/03004430802666932

Schmidt, F. & Lahroodi, R. (2008). The Epistemic Value of Curiosity. *Educational Theory.* 58(2), 125–148.

Schroeder-Yu, G. (2008). Documentation: Ideas and applications from the Reggio Emilia approach. *Teaching Artist Journal*, 6(2), 126–134.

Schulz, M. (2015). The documentation of children's learning in early childhood education: Children and society. *Special Issue: Documentation in childhood*, 29(3), 209–218.

Semenec, P. (2018). Re-imagining research with children through an engagement with contemporary art. *Childhood*, 25(1), 63–77.

Semple, R., Lee, J., Rosa, D., & Miller, L. (2010). A randomized trial of mindfulness based cognitive therapy for children: Promoting mindful attention to enhance social-emotional resiliency in children. *Journal of Child & Family Studies, 19*(2), 218–229. DOI: 10.1007/s10826-009-9301-y.

Semple, R., Reid, E., & Miller, L. (2005). Treating anxiety with mindfulness: Open trial of mindfulness training for anxious children. *Journal of Cognitive Psychotherapy: An International Quarterly, 19*(4), 379–392. DOI: 10.1891/jcop.2005.19.4.379

Sheridan, S. & Pramling Samuelsson, I. (2001). Children's conceptions of participation and influence in pre-school: A perspective on pedagogical quality. *Contemporary Issues in Early Childhood*, 2(2), 169–194.

Sierra-Cedillo, A., Sánchez, C. Figueroa-Olea, M., Izazola-Ezquerro, S & Rivera-González, R. (2019). Children's participative citizenship within the context of integral care and daily life. *Early Child Development and Care*, 189(6), 883–895. DOI: 10.1080/03004430.2017.1345897

Singer, A. (2014). Voices Heard and Unheard: A Scandinavian Perspective. *Journal of Social Welfare and Family Law*. 36(4): 381–391. DOI: 10.1080/09649069.2014.967986.

Smith, A. (2007). Children's rights and early childhood education. *Australian Journal of Early Childhood*, 32(3), 1–8.

Sommer, D., I. Pramling Samuelsson, and K. Hundeide. (2013). Early childhood care and education: A child perspective paradigm. *European Early Childhood Education Research Journal* 21(4), 459–475. DOI: 10.1080/1350293X.2013.845436

Southcott, L. H. (2015). Learning stories: Connecting parents, celebrating success, and valuing Children's theories. *Voices of Practitioners*, (Winter), 10, 33–50.

Stegenga K. & Ward-Smith P. (2008). The adolescent perspective on participation in treatment decision making: a pilot study. *Journal of Pediatric Oncology Nursing*, 25, 112–117.

Stephenson, A. (2009). Horses in the sandpit: photography, prolonged involvement and 'stepping back' as strategies for listening to children's voices, *Early Child Development and Care*, 179(2), 131–141. DOI: 10.1080/03004430802667047.

Sussman, R. (1989). Curiosity and exploration in children: where affect and cognition meet. In K. Field et al. (Eds) *Learning and education: psychoanalytic perspectives*, (pp. 245–266). International Universities Press.

Sylva, K., Melhuish, E., Sammons, P. , Siraj-Blatchford, I., & Taggart, B. (2004). *The effective provision of preschool education (EPPE) project: Technical paper 12 - The final report*. DfES/Institute of Education, University of London.

Taft, J. (2015). Adults talk too much: Intergenerational dialogue and power in the Peruvian movement of working children. *Childhood*. 22 (4), 460–473.

Taggart, B. (2010). Making a difference: How research can inform policy. In K. Sylva, E. Melhuish, P. Sammons, I. Siraj-Blatchford, & B. Taggart (Eds.), *Early childhood matters: Evidence from the effective pre-school and primary education project*. Routledge.

Tay-Lim, J. and Lim, S. (2013). Privileging Younger Children's Voices in Research: Use of drawings and a co-construction process. *International Journal of Qualitative Methods*. 12, 65–83.

Theobald, M., Danby, S., Einarsdóttir, J., Bourne, J., Jones, D., Ross, S., Knaggs, H., & Carter-Jones, C. (2015). Children's perspectives of play and learning for educational practice. *Education Sciences*, 5, 345–362.

Theobald, M., Danby, S. J., & Ailwood, J. (2011). Child participation in the early years: Challenges for education. *Australasian Journal of Early Childhood*, 36(3), 19–26.

Thompson, M., & Gauntlett-Gilbert, J. (2008). Mindfulness with children and adolescents: Effective clinical application. *Clinical Child Psychology and Psychiatry*, 13(3), 395–407. DOI: 10.1177/1359104508090603.

Thomson, P. (2008). Children and young people: Voices in visual research. In P. Thomson (Ed.), *Doing visual research with children and young people* (pp. 1–19). Routledge.

Tisdall, E. K. (2012). The Challenge and Challenging of Childhood Studies? Learning from Disability Studies and Research with Disabled Children.*Children & Society*, 26(3), 181–191. DOI: 10.1111/j.1099-0860.2012.00431.x

Tisdall, E. K. M. (2016). Participation, rights and 'participatory' methods. In A. Farrell, S. L. Kagan, & E. K. M. Tisdall (Eds.), *The Sage handbook of early childhood research* (pp. 73–88). Sage Publications.

Tobin, J., Adair, J. K., & Arzubiaga, A. (2013). *Children crossing borders: Immigrant parent and teacher perspectives on preschool for children of immigrants*. Russell Sage Foundation.

Tobin, J. J., Wu, D. Y., & Davidson, D. H. (1991). *Preschool in three cultures: Japan, China, and the United States*. Yale University Press.

Trevarthen, C. (2011). What young children give to their learning, making education work to sustain a community and its culture. *European Early Childhood Education Research Journal*, 19(2), 173–193. DOI: 10.1080/1350293X.2011.574405

Turner, T. & Gray Wilson, D. (2009.) Reflections on Documentation: A discussion with thought leaders from reggio emilia, *Theory Into Practice*, 49(1), 5–13. DOI: 10.1080/00405840903435493.

United Nations. (1989). *The United Nations convention on the rights of the child*. New York: UNICEF.

Viglas, M. & Perlman, M., (2018). Effects of a Mindfulness-Based Program on Young Children's Self- Regulation, *Prosocial Behavior and Hyperactivity. Journal of Child & Family Studies*. 27, 1150–1161. DOI: 10.1007/s10826-017-0971-6.

Vygotsky, L. S. (1986). *Thought and language*. MIT Press.

Waller, T. (2006). 'Be careful – don't come too close to my Octopus Tree': Recording and evaluating young children's perspectives of outdoor learning, *Children Youth and Environments* 16(2), 75–104.

Waller, T. & Bitou, A. (2011). Research with children: Three challenges for participatory research in early childhood. *European Early Childhood Education Research Journal*, 19(1), 5–20.

Warming, H. (2005). Participant observation: A way to learn about children's perspectives. In A. Clark, A.T. Kjørholt, & P. Moss, (Eds.). *Beyond listening: Children's perspectives on early childhood services*. (pp. 51–70). Policy Press.

Warneken, F. & Tomasello, M. (2007). Helping and cooperation at 14 months of age. *Infancy*, 11(3), 271–294.

Weare, K. (2013). Developing mindfulness with children and young people: A review of the evidence and policy context. *Journal of Children's Services.* 8(2), 141–153. DOI: 10.1108/JCS-12-2012-0014.

Wenger, E. (1998). *Communities of Practice.* Cambridge University Press.

Wessel-Powell, C. Kargin, T. & Wohlwend, K. (2016). Enriching and Assessing Young Children's Multimodal Storytelling. *The Reading Teacher* 70(2), 167–178.

Whitebread, D. (2013). Self-regulation in young children: Its characteristics and the role of communication and language in its early development. In D. Whitebread, N. Mercer, C. Howe & A. Tolmie (Eds.). *Self-regulation and dialogue in primary classrooms. British Journal of Educational Psychology Monograph Series II: Psychological Aspects of Education – Current Trends, No. 10.* (pp. 25–44). Leicester: BPS.

Whitebread, D., Coltman, P., Pino Pasternak, D., Sangster, C., Grau, V., Bingham, S., Almeqdad, Q. Demetriou, D. (2009). The development of two observational tools for assessing metacognition and self-regulated learning in young children. *Metacognition and Learning*, 4(1): 63–85.

Whitebread, D. (2012). *Developmental psychology and early childhood education.* Sage Publications.

Whitty, G., and E. Wisby. (2007). Whose Voice? An Exploration of the Current Policy Interest in Pupil Involvement in School Decision-Making. *International Studies in Sociology of Education.* 17 (3): 303–319.

Wien, C. A., Guyevskey, V., & Berdoussis, N. (2011). Learning to document in Reggio inspired education. *Early Childhood Research and Practice*, 13(2), 1–12.

Wiltz, N. W. & Klein, E. L. (2001). 'What do you do in child care?' Children's perceptions of high and low quality classrooms. *Early Childhood Research Quarterly.* 16(2), 209–236.

Wood, E. (2014). Free choice and free play in early childhood education: Troubling the discourse, *International Journal of Early Years Education*, 22(1), 4–18. DOI: 10.1080/09669760.2013.830562.

Wood, L, Roach, A.T., Kearney MA, & Zabek, F. (2018). Enhancing executive function skills in preschoolers through a mindfulness-based intervention: A randomized, controlled pilot study. *Psychol Schs.* 55, 644–660. DOI: 10.1002/pits.22136.

Woodhead, M. (2008). Respecting rights: implications for early childhood policies and practices. In Glenda Mac Naughton, Patrick Hughes and Kylie Smith (Eds). *Young Children as Active Citizens: Principles, Policies and Pedagogies.* (pp. 15–30). Cambridge Scholars Publishing.

Wright, C., Bacigalupa, C., Black, T. & Burton, M. (2008). Windows into Children's Thinking: A Guide to Storytelling and Dramatization, *Early Childhood Education Journal*, 35, 363–369. DOI: 10.1007/s10643-007-0189-0.

Wright, C., Diener, M. & Kemp, J. (2013). Storytelling Dramas as a Community Building Activity in an Early Childhood Classroom. *Early Childhood Education Journal*, 41, 197–210. DOI: 10.1007/s10643-012-0544-7.

Wright, S. (2003). *The Arts, Young Children, and Learning*. Old Tappan: Pearson Allyn Bacon Prentice Hall.

Wright, S. (2007). Graphic-narrative play: Young children's authoring through drawing and telling. *International Journal of Education and the Arts*. 8(8), 1–28.

Wyness, M. G. (2013). Children's participation and intergenerational dialogue: Bringing adults back into the analysis. *Childhood* 120 (4), 429–442.

Wyness, M. G. (2012). *Childhood and society: An introduction to the sociology of childhood*. Basingstoke: Palgrave Macmillan.

Yelland, N. J. (2018). A pedagogy of multiliteracies: Young children and multimodal learning with tablets. *British Journal of Educational Technology*, 49(5), 847–858.

Young, L., and H. Barrett. (2001). Adapting Visual Methods: Action Research with Kampala Street Children. *Area* 33: 141–152.

Young, S. (2005). Changing Tune: Reconceptualizing Music with under Three Year Olds. *International Journal of Early Years Education*. 13 (3): 289–303. DOI: 10.1080/09669760500295987.

Zelazo, P., & Lyons, K. (2012). The potential benefits of mindfulness training in early childhood: A developmental social cognitive neuroscience perspective. *Child Development Perspectives*, 6(2), 154–160. DOI: 10.1111/j.1750-8606.2012.00241.x

Zhang, Z. (2017). Gifted education in China. *Cogent Education*, 4(1). DOI:10.1080/2331186X.2017.1364881

Zoogman, S., Goldberg, S. B., Hoyt, W. T., & Miller, L. (2015). Mindfulness interventions with youth: A meta-analysis. *Mindfulness*, 6, 290–302. DOI: 10.1007/s12671-013-0260-4.

Zwaanswijk, M, Tates, K, van Dulmen, S., Hoogerbrugge, P, Kamps, W & Bensing, J. (2007). Young patients', parents', and survivors' communication preferences in paediatric oncology: Results of online focus groups. *BMC Pediatrics* 7; 35.

Index

A

ability/disability 205–208
abstract thinking 107, 140
accessing children's perspectives in research: Mosaic approach 14, 20–22, 52, 83, 86–87, 102, 126, 147, 159, 201–202, 216; multi-modal approaches 19–20, 83, 95–96, 104, 111, 176, 192–193, 198, 203, 214; Reggio Emilia 23, 46–47, 50, 64, 126, 180, 193; Steps for Engaging Young Children in Research 2–3, 22–23, 31–33, 106, 126, 162, 193–196; Young Children as Researchers study (YCAR) study 23–24, 209
accountability to each other 50
accountability to self 50
accountability to the larger community 51
adaptable approach 20
adult cultures 41
adult-initiated, shared decisions with children 7
affordances 130, 148
agency in childhood 4, 26, 52, 68, 177, 184, 204–206, 209, 211, 216, 223
Albon, D. 96
Alcock 65, 68
Ames, P. 194
analysis 43, 47, 57, 134; children's data 121; children's drawings 136, 141, 142–146; children's photos 155–158; children's storytelling 190–192; framing analysis 143, *144*, *145*, 146
Article 12 of UNCRC 5, 6, 204
assembled signs 130
attunement 49, 80

B

Bacon, K. 204, 205
Banaji, M.R. 18
Barblett, L. 2, 220, 222
Barnes, J. 176
Barratt-Pugh, C. 2, 220
Bath, C. 201
behaviour consequences 88, **89**
Bergen-Cicco, D. 167
Bitou, A. 25, 42, 43
Booth, A. 133
Breathnach, H. 99, 100
Brown, V. 187
Buckley, L. 36, 37
Burke, A. 115–118
Bus journeys to Polka 182–187

C

calming and relaxing activities: mindful breathing 171–172; mindful listening 174–175; mindfulness jars 173–174
Car 199
Carelse, B. 169
Carr, M. 58, 59, 199, 200
Carter, C. 123
checklists 90, **91**

248

child-centred model 213–214
child-centred research 1–25, 74, 80, 213–219
child-led tour approach 110–114, 153–154
children's decision-making 1–6, 26, 28, 31, 42, 165, 204, 209, 223
Children's Play Narratives (CPN) project 10
child–researcher relationship 25, 45, 99–100, 106, 108–109, 163–164, 213, 224
child-to-child interviews 108–110
Christensen, P. 97
Chubb, E. 216
citizenship in childhood 5, 28, 204–205, 208–211
Clark, A. 14, 21, 52, 83, 84, 103, 105, 148, 154, 207
Claxton, G. 199
Clayton, P. 79
Coates, A. 139
Coates, E. 139
co-constructions of meaning 7, 12–13, 45, 46, 131, 139–140
Colliver, Y. 2, 44
Colwell, J. 2, 3, 29, 31, 163, 195
communication 1, 3, 4, 44, 60, 80, 103, 110, 126, 223; drama as communication 181; multi-methods in communication 216; multi-modal communication 176–177; visual communication 130–132
complete observer 95–97
complete participation 94, 96, **97**
compositional modality 156, **157**
construction of measnings 8–12
constructions of children and childhood 3–5
contextual intersubjectivity 44
continuous narrative records 91–92, **92**
conversations with children 17, 31, 43, 54, 70–71, 81, 96, 98, 108–113, 111–112, 139, 142, 156, 158
Cook, T. 43, 44
Cooper, M. 81
Coyne, I. 216
culture, cultural context 4, 37, 77, 98, 118, 130, 136–137, 143–144

D

Dahlberg, G. 60
Dalli, C. 104
DCYA *see* Department of Children and Youth Affairs (DCYA)
Deans, J. 178, 180
decision-making 1
deficit narratives 8–12
Department of Children and Youth Affairs (DCYA) 215
Developmental Psychology 80
dialogical process 12
Diener, M. 191
digital media and meaning-making 192–193
digital technology 99, 148
digital and disposable cameras 148–150
Dockett, S. 33, 131, 134, 147, 152, 156
Doyle, O. 133
drama: additional resources and props 181; bus journeys, sandwiches and play 182–186; process drama 187–188; storytelling dramas 188–192; theatre in the early years (TEY) 181; theatre as experience 182; theatre as performance 182; workshops 181
dramatic play 119–122, **122**
draw-and-talk methods: annotating children's expressions 142; co-construction in children's drawing 139–141, *141*; framing analysis 143, *144*, *145*, 146; interactive process 132; narratives 134; off-task conversations 139; open-ended approaches 134–136, *135*; prompted drawings and free drawings 137–139; socio-economic disadvantage 133; technical principles 142; thematic analysis 143; thoughts and feelings 132–133
Duncan, P. 8, 130, 137, 142, 146

E

Early Years Professionals/Practitioners (EYPs) 13, 40, 50, 52, 53, 71, 80–82, 88, 104, 174

The Ecology of Role Play 120
Edmiston, B. 121
Effective Provision for Preschool Education (EPPE) study 51, 52
egocentrism 17
Einarsdóttir, J. 131, 134, 152
EPPE study *see* Effective Provision for Preschool Education (EPPE) study
ethical challenges in research with young children: confidentiality and privacy 39–40; gaining consent 27, 39; informed assent 33–34; informed decisions 28, 29; interactive narrative approach 36; reflexive engagement 40–41; relational process 29; roles and responsibilities 29; seeking assent 30–31, 33; steps for engaging children 31–32; token participatory methods 28; unanticipated issues 40
ethnicity 205
Etzioni, A. 211
event sampling 88, **89**
exhibitions of children's learning 67–69, *68, 69*
EYPs *see* Early Years Professionals (EYPs)

F

facilitated conversations 106–107
Fan of the Child 75–77, **76**
Fargas-Malet, M. 149
Fawcett, M. 79
Ferraris, M. 60
Ferris, J. 178, 180
Fleer, M. 44, 214, 215
Fleet, A. 112, 128, 150
Fochi, P. 223, 224
focus group interviews using circle time format 114–115
Forman, G. 16
Frankel, S. 204

G

Gelman, S.A. 18
generational social order 101
Giardiello 82

Global Play Memories Project (GPMP) 10
Gorman, G.E. 79
Graham, A. 40
Gray, C. 206, 207

H

Haiman, P.E. 85
Hall, E. 16
Hammersley, M. 205
Harcourt, D. 224
Harrison, L. 92
Hart, R. 2, 3, 5, 7, 29, 31, 163, 195
Hayes, N. 19, 48, 162
Hedges, H. 81
Hess, E. 43, 44
hierarchical model of participation 5–8, 205
Holm, G. 147
Howitt, C. 7
The Hundred Languages of Children 46, 47

I

informal conversations 110–111, 142, 202
information, understanding, voice and *influence* 6, 205–207
innovative research methods 51, 53, 108, 149–150, 207, 208, 223–224
intellectual skills 222
intergenerational learning (IGL) 138–139
internal listening 102–105
interpreting children's meanings: awareness of adult assumptions 43–44; open attitude 44
interval recording 89, **90**
interviews with children 102, 107–115, 121–123, 142, 196
Irwin, L.G. 106

J

Jevgjovikj 9
Johnson, J. 106
Johnson, V. 2, 3, 13, 29, 31, 106, 113, 163, 176, 181, 188, 195
Jordan, B. 140

K

Kashin, D. 58
Kearney, E. 33
Kellett, M. 205
Kemp, J. 191
Kjørholt, A.T. 52, 207
Krechevsky, M. 47, 50, 51, 61, 63, 64, 65, 67, 72, 73, 82, 127
Kurnik 9

L

Langhout, R. 212, 213
Larkin, E. 149
learning stories 58–59, 200–201
Lee, W. 58, 59
Levy, R. 109
Li, L. 214, 215
Lim, S. 140
Lipponen, L. 75
listening to young children outdoors: conversations 54; observations 54; photography 55, 55–56, 56
Listening to Young Children study 83–84
The Living Spaces Study 21, *22*, 83
London on your doorstep project 149–150

M

Maagerø E. 136, 143
magic carpet 158–159
The Magic Flute 178–180
making learning visible 23, 50, 59, 67, 72, 73, 82
Making Learning Visible project 50–51
Mallon, D. 216
Mardell, B. 73
Marshall, N. 14
Martin, S. 36, 37
Maxwell, T. 146
Mayall, B. 4
Mayne, F. 5, 7, 36, 205, 206
McCormick, K. 202
McSherry, D. 149
meaningful communication 13
meaning-making abilities 8; cameras and photographs *see* photographs; discourse of 130; draw-and-talk methods *see* draw-and-talk methods; drawing process 130–132; multiple media and modes 126–127; visual research methods 127–130
Merewether, J. 57, 96, 111, 112, 128, 150
Miles, E. 2, 44, 182, 186
mindful moments and performance: attentional skills 167–168; attention and focus 165–166; breathing and hearing 161, 166, 169, 170–175; calming and relaxing activities 171–175; child-peer relationships and co-operation 164–165; curiosity and openness 165; developmental considerations 169–170; multi-modal approaches 176; music 177–181; performance of understanding 176; positive and trusting relationships 163–164; safe and stimulating environment 162; self-regulation skills 166–169; verbal expression and speech 163; wellbeing exercise 193–194
Mini-Mind 166
Mosaic approach 14, 20–22, 52, 83, 86–87, 102, 126, 147, 159, 201–202, 216
Moss, J. 52
Moss, P. 14, 47, 154, 207
Mukherji, P. 62, 88, 91, 96, 107, 114, 121, 151, 152
multi-method approach 20
multi-modal methods: agreement in pre-school areas/aspects 208; children's agency 205–207; citizenship 208; documenting everyday moments 199–201; educators and researchers 201–204; equitable reality 222–224; power sharing 219–222; rights based policy and practice 208; thinking and learning 197–199; transformative potential *see* transformative potential; Young Children as Researchers (YCAR) study 209; Young children's everyday civics 210–211
multiple listening 105
Murray, J. 205

N

narrative approaches 115–119, *118*
national consultation with young children 216–219
naturalistic observations 91–92
Nicholson 9, 12
Nilsen, B. 106, 107
non-participant observation 96–98
Nutbrown, C. 123
Nyland, B.A. 178, 180

O

observation skills: aims and objectives 82; behaviour patterns and difficulties 85–86; benefits 78; curiosity 84–85; documentation 82–83; early years practitioners 79–82; gateway to children's interests 83–84; non-participant observation 96–98; participant observation *see* participant observation; planned and spontaneous observations 82; structured observations 88–90; symbolic play 85; technological media 99–101; unstructured observations 90–91; young children aged 1 to 2 years 86–87
observer as participant 92–94, **97**
O'Farrelly, C. 133
Office of the High Commissioner for Human Rights (OHCHR) 5
off-task conversations 139
OHCHR *see* Office of the High Commissioner for Human Rights (OHCHR)
O'Rourke, C. 133, 134

P

pain discomfort 203
Papadopoulou, T. 98, 119
The Paper Bag Princess 116–117
Participant and non-participant observation 9
participant as observer 94–95, **97**
participant observation 79; complete observer 95–97; complete participation 94, 96, **97**; depth of involvement 92; environment aspects 92; insider 91–92; observer as participant 92–94, **97**; participant as observer 94–95, **97**; role-play 98
participation in childhood 2, 5–8, 12, 13–15, 27, 28–30, 36, 41–43, 52, 128; adult supporting 201; community 164, 184, 191; mindful 162; participation and children's citizenship 204–206
participatory approach 20, 41, 42
participatory research 205–207
Payne, K. 210
Peacock, J. 165, 169, 170, 173, 175
pedagogical documentation: benefits and challenges 73–75; contextual knowledge 71; documentation book 57; effective documentation 60–61; engaging families 66–67; EPPE study 51, 52; Fan of the Child 75–77, **76**; handwritten field notes 57; Horses in the sandpit 70–71; interpretation and analysis 47; interpreting documentation 64–65; learning stories 58–59, *59*; listening to young children outdoors 54–57; material-discursive entanglement 57; negotiating and contesting 72; notion of sharing data 65; observing and recording 62–63; practitioner-researchers 52; practitioner's role 46; principles of learning 73; public exhibitions and products creation 67–69, *68*, *69*; reciprocal learning 46; Reggio Emilia approach 46, 48, 65; sharing meanings, within and across classrooms 66; slowed-down process 49; space and time 47; spontaneity and naturalness 49; tangible artifacts 63; visible learning and meanings 50–51; watchful attentiveness 49; writing 57
Pedagogy of Friendship 125, **125**
pedagogy of listening: communicative idiosyncrasies 104; internal listening 105; invitation to conversation 105–107; language expression and comprehension 104; multiple listening 105; visible listening 105

Pence, A.R. 47
Pence, M. 60
Perlman, M. 166
Perry, B. 33, 131, 134, 152
persona doll interviews 123–125, **125**
photobooks 153–155
photo elicitation 151–153
photographs: data and documentation 146–147; digital and disposable cameras 148–150, *151*; ethical issues 159–160; interpretations 155, 156, **157**; magic carpet 158–159; map-making 158; photobooks 153–155; photo elicitation 151–153; pre-existing images 147; researcher-produced images 147; subject-produced images 147; value of 147–148
Playing at Polka 184
Portugal, T. 194
positive emotion 203
Power, M. 40
power sharing with children 219–222
progressive filter of early years teaching 59, *59*
problem-solving skills 141
process drama 187–188
Project Zero 50

R

Raymond, K. 167
Razza, R.A. 167
reasoning/logical thinking 141
refining research methods 1
Reggio Emilia and Project Zero 23
Reggio Emilia approach 23, 46–48, 50, 64, 65, 126, 180, 193
reification 199
relational pedagogy 81, 222–223
research with children and adults: capturing sense of curiosity 15–16; children's working theories 16–17; concentration and distraction 14; ethical protocols and procedures 13; language 14; memory 14; metacognitive skills 19
Mosaic approach 14, 20–22, 52, 83, 86–87, 102, 126, 147, 159, 201–202, 216; naturalistic settings 14; visual and narrative approaches 13

research with young children 1–25, 74, 80, 213–219; child-adult researcher relationship 25; child-adult perspectives 9–12; children as informants 100; children's assent 33–36; children's caring expressions 202; children's friendships 123; confidentiality and privacy 25; consulting with children 216–219; early childhood educators 25; empowering children's voices 116–119; equal partners 26–27; ethical challenges 27–35; experiences of opera 178–180; experiences of theatre 182–187; exploring children's views of citizenship 210–211 feelings of sadness and fear in childhood 136, 143, 194; infant abilities 93–94; interpreting children's meanings 43–45; listening to young children outdoors 136–137; methodological challenges 41–43; mindfulness 167–169; quality in early years settings 37; school experiences 133–134; stepping back to listen to children 123; views on early childhood settings 154–155; views on learning 220–222; views on outdoor spaces 112–113; wellbeing in different cultural context 194
Reunamo, J. 75
Reunamo, L. 60
Rinaldi, C. 53, 77, 83, 105
Rintakorpi, K. 60, 73, 75
Rivard, M. 73
Roberts-Holmes, G. 159
Robinson, C. 149
Rojas, V. 194
role-play 119–122, **122**
Rose, G. 156
Ruscoe, A. 220, 222

S

Salamon, A. 92
self-care habits 203–204
semi-participatory roles 7
sensory preferences 80
shared resources 204

small world play interviews 121–122
Smith, Kylie 178, 179
social constructionism 4
social modality 156, **157**
social relations 143, *144*, *145*
social skills 222
sociology of childhood 3
spaces for childhood 42
Spaces to Play study 83
Stephenson, A. 71, 186
Steps for Engaging Young Children in Research 2–3, 22–23, 31–33, 106, 126, 162, 193–196
storytelling 36, 115–119, *118*
storytelling dramas 188–192
structured observations: checklists 90, **91**; event sampling 88, **89**; rating scales 90; time sampling 89, 90
Sunde, T. 136, 143
sustained shared thinking 164

T

tangible artifacts 63
Tay-Lim, J. 140
Taylor, N. 40
technological media 99–101
technological modality 156, **157**
Theatre for Early Years (TEY) 181
Thomas, E. 212, 213
Thompson, P. 109
time sampling 89, **90**
Tisdall, E.K.M. 43
Together Old and Young (TOY) project 138
Tomasello, M. 18
transformative potential: active participants 212; child-centred model 213–214; children's perspectives 215; competent interpreters 212; early childhood settings 213, 215; national consultation with young children 215–219; participatory action research 212–213; photographs 215; research context 212; research-for-transformation 215; skill set and competencies 212
Trevarthen, C. 219

U

Ufoegbune 9
UNICEF 197
United Nations Convention for the Rights of the Child 5, 8
unstructured observations 90–92

V

value of listening: child-led tours 110–114; child-to-child interviews 108–110; circle time format 114–115; dramatic play 119–122, **122**; effective listening 103–104; egocentrism 108; narrative approaches 115–119; pedagogy of listening 104–107; persona doll interviews 123–125, **125**; power dynamics 107; short attention span 108; small world play interviews 121–122; storytelling 115–119; strategies and research tools 102–103; walk-around interviews 110–114
Viglas, M. 166
Visible Learners: Promoting Reggio-Inspired Approaches in All Schools 23
visible listening 64, 105
visible thinking 198
visual research methods: children's ideas and views listening 127–128; encouraging and supporting 127; focus of each weekly visit *129*, 129–130; selection, design and development 128–129
Vivian Paley's storytelling 190
Vygotsky, L.S. 81, 162

W

walk-around interviews 110–114
Waller, T. 25, 42, 43
Warneken, F. 18
wellbeing exercise 193–194
Wenger, E. 199
White, E.J. 104
whole-of-Government strategy 215–219

Wien, C.A. 15, 49, 50, 63, 68, 126
Wilson, D. 73, 79
Winter, E. 206, 207
Wright, C. 189, 190, 191
Wright, S. 160
Wyness, M.G. 7, 12

Y

Yelland, N.J. 95
The Young Children as Researchers (YCAR) study 23–24, 209

For Product Safety Concerns and Information please contact our EU representative GPSR@taylorandfrancis.com
Taylor & Francis Verlag GmbH, Kaufingerstraße 24, 80331 München, Germany

www.ingramcontent.com/pod-product-compliance
Lightning Source LLC
Chambersburg PA
CBHW061710300426
44115CB00014B/2629